PRAGMATIC CAPITALISM

PRAGMATIC CAPITALISM

WHAT EVERY INVESTOR NEEDS TO KNOW ABOUT MONEY AND FINANCE

CULLEN ROCHE

palgrave
macmillan

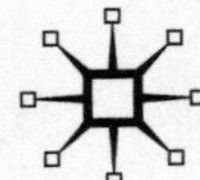

PRAGMATIC CAPITALISM

First published in 2014 by PALGRAVE MACMILLAN ® in the U.S.—a division of St. Martin's Press LLC, 175 Fifth Avenue, New York, NY 10010.

Where this book is distributed in the UK, Europe and the rest of the world, this is by Palgrave Macmillan, a division of Macmillan Publishers Limited, registered in England, company number 785998, of Houndmills, Basingstoke, Hampshire RG21 6XS.

Palgrave Macmillan is the global academic imprint of the above companies and has companies and representatives throughout the world.

ISBN: 978-1-137-27931-6

Library of Congress Cataloging-in-Publication Data

Roche, Cullen.
Pragmatic capitalism : what every investor needs to know about money and finance / Cullen Roche.
pages cm
ISBN 978-1-137-27931-6 (alk. paper)
1. Monetary policy. 2. Economic development. 3. Economic policy. 4. Finance, Personal. I. Title.
HG230.3.R63 2014
339—dc23

2013047126

A catalogue record of the book is available from the British Library.

Design by Letra Libre, Inc.

First edition: July 2014

10 9 8 7 6 5 4 3 2 1

Printed in the United States of America.

CONTENTS

ACKNOWLEDGMENTS

THIS BOOK IS THE RESULT OF DECADES OF PERSONAL DEVELOP-ment and learning that I could have never achieved entirely on my own. A great number of people have helped me develop the understandings and personal knowledge that made this book possible.

First and foremost, I want to thank everyone at Palgrave Macmillan who made my idea for the book a reality. In particular, I want to thank Laurie Harting, whose tireless editing and coaching helped make my writing intelligible.

To the many colleagues in the field of finance and economics—my understanding of the financial world would be far more deficient were it not for my interactions with Jeff Howlett, Brett Fiebiger, Mike Sankowski, Carlos Mucha, Michael Peckham, James Montier, Ramanan V, Warren Mosler, Marc Lavoie, Josh Brown, Meb Faber, John Carney, and many others involved in the world of finance and economics.

To the many friends and readers at the Pragmatic Capitalism website—thank you for always pushing my learning curve and helping me develop an environment of learning and improvement.

To my seven best friends in the world, my brothers and sisters—thank you for never being too upset with me for being better looking than you. And thank you for always being there for me, no matter what. I wouldn't be half the person I am without you (although that half would still be better looking than you).

To my dog, Callie, who might benefit from this book more than anyone (she very much enjoys eating paper)—thank you for always reminding me that every day is the best day to be alive.

To my mom and dad—I definitely won the amazing parents lottery. How could I have possibly asked for more love and support through the years?

And to Erica—you are everything to me. Every day I wake up the wealthiest man in the world.

WHAT I HOPE TO ACCOMPLISH

THE GLOBAL FINANCIAL SYSTEM IS UNDERGOING A SEISMIC shift as I write. What was once a localized and domestic system is quickly being transformed into a complex, interconnected, and interdependent global macroeconomic system. This transformation is changing the way we do everything—from the way we transact with one another, to the way we invest, to the way governments implement policy.

Although the global financial system is rapidly evolving and becoming increasingly complex, most of its participants remain woefully ill equipped to navigate this system. According to a 2012 study by the Securities and Exchange Commission:

> U.S. retail investors lack basic financial literacy . . . have a weak grasp of elementary financial concepts and lack critical knowledge of ways to avoid investment fraud.[1]

The good news is that we have the tools needed to better understand and adapt to this changing macroeconomic monetary system. To be better prepared to benefit from this system, we have to want to learn about it.

Pragmatic Capitalism is a series of principles and understandings intended to piece together the puzzle of the global financial system so you can be better prepared to invest, save, and participate within this rapidly evolving system. The text covers a substantial amount of ground and as a result it will read much like many separate sections each with their own important principles. It is my hope that this book will provide you with a superior understanding of the world of money, finance, and economics so you can prepare for the new macroeconomic world and better navigate your path to financial success.

CHAPTER 1

WHAT IS MONEY?

The person who mistakes "money" for "wealth" will live a life accumulating things, all the while mistaking a life of owning for a life of living.

IF YOU PICK UP A FINANCE OR ECONOMICS BOOK THESE DAYS, you will rarely find a thorough explanation of what *money* is. In fact most modern economists do not even agree on a set definition of money, and many do not include money in their models of the economy. Of course we all have a vague concept of money, but do any of us truly understand what it really is? I think that any book about finance and economics is incomplete if it does not begin by explaining what money is. After all, how can you understand the economy if you don't understand the primary tool with which we interact in that economy? A finance or economics book without an understanding of money is like a car manual that lacks an explanation of how to refuel your car. Even worse, it is like a car manual that doesn't even tell you what type of fuel your car should use. Unfortunately money is a far more dangerous construct than fuel so it would be imprudent to write a book about money that does not first explain what it is.

From an economic and financial perspective understanding precisely what money is and how it influences the economy is crucial. Why? Because money is the most important tool we use in modern life. Money is at the heart of every financial transaction, including our calculations of output, profits, and every measurement of our financial health. Understanding how this tool works is central not only to understanding how the monetary system and the economy works but to understanding modern human life.

WHY DO WE USE MONEY?

Before we can say what money is, it's helpful to understand first why money even exists. To answer that question, and really begin to understand money and the history of money, it might help to understand the most basic purpose that money serves. As highly socialized and intelligent animals, we humans have created various tools that improve our ability to trade and interact. A barter system is relatively primitive and insufficient because it forces you to be able to obtain something that someone else will want in exchange for the things you might need. Creating a universal medium of exchange is the bind that ties all goods and services together by making all goods and services exchangeable. At its core money is simply a social construct that allows for the exchange of goods and services.

Money, within a modern human society, is highly evolved, formal, and even institutionalized. The true history of money is lost in time, but it's likely that money started in the form of unspoken promises, evolved through a barter system of some type, and has expanded over time into formal promises and legal contracts. Today most money is defined and protected by laws. Modern money has evolved primarily into the electronic records of account.

We live in a highly advanced and sophisticated economic system that is predicated on the social interaction of trading goods and services for money. Said differently, money is the medium by which we gain access to the things we desire. You can't always trade a back scratch for a back scratch, but humans have resolved that issue by creating something that facilitates the exchange of most goods and services. For instance, if I want a back scratch, but I don't want to scratch your back, it's not a problem. Instead you scratch my back in exchange for $10, thereby voiding my need to provide you with an equivalent back scratch, and you can go buy whatever you want.

At its most basic level money is just a tool that is created to facilitate exchanges among highly socialized animals—a social tool that acts as an intermediary in transactions. So now we can arrive at our first understanding of money:

1. *Money is a social construct.*

But this still doesn't tell us why money exists. Why do you work such long hours to acquire pieces of paper or electronic credits in a bank account? Why do we stress and worry about money? It might help a bit to think of money as a theater ticket.[1] If the economy (and our access to goods and services) is the theater, then we can think of money as the ticket that gains us entry to the show. In a modern monetary system a specifically designated form of money is little more than something that gains you entry to be able to transact within that economy. And we work because of and stress about our ability to obtain money because our access to the goods and services that we need ultimately relies on obtaining this tool.

At times in human history money has been many things, including unspoken bonds, sticks, rocks, precious metals, pieces of paper, or records on the Internet. Technically, many things can and do meet the various properties of money. These things generally represent something of a certain value that can be easily measured. In other words we have developed a system of using items of particular value that represent the right to claim a certain amount of goods and services. It is, in essence, a way of recording a deferred promise. But we should be careful not to always think of money as a physical thing or something that has intrinsic value. Money represents a certain value, but the money thing itself (like a cash note) does not necessarily have intrinsic value.

Money in a modern society is largely made up of electronic records and numbers in computer systems. Your bank account exists primarily in a computer system as a record of account and not as a bar of gold in a vault. The electronic money system has come to dominate the way we transact and use this social tool. This brings us to our second crucial understanding about money:

2. *Modern money is not necessarily a physical item or something with intrinsic value but is merely a medium of exchange and a record of account.*

But what is the primary purpose of money? As I mentioned briefly earlier, the primary purpose of money is to provide us with a convenient medium of exchange for access to goods and services. That is, instead of toting around bars of gold to buy groceries at Walmart or relying on a barter system, we have created convenient ways to record our payments in order to obtain goods and services that we might desire. This gives us access to the ability to feed our families, send our children to school, maintain our health, enjoy ourselves, and so on.

Money, while important, should never be confused with true wealth. Remember, money is merely the medium of exchange. It is a tool like many other tools humans create, and it provides us with a means to an end. While the ticket gets you into the theater, what you want is not the ticket. The ticket simply gives you access to the show, which is the true end. Money is merely the means to that end. Although money is a necessary component of modern life, it is not a necessary component of acquiring true wealth.

Now, *true wealth* has different meanings to different people, but in most cases it involves the addition of companionship, good friends, good family, good health, access to food, access to water, security, et cetera. More money might make it more convenient to achieve certain things, but money and true wealth should not always be thought of as the same thing. Confusing money with true wealth is like confusing the theater ticket with the performance. Although we need some amount of tickets to enter the theater, the quality of that show is not necessarily dependent on the number of tickets we obtain throughout our lives. While money can certainly make it easier to obtain material goods, and perhaps even some level of happiness, it is always a means to some other end and should not be confused with *the* end.

This brings us to what might be the most important lesson we can learn about money:

3. *Money is not necessarily true wealth.*

Almost anything can serve as money. You could take toilet paper to the local pawnshop and trade it for something of equal value, assuming the pawn shop will find it valuable. More commonly we tend to see people view precious metals like gold as money. This is not incorrect.

Anything can serve as a medium of exchange. It's just that gold is a rather inconvenient form of money. It's heavy, hard to value in real time, and not widely accepted as a medium of exchange. So it's a fairly inconvenient means of purchasing goods and services.

Most of the money in a modern monetary system is what's called fiat money. *Fiat money* is money that has no intrinsic value but is used as a medium of exchange because a specific government deems it so. In Latin *fiat* means "let it be." Today's monetary systems are designed as social systems that institutionalize and organize money under specific laws within specific societies. Governments regulate these monetary systems and identify the entities that may issue specific types of money. The US government regulates the US monetary system, which is designed around the private banking system. You can think of the private banking system as the playing field upon which the US payments system works. The government is the referee (regulator), and we are the players trying to obtain balls (money) to score goals (consume and produce). But if you want to play on the field designated and regulated by the US government, then you must use the ball that it deems to be acceptable, and that means engaging the playing field that is the US banking system.

In the United States the dollar is the unit of account in which all money is denominated. *Unit of account* is the measuring stick we use for money. Much like the metric scale, money is measured according to its unit of account. So one dollar can buy you X number of sandwiches or whatever goods or services you desire. The unit of account is different in different countries, but the concept is always the same—a government has designated a specifically denominated money as the unit of account (for instance, the yen in Japan, euros in Europe, or pesos in Mexico), and the government regulates the playing field upon which that unit of account is used. If you want to participate in the US economy, you must generally obtain money that is denominated in US dollars, which is the standard form of payment accepted for goods and services. In most cases that means participation in the US banking system using bank deposits denominated in dollars.

This brings us to the next important understanding about money:

4. *Modern money is a specifically defined unit of account.*

For the purposes of this book I will focus primarily on the economic purpose of money. At its most basic purpose, money is simply a medium of exchange, the tool that gains us access to goods and services. Today's primary tool of exchange is bank deposits. The modern monetary playing field exists primarily within the banking system, which processes trillions of dollars in payments every single day. When you buy a sandwich with your debit card, your bank is processing a payment on your behalf. You are transferring bank deposits from your bank account to that of the seller. When you take money out of the ATM to make a purchase, you are drawing down a bank account in order to transact with physical money more conveniently. All these transactions are centered around the banking system and the deposit system. Today's monetary system exists primarily on spreadsheets as numbers in computers recorded by banks as bank deposits. Bank deposits are created when banks make loans; then these deposits are used as the primary means of transacting business at the point of sale. Modern money is both someone's asset and someone else's liability, existing primarily in computer systems as records of this basic accounting. For instance, when a bank creates a loan, the loan generates four specific accounting entries. The loan is an asset for the bank; when the recipient of the loan deposits the money, the deposit creates a liability for the bank. For the borrower the loan is a liability and the deposit is an asset.

I will cover the creation and structure of the banking system in detail later, but understanding that most modern money is based on the electronic deposit system controlled by the banking system, and that this money is created as credit through the loan creation process, is crucial. This sophisticated banking system allows us to conveniently and efficiently exchange goods and services by establishing a money supply that is elastic. This means the money supply can expand and contract according to the needs of its users.

This brings us to an essential understanding of modern money:

5. *Most modern money is credit.*

In today's electronic money system most money exists as a record of account on spreadsheets as a result of the accounting relationship that created the money through the loan creation process.

This is a crash course in the basic concept of modern money. I will elaborate later on some details as they pertain to particular monetary systems, but you now have enough information to get into the interesting parts of money, finance, and economics and begin to see why understanding all this really matters.

CHAPTER 2

WHY THE NEW MACROECONOMY MATTERS MORE THAN EVER

It's easier to look like a great swimmer if you know the direction of the current.

I'VE WRITTEN THIS BOOK PRIMARILY FROM WHAT'S CALLED A top-down approach—the 30,000-foot view of the world. If we think of the global economy as one massive entity, then navigating the economy or understanding it requires not only a micro "small picture" understanding but also a macro "big picture" understanding. And if you can understand the major influences on an economy, you're likely to be much more informed about the smaller trends.

Understanding the global economy is not unlike sailing across an ocean. It's important to understand the small details, but if you know which direction the current is going, which direction the winds are blowing, and where the big storms are, and have established the general direction of your destination, you've taken care of many of the most important parts of the trip. Understanding the big picture will allow you to reach your destination, while the smaller details may assist in the speed and ease of your trip. If you get the big ideas right, the small details tend to fall into place more easily. When we think of the global economy, we should approach it with much the same mentality. This doesn't mean the small details don't matter; it just means that understanding the microeconomy can be easier if we also understand how the macroeconomy influences it.

The great financial crisis of 2008 proved that understanding the big picture matters more than it ever has. The crisis was global in scope and led to widespread government intervention. Comprehending and reacting to the crisis required an understanding of these global macroeconomic dynamics. The crisis might feel like a distant memory to some, but it showed how much more integrated the entire global economic machine has become. To succeed we can no longer understand only the domestic local economies. We have to understand the changing global macroeconomic picture. And perhaps more important, we have to understand the institutions and entities that operate within this system so we can properly understand how to navigate their increasingly involved policy decisions. This isn't just changing the way we view politics, understand money, or engage in the economy on a daily basis—it is changing the way we use money. Perhaps most notably it is changing the way we engage in financial markets.

Before his death the famous value investor Benjamin Graham said:

> In general, no. I am no longer an advocate of elaborate techniques of security analysis in order to find superior value opportunities. This was a rewarding activity, say, 40 years ago, when our textbook "Graham and Dodd" was first published; but the situation has changed a great deal since then.[1]

The world is a very different place than it was in the last quarter of the twentieth century during the heyday of Warren Buffett and Benjamin Graham when economies were highly localized and information was difficult to obtain. This era was truly the golden age of the value, or microeconomic, investor. Securities analysis was a highly rewarding endeavor as markets were starved for information, and competitive analysis of information created vast opportunities. But we no longer live in the age of Buffett and Graham. The world today is a global economy in which information moves fast and the competition in search of information is greater than it's ever been. Computer algorithms scour every bit of news and data for any potential price discrepancy, and armies of PhD mathematicians now populate financial firms to compete with the everyday person in search of value. I think Benjamin Graham was beginning to see this trend unfolding during his career, but the world has been slow to catch up.

With the value creation of stock picking and security analysis waning for the average market participant, an understanding of the macroeconomy's environment matters more than it ever has. It is increasingly important with regard to how we will analyze economies, markets, finance, and money. If you're going to understand the rapidly changing global economy, you need to understand the macroeconomic environment—that's something I cannot stress strongly enough. The problem is, as we transition to a new macroeconomic world, most of us are still living in a microeconomic world. It's estimated that 71 percent of the movements in the financial markets are the result of macroeconomic trends, yet 69 percent of all market participants still focus their approaches on a company-specific microeconomic view.[2] That macroeconomic trends drive the markets has only become more pronounced in recent years. This became obvious when the central banks and governments of the world were forced to coordinate policy in 2008–2009 because they realized how interconnected all their actions were.

It's not surprising that most of us still focus on our local economy's, or microeconomic, trends. From a personal perspective we tend to think more locally and without regard to our global surroundings. We live in local communities, states, or countries. But our actions increasingly impact, or rely on, the interdependence of the global economy. And when it comes to financial markets many are still convinced that microeconomic analysis and company-specific analysis is the best way to approach the financial market. If you turn on financial news these days, you are inundated with company-specific news and analysis of the microeconomy. Understanding these details matters, but the big picture is often universally overlooked. One of the big lessons of this book is why I think the macroeconomic matters more than ever. Whether we're stock pickers, asset allocators, politicians, or just everyday people, the macroeconomy matters to our lives, and understanding it can only help us better navigate the world.

THE CONVERGENCE CHANGING THE GLOBAL ECONOMY

As the world has evolved, economies have transitioned from small localized markets to markets that now span the globe. This particular time in human history is unlike any other with respect to the transformation that is occurring in the global economy. We are experiencing what some experts refer to as a hyperglobalization.[3] *Hyperglobalization* is a fantastically rapid change in globalization resulting from growth in global trade, global financial transactions, migration, and dissemination of knowledge.

Two primary trends are changing the way we all live: a huge expansion in the human population and the middle class of emerging markets; and the rapid pace of accessible technological advancements. The convergence of demand for information and knowledge with the rapid pace of technological change is making the world a very small place as technology becomes more accessible and demand for this technology grows rapidly.

To put this change in perspective, it's helpful to look at a bit of history. The human population grew from two hundred million people in 1 AD to 1.6 billion people 1900 AD. In the hundred-plus years since 1900, the human population has more than quadrupled, to more than seven billion people (see Figure 2.1). This incredibly powerful trend is changing the way we produce and consume almost everything on our planet.

Within this population growth we see quickly shifting demographic trends as well. The developed world is aging rapidly and, according to

Figure 2.1: Global Population Since 1 AD (millions)

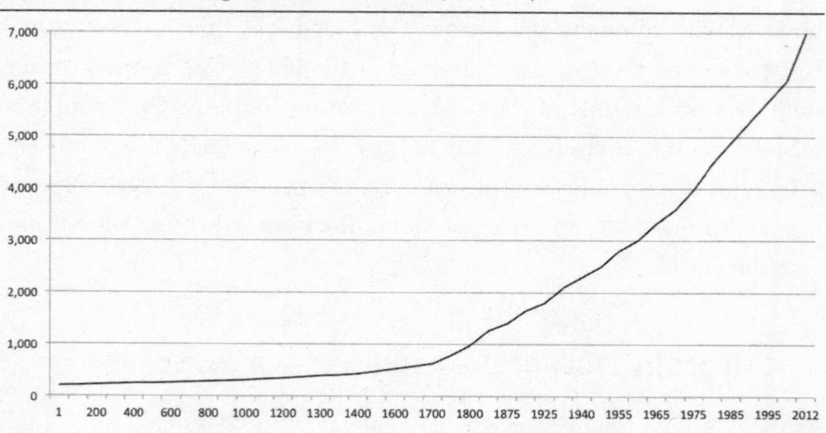

Source: US Census Bureau, World Population Summary, *1–2012, http://www.census.gov/population/international/data/idb/worldpopinfo.php.*

the US National Intelligence Council's *Global Trends* report, the median age of people in the developed world will be 43 in 2030 compared to 38 in 2012.[4] Emerging markets, on the other hand, are much younger and much larger; they also will be developing growing needs as these countries transform their middle classes. This means the technological developments of the developed world are going to be in increasingly high demand from the emerging world. This convergence is going to fuel global growth and change for decades to come.

The broader trend in population growth has been met with an equally impressive surge in overall production. As of 2012 gross world production was more than $71 trillion (see Figure 2.2). That's up from $41 trillion in 2000 and $27 trillion in 1990. We have produced almost as much in the last twenty-five years as we did in the previous 1,900 years.

What is occurring is a global middle-class population that is becoming much larger in a world that is becoming much more productive. If we use a simple model of future Gross Domestic Product (GDP) growth, population plus growth rate of GDP per capita should continue to expand as this hyperglobalization trend plays out. In other words we are a long way from maximizing our human potential.

Figure 2.2: Gross World Product Since 1 AD (millions)

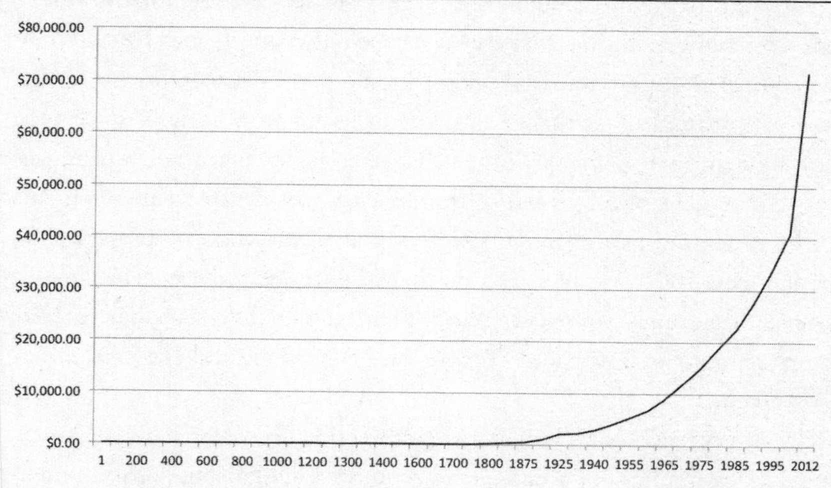

Source: U.C. Berkeley, Bradford De Long, Estimates of World GDP, *1–2012, http://delong.typepad.com/print/20061012_LRWGDP.pdf.*

In addition to the population boom and production boom, we are experiencing a rapid pace of technological change. As Moore's Law states, during the history of computer technology the number of transistors on integrated circuits has doubled every year. We're producing new technologies so rapidly and in such massive quantity that consumer demand can't keep up with the latest gizmo or gadget before the next one has been released.

The new macroeconomic world isn't about consumer gadgets, though. It's about a proliferation of information and data across the global economy. The developed world has seen tremendous advances in living standards in the last hundred years, and the emerging markets want a piece of this standard of living as their middle classes expand. Most important, this access to technology is causing a huge change in the way undeveloped economies are being transformed. Developed economies are making their technologies accessible to the entire global community; through this process the emerging world is able to provide its massively expanding population with a better standard of living.

These trends are perhaps most apparent in corporate income statements. US stock market indexes once were made up of truly American companies. That is, the vast majority of revenues came from the domestic economy. But as technology has opened doors to new markets, we've seen local companies become national companies and then become multinational companies. Since 1990 S&P 500 companies have grown from generating 22 percent of their revenue from abroad to 30 percent. Although data don't exist for the early decades of the 1900s, one can presume that this revenue figure is up substantially since then and likely only to increase. In fact, if we consider that the US produces just 22 percent of all global output, a vast world of revenues remains to be generated from foreign markets that have yet to be tapped. And if the S&P 500 were taken to its logical extreme, where it becomes a truly international index, we should expect that international revenue number to go well north of 50 percent, 60 percent, and even as high as 70 percent.

The S&P 500 is no longer a US index. It is becoming a global index, and understanding its constituents requires a global big-picture understanding as never before. The big picture matters to market participants because US stock markets are becoming increasingly dependent on a stream of foreign revenues as they tap into foreign markets for business expansion. And that means we're all becoming more and more interconnected in more ways than we think. This global influence can also be seen in the way assets are responding in tandem with increasing frequency. From 1990 to 1995 the average correlation in global equities was just 29 percent. From 2005 to 2010 the average correlation in global equities surged to 73 percent. This hyperglobalization effect isn't just changing trade. It's altering financial markets.[5]

It's estimated that China's economy will be $9 trillion in 2014. That's twice as large as it was in 2008. The McKinsey Global Institute estimates that emerging markets will account for 239 companies, 120 of which from China alone, in the Fortune 500 by 2025. As of 2010 this figure was 85.[6] This is an incredible shift in the way the global economy operates. The point is that we're living in a world that is growing by reach but shrinking in size. What happens in China matters in the United States. What happens in Europe matters in China. And what happens in the United States matters in Europe. Understanding your local economy or your domestic economy is not good enough anymore. If you don't understand the global macroeconomic trends at work, you're at a substantial competitive disadvantage to those who do. And this trend is only becoming more pronounced.

Another way of looking at this trend is to study Gross World Product (GWP) relative to stock market size (market capitalization). As of 2012 emerging market economies represented 51 percent of GWP but accounted for just 12 percent of global stock market capitalization.[7] One could easily argue that this divergence will shrink in the coming decades as more and more corporations in emerging markets become globally recognized names and market capitalization converges with global output share. If McKinsey is right, and I think they are, then that stock market capitalization figure for emerging markets is headed up.

Perhaps most important, this hyperglobalization is causing huge changes in the way governments operate. This increasingly informed and interconnected world is forcing governments to become more cognizant of one another's policies. The global financial crisis that led to the coordination of government policy is not a once-in-a-generation phenomenon. It is merely a reflection of how interconnected our world is becoming. And understanding these government institutions and policies is becoming more and more important. What the European Central Bank and the Federal Reserve do matters more than ever now. Foreign economies can and will increasingly influence US economic output and US corporate performance. And understanding these foreign institutions and economies and their impact on the world requires a sophisticated understanding of the macroeconomic world. And that means we all need to start using a macroeconomic mind-set.

BEGINNING TO THINK IN A MACROECONOMIC WAY

What does it mean to take a macroeconomic view of the world? Macro is just a big-picture view of things. If we're going to start understanding how the microeconomy is impacted by the macroeconomy, we need to start thinking about the world in terms of how it's changing. We need to start understanding that we're all part of something much bigger than we are. For instance, if you want to understand how the tides change on Earth, you have to understand that Earth is a microplanet in a macrosystem. You can't just study Earth's weather patterns or other more microclimate trends on the planet alone. To fully comprehend the micromovements of Earth's tides, we have to understand the macrotrends that influence these changes. That means understanding the solar system in which Earth exists and the ways that various elements impact these tide changes. The macroeconomic view is about understanding how large trends contribute to microeconomic occurrences.

Thinking this way requires some relatively basic big-picture understandings. When I think about the macroeconomy, I see progress. That progress is something that transcends economic understanding. I am quite confident that more people wake up every morning saying, "I am going to do better than I did yesterday," than people who wake up saying, "I am going to do worse than I did yesterday." Progress is inherent to the human species. We are always striving to find answers to life's most important questions, and this innate drive has resulted in incredible progress in a relatively short time on this planet.

When we study the macroeconomy and the big picture, understanding this basic premise is crucial. Yes, the rate of change might alter and shift from time to time (it might even become negative for periods of time), but the long-term trend is undeniable—we've come a long way from the days when we were scurrying along the plains, trying to avoid becoming another animal's dinner.

Figure 2.3 shows a log scale of global growth over the past 2,000 years. The post-industrial revolution era (since 1750) has experienced an average annual growth rate of 2.4 percent.

Now, I don't think it's prudent to build a model of perpetual 2.4 percent global growth, but this provides some directional understanding of this powerful long-term trend. The human species tends to make economic progress. History shows that betting against this has been a bad bet for hundreds of years. So a macroeconomic view should start with at least a moderately optimistic view of the world. But I like to say that we should approach the world with measured optimism. That is, we can and will encounter periods of turbulence along the way, and the measured optimist is likely to be better prepared for these periods than the eternal optimist. Permabulls are guaranteed to be disappointed for periods during their lives, but the measured optimist can approach the macroeconomic world with the understanding that humans are likely to make progress if given enough time but will at times encounter difficult periods.

Figure 2.3: Gross World Product Log Scale Since 1 AD (millions)

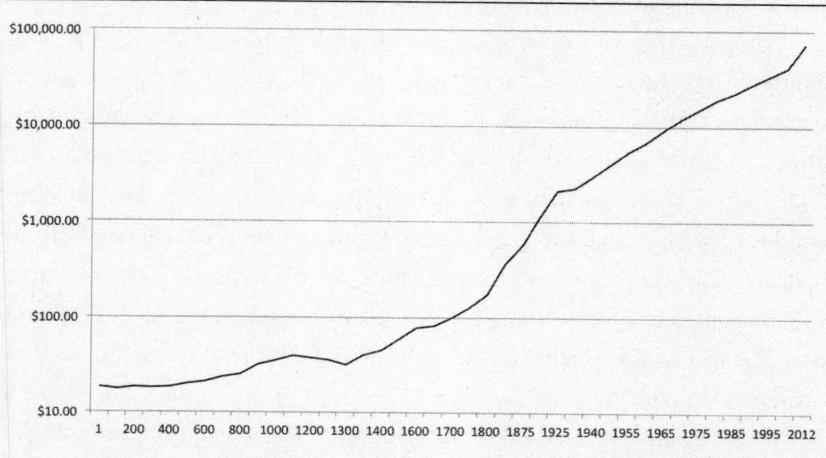

Source: U.C. Berkeley, Bradford De Long, Estimates of World GDP, *1–2012, http://delong.typepad.com/print/20061012_LRWGDP.pdf.*

HOW THE FLOW OF FUNDS DRIVES THE MONETARY MACHINE

Thinking in a macroeconomic sense requires an understanding of the drivers of the economic system. I like the way Ray Dalio, the founder of the world's largest and most successful global macro hedge fund, Bridgewater Associates, has referred to the economy as a machine.[8] Like any machine, the economy has parts and pieces that come together to create a particular result. I like to think of the economy in terms of one of the world's most sophisticated machines, the human body. What makes the human body operate? What makes it grow, thrive, and even die? Well, the economy, like the human body, thrives on a series of flows. What does that mean? An economy is made up of monetary transactions. Humans, in their desire to achieve progress and improve their living standards, produce and consume goods and services using money. The macroeconomy is just a much larger example of millions of these microeconomic transactions.

All the monetary transactions in the world are what economists call a flow of funds. And, like blood flowing through the human body, this flow of funds keeps the system moving forward. If the economic machine has no flow, it suffers the equivalent of a heart attack. So the most basic component of the economic machine is this series of flows through the system that help generate revenues for businesses, incomes for households, and tax revenues for governments.

And here we can begin to see why understanding money matters. Money is the blood flow in our economic machine. It is the thing that is used to transact and keep the flow going. Remember, the macroeconomic machine is just the sum of all these microeconomic transactions. GDP is just the monetary value of all the finished goods and services produced within a country in a specific time period. This is one way to measure the success of a particular economy. I'll cover the details of this calculation in a later section, but for now it's important to understand that the monetary machine is largely driven by the flow of funds that produces this output.

At this point it's helpful to understand some basic functions of the economy. When thinking about this system of flows, it's vitally important to understand that one person's spending is another person's income. *I'll say it again because it's so important: One person's spending is someone else's income.* Someone spends, another person earns this income; the income recipient invests, the entity in which the investment is made spends, and the cycle goes on. When the cycle of spending dies, the economy essentially dies (or goes into what economists might call a recession). Incomes decline, profits dry up, output goes unsold, workers get fired, and so on. It's similar to the way the human body works. So long as the blood flows, the body receives the nutrients necessary for survival and every day operation. But the flow is not necessarily enough on its own to sustain the system. The system must be properly nourished and taken care of. Human beings who sit on the couch every day eating pizza are likely to experience an interruption in this flow at some point as the health of their system deteriorates over time. And when the flow stops (for whatever reason) the system dies.

In the economy the health of the system is based largely on how this flow results in an improvement in living standards over time. Are the economic agents using this flow to create goods and services that improve the overall standards of living for the system as a whole? For an economic system the equivalent of sitting on the couch and eating pizza is a system in which the economic agents are unable to find productive uses for the flow of goods and services. In this scenario living standards stagnate, the flow stagnates, and the system deteriorates.

Beginning to think in a macroeconomic way is all about this basic foundation. People consume and produce in order to try to improve their living standards. So the foundational assumptions of thinking in a macroeconomic way include the basic understanding that one person's spending is another person's income and that, to try to improve their living standards, humans consume and produce using the tool of money. Understanding this basic assumption leads to a better understanding of why the macroeconomy matters to our everyday lives.

CHAPTER 3

ARE YOU AN INVESTOR, SAVER, OR BOTH?

The best investment you'll likely ever make is in yourself.

ONE WAY TO LOOK AT THE ECONOMY IS AS THE SUM OF MILLIONS of transactions. And while we have to be careful about extrapolating the microeconomic aspects of these transactions to the larger context, exploring microeconomic transactions in more detail can be helpful in understanding how these seemingly individual acts influence the broader economy. In this chapter I cover some basic specific aspects of the underpinnings of the macroeconomic machine.

At the most basic level the monetary system is made up of spending, which creates someone else's income. For simplicity I'll break down the income component of this concept. There are three basic things you can do with your income. You can consume, invest, or save. Let me be more specific.

We obtain money in part because we need to use it to accommodate our current or future needs. Most of our income goes into consumption, accommodating our current needs. Consumption is the final sale of goods and services. You consume things like housing, food, or a new TV.

Consumption—the final sale of goods and services

You could also use your income to produce more in the future. Production is the creation of value by turning out goods and services.

Production and consumption are two sides of the same coin: producers ultimately require consumers to purchase output (producers need consumers). When we spend in order to produce, we are making an investment. Using the word *investment* requires precision because it generally is associated with the purchase of something like a share of stock on the New York Stock Exchange. But that's not always accurate. Investment is actually spending, not consumed, for future production. Say that a bunch of times so it sinks in. *Investment is spending not consumed for future production.* Examples include building a factory or going to college. You're making an investment in something in the hope that it will generate future production.

Investment—spending not consumed for future production

You can use your income in a third way, too. You can do nothing with it. This is called saving. *Saving* is simply income not consumed.

Saving—income not consumed

When you save, you're not really doing nothing with your savings. In a monetary world you are by definition allocating your savings to some financial instrument. Many of us simply keep our savings in a bank account, where it is held as bank deposits that earn no interest but are available to be tapped when we want or need to consume. Technically all income is saved, at least for a brief moment, before it is used for consumption or investment.

In a monetary world you have options for saving your income if you should choose to do. You can allocate your savings however you like. You might move your savings into a savings account, where it earns a little interest. You might allocate it to something a bit more risky, such as a government bond. Or you might allocate it to stocks, corporate bonds, real assets, or other monetary vehicles that allocate your savings for you (for example, exchanged traded funds or mutual funds). These are all ways of allocating your savings. But I don't want you to always think of this as investment as it is traditionally portrayed in the media. Let me explain why.

Most of us think of investment in the stock market sense. Most of us think we invest in stocks and bonds. But we are not actually investors in the purest sense of the word when we buy stocks and bonds. Most of us are simply savers who allocate our assets to certain financial instruments. To understand this point it is necessary to understand exactly why these financial instruments exist. When a new corporation is formed, it might raise money in a number of different ways. The most traditional form is a simple bank loan or the issuance of corporate debt. But it could also raise money by selling equity, or ownership, in the company. When someone provides funding for a corporation in this manner, it will issue them the equivalent of a stock certificate, which gives the investor a legal claim on a certain ownership portion of the business. In making this investment the investor has provided the corporation with current capital that will help it create future production. The investor has made a real *investment* in the company. Remember: Investment is spending not consumed for future production. The investor in this example has spent but not consumed in order to fund the future production of the firm.

Now, what if that initial investor no longer wants to own that stock certificate and sells it to a neighbor, Sue, who thinks the company is a good value? In this case Sue will exchange cash for the stock certificate, which results in a change in ownership of the stock certificate. When Sue buys shares in this manner, she is allocating savings. The buyer is not an investor in the same sense that the initial investor was because the underlying company has no real involvement in the transaction. This purchase of stock does not actually fund future production of the company. It simply changes the legal ownership of the outstanding stock from one person to another. An exchange or reallocation of savings has occurred, but no funding of future production has occurred.

UNDERSTANDING SECONDARY MARKETS AND PRIMARY MARKETS

This brings me to the concept of secondary markets and primary markets. Shares of stock, like the one I just discussed, are issued in a primary market in which real investors provide funding to a corporation in exchange for shares. *Primary markets* provide funding for future production. They are more widely known as the place where an initial public offering (IPO) occurs. An IPO provides funding for a corporation, but as soon as the shares are issued, they will trade on a secondary market, in which buyers and sellers exchange them. The New York Stock Exchange is so called because it is where buyers and sellers meet to exchange ownership of shares. When you buy a share of stock, you are obtaining someone else's stock, and someone else obtaining your cash in exchange. Buyers and sellers are exchanging ownership of assets by allocating their savings to specific instruments. You can think of primary markets as the place where investment is made to provide firms with capital for future production, and you can think of secondary markets as the place where savers reallocate their savings by exchanging financial assets.

A SIMPLE CONSUMPTION, PRODUCTION, AND SAVING SYSTEM

Let me give you a real-world example to illustrate how the pieces of the puzzle work here. First I'll explain exactly how a firm goes about operating—how it produces goods and services, how its consumers consume, how the business generates a profit, how it grows, and how others can benefit from either investing in the corporation or allocating their savings to it.

Step 1—Starting a company. My friends and I are creating a corporation that hopes to produce computers. So we file regulatory documents, name the corporation (call it MacroSoft), and start operating out of my garage. We have great ideas for designing the software and hardware for these computers (we'll just copy the hardware design from the Granny Smith Corporation), but we don't have the capital to begin building the computers. So we need to raise capital.

Step 2—Raising capital. Assume we have $10,000 that we've invested in the company ourselves, but we think it will take $20,000 to build the first few computers to sell and comfortably manage the first year of operations. So we need to convince someone else to give us $10,000 more.

We could raise capital in a number of different ways. The most common way is to obtain a bank loan. But banks don't generally like to loan money to a new company with no revenues and no collateral, so we will look elsewhere. We'll start by selling corporate debt to private investors. We convince our friend Gill Bates to provide $2,500 at a rate of 10 percent ($250) interest per year for one year. But we're still $7,500 short of our capital-raising goal. We are worried we can't afford the interest payments on $7,500 more in corporate debt, so we decide to sell part of the company. We decide to raise money by selling equity in the firm, and someone named Allen Paul agrees to provide $7,500 in exchange for 37.5 percent of the company. This is a less risky way to raise capital now (because the 10 percent interest rate is expensive) but could turn out to be a more expensive option if our company is wildly successful (because that 37.5 percent ownership is an ownership share we are foregoing). So, now we have our $20,000 in cash as well as $20,000 in outstanding securities ($2,500 in corporate debt and $17,500 in private stock—we still own 62.5 percent of the company, but that's not important for now).

Step 3—Understanding our corporate balance sheet. Because money is a record of account (see chapter 1), my friends and I will have to understand basic accounting in order to understand how money works. A sound understanding of modern money requires a basic understanding of accounting.

From here we can begin to see what our corporation looks like on paper before it has actually produced anything. A simple balance sheet shows our assets, liabilities, and net worth, as shown in Figure 3.1.

Assets–liabilities = net worth (shareholders' equity). That's simple, right? Balance sheets must balance. Our simple balance sheet shows total assets of $20,000 in cash, $2,500 in corporate debt, and $17,500 in shareholders' equity (which includes our initial $10,000 investment in addition to Allen Paul's $7,500 investment). *Shareholders' equity,* another term for *net worth,* is the shareholders' claims on the company's assets. If we sell the business today and pay off all creditors, the shareholders' equity is what would be left over.

Step 4—Starting operations. To start operations we need to invest in any supplies that will go into the production process. Say we purchase a production line for $1,000 and install it in my garage. This is a fixed asset for our business. We also need any supplies that will go into the actual production of the computers. Say these supplies cost $5,000. After all these investments our balance sheet looks like Figure 3.2.

Figure 3.1: MacroSoft Balance Sheet—Raising Money

Assets		Liabilities	
Cash	$20,000	Corporate Debt	$2,500
		Shareholders' Equity	$17,500

Figure 3.2: MacroSoft Balance Sheet—Starting Operations

Assets		Liabilities	
Cash	$14,000	Corporate Debt	$2,500
Fixed Assets	$1,000	Shareholders' Equity	$17,500
Supplies	$5,000		

Step 5—Generating income and understanding the income statement. We make some simple assumptions about how our business operates in year one. We produce and sell 20 computers at a price of $2,000 each, and each computer costs us $250 to make. We have no employees other than ourselves, so we're building the computers, and only our labor goes into developing the final product. Being an entrepreneur isn't always easy.

Now we can look at another important accounting statement, our income statement, which shows the revenues, costs, and profits for our business in the current period (see Figure 3.3).

We have revenues of $40,000 from selling 20 units at $2,000 each. We also have $5,000 in expenses from the cost of production ($250 for each of 20 units) and interest expense of $250 (don't forget the debt we sold to fund the company). So we have pretax earnings of $34,750 after year one. Nothing too complex here so far, but I've covered a lot of the basics. We've invested in our future production, we've raised capital from outside investors, we've produced goods (supply), and we've seen

Figure 3.3: MacroSoft Income Statement

20 Units at $2,000 Each	
Revenues	$40,000
Minus	
Cost of Goods Sold	$5,000
Interest Expense	$250
Pre-Tax Earnings	**$34,750**

how our consumers (demand) are essential to our success. Now it's time to look for the exit strategy from this successful business.

Stage 6—Selling on the secondary market. At this point we've had a pretty good run with our business. We've been around for only one year, but we've created a product that generated a profit, helped people enhance their lives, and made the owners of the company better off. So let's cash out. If we look at our balance sheet now, it looks like Figure 3.4.

Remember, we began with $20,000 in cash and invested $6,000 in the production line and supplies to build our computers. Those supplies went out the door in the final product, but the fixed asset in the production line remains part of the business (ignore depreciation for now since that just muddies things). So we now have $14,000 in cash ($20,000–$6,000) *plus* the $1,000 production line *minus* the interest expense of $250 paid to our bond investor *plus* the final annual revenue of $40,000. So our balance sheet after year one shows $53,750 in cash,

Figure 3.4: MacroSoft Balance Sheet—One Year Later

Assets		Liabilities	
Cash	$53,750	Corporate Debt	$2,500
Fixed Assets	$1,000	Shareholders' Equity	
		Capital Stock	$17,500
		Retained Earnings	$34,750

$1,000 in fixed assets, $2,500 in corporate debt, retained earnings of $34,750, and our original capital stock of $17,500. This leaves us with total assets of $54,750, liabilities of $2,500, and, once we pay back our corporate debt, shareholders' equity of $52,250 (assets–liabilities = net worth). In other words, if we sold the whole business today and paid back our debtors, the shareholders would get $52,250 to divide among themselves. Not bad.

In order to cash out we might sell our shares to someone else in a secondary market. In doing so we would simply be exchanging the existing ownership claim in the business for money from whomever becomes the new owner. The new owner, however, is not injecting new capital into the firm. The new owner, Tony, is simply reallocating his cash into the stock of this company, and we are reallocating our stock into cash. We've exchanged stock for cash, and Tony has exchanged cash for stock. Tony is not an investor in the traditional sense of the word. He is merely allocating his savings. It's that simple.

Before I conclude here, I want to revisit an earlier discussion. Remember when my friends and I sold the corporate debt and the equity to fund the firm? We sold 37.5 percent of the company to an equity investor because we were worried that the debt might be too expensive. That debt ended up costing us $250 during the one year. But when we sold the company, we paid out 37.5 percent to our equity owner. That means 37.5 percent could have gone to us if we'd been willing to sell more corporate debt. In other words, the equity cost the founders quite a bit of money.

This simple business shows how investment works (spending to generate future production) and how consumption works (someone had to buy the computers). It also illustrates the workings of a primary market, whereby some investors seeded capital to help us start our company. And the business demonstrates how a secondary market works: the ownership of the business changed hands, and a reallocation of savings occurred.

SAVER OR INVESTOR? WHICH ONE ARE YOU?

When confronting the world of money and how you will participate in the economy, nothing is more important than understanding when you are an investor, when you are a saver, or when you are both. *Remember: Real investors seed future production by providing capital for future production. Savers merely allocate their unconsumed income to financial assets.*

When you think about your overall portfolio, you should try to think of your asset allocation in terms of this breakdown. If you are a true investor in the sense that you seed capital for the purpose of future production, you're playing a different role than someone who is simply exchanging shares on a secondary market and allocating savings. It's a nuanced point but an important one that will guide your understanding of how you obtain money, how you use it, and how you protect it. Figuring out whether you're an investor, saver, or both is how you'll make many of your most important financial decisions.

THE BEST INVESTMENT YOU'LL EVER MAKE

Most of us go through life thinking of investing as something you do in the stock market or in other companies. We don't always think of it as something personal. But the reality is that the best financial investment most of us will ever make is in our own future production. The key to understanding our value in a monetary system is understanding how each of us is uniquely valuable to other people. In this interconnected monetary world we all have something that other people can find value in. And one thing you have to figure out is what that means to you. Of course it means different things to different people. We all have different talents and different specialties. The best investment you'll ever make is in trying to understand and maximize the value you can contribute to other people.

A capitalist system is often portrayed as an individualistic and selfish construct. But I think the best capitalist systems are those built on the simple understanding that we serve ourselves best by serving others. This means that most of us will make our true investments in things like our educations, skills, training, and so on so we can provide something even more valuable to others. This is where we will spend our own capital in the hope of generating future production.

This future production will generate an income that finds its way into a repository we call our savings. From there we need to decide how we will spend that capital. Will we simply consume it all on goods and services? Will we invest it in the hope of generating future production? Or will we simply allocate it to existing assets in the hope of protecting it? Answering these questions is personal, something each of us needs to explore on our own. Some of us will choose to maximize our investment in our primary expertise while choosing to allocate our savings in a prudent and methodical manner, whereas others might choose to use their savings for purposes that more closely resemble pure investment. But remember: your income is your monetary lifeblood. So before you go thinking that the best investment you'll ever make is in shares on a stock exchange or in instruments issued by some other entity, first consider that the best investment you'll ever make is in yourself.

UNDERSTANDING YOUR TOTAL PORTFOLIO

By now I hope you're beginning to see why I stress the difference between saving and investing. Investing, the pursuit of generating future production by spending your capital, can be highly rewarding but can also be dangerous in many cases because it often involves fronting our own capital for this future production.

Most of us are already making investments in ourselves over time and are generating an income stream that helps us build savings. We invest in ourselves to maximize our future production. We are experts in something in which we have made these real investments. So we have to understand how we then decide to allocate our capital in what I like to think of as a "total portfolio." You should think of your personal balance sheet and income statement in much the same way our computer company built its accounting records. I want you to think about your primary source of income, your expenses, and your bottom line as though you are a business that comprises a flow through a "total portfolio."

From there the question you need to ask is how you think it's most prudent to go about allocating your assets so that they can help you achieve particular goals. For most of us the goal is rather simple. We are trying to maximize our income by making sound investments in our primary expertise. If you're a doctor, you should invest in becoming the best doctor. If you're a teacher, you should invest in becoming the best teacher. You get the point. This is how most of us maximize our financial wealth. In fact, if you look at the list of the wealthiest people in the world, you'll find that an overwhelming majority are on that list because they maximized a personal expertise. Many own their own companies or helped build companies that produced something extraordinary. These people made huge investments in themselves and were rewarded by providing something other people found value in.

When thinking about this total portfolio, you should think about the role various financial assets play in your life and how they can help you achieve particular goals. I want you to think of the things you make real investments in, like your primary area of expertise, as your investment portfolio. And I want you to think of your savings as a savings portfolio. *Your investment portfolio is the portion you're willing to invest in your personal area of expertise.* This could even include a side passion of yours that you feel confident pursuing. It's important to note

Figure 3.5: The Flow of Funds Through the Total Portfolio

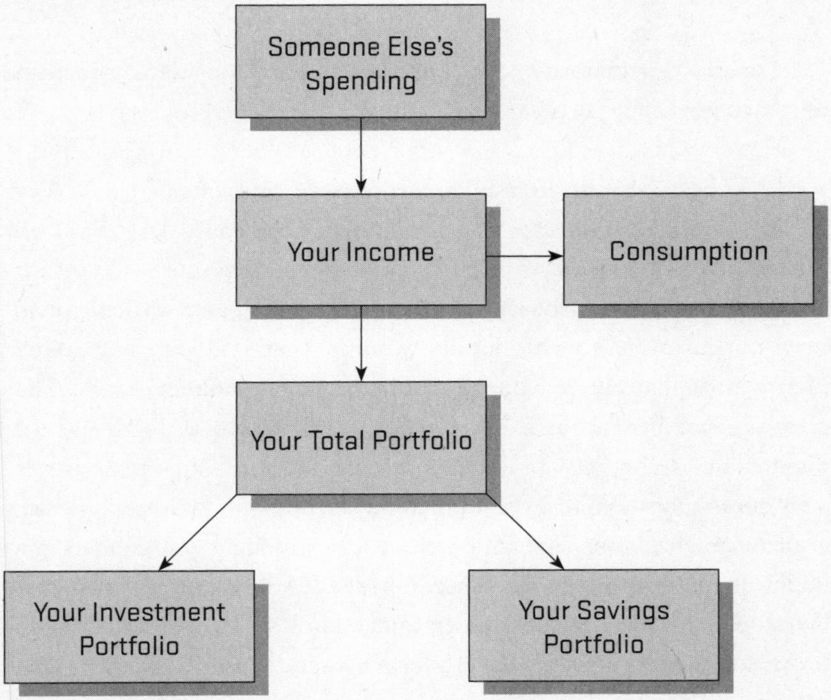

that you should be willing to forgo a substantial portion of this. These are the funds that are most likely to generate the highest personal return for you. The savings portfolio is different. *Your savings portfolio is money set aside for specific future requirements and must be available at specific dates in the future. These funds should be allocated in a fairly safe manner to ensure that they will be there when you need them.* How you allocate this total portfolio depends entirely on who you are and what your goals are. Many of you could find that your investment and savings portfolios overlap, but try your best to break them down individually, as in Figure 3.5.

As I've already stated, most of us are making our most important investment in our primary source of income. If we can maximize and generate a substantial return on that primary income source, our residual of savings begins to serve a different purpose, allowing us to better allocate funds for our savings portfolio and better plan for future needs.

Our investment portfolio has one primary goal:

To help maximize future production.

For the vast majority of us our savings portfolio needs to achieve only two goals:

To protect us from the loss of purchasing power.
To protect us from permanent loss of funds.

The mistake many of us make is assuming that our savings portfolio *is* our investment portfolio, and we improperly allocate our savings in a manner that exposes our portfolios to huge amounts of risk. That creates instability in our lives and our overall portfolios. This in turns disrupts our ability to plan for the future and creates unnecessary stress. This doesn't mean your savings portfolio is a no-risk portfolio. It doesn't even mean that your savings portfolio can't include components that might be investments (for instance, a hedge fund making private equity investments). It just means that to understand the proper construction process for a portfolio, it helps to have a sound understanding of what savings and investment are. Then you can apply these concepts properly to your personal portfolio's needs and goals.

A concept you'll see repeated in this book is the idea of the "optionality of cash." Warren Buffett has said that cash should be thought of as a call option with no expiration date.[1] In other words, cash is something that gives you flexibility to exercise new ideas, whether you are making a true investment in the sense that it might generate future production, or whether you are allocating your savings. One primary goal of the total portfolio is to create a cash-flow machine that maximizes the optionality of cash. This is why I focus on the need to make our true investments in our primary form of expertise—because this is where you will most likely maximize the cash flow that is your income. Your investment portfolio is where you will likely generate your highest returns.

By now you're probably curious about how you should go about allocating these assets along these lines, right? After all, most of us are concerned with allocating assets in the secondary markets like the stock markets and bond markets. Not so fast. I've covered a lot of the basics already, but I need to lay the foundation for a better understanding of the markets first. Unfortunately there are many myths about money, finance, and markets, so you need to try to unlearn some things you think you already know.

CHAPTER 4

MARKET MYTHS THAT PERSIST

Progress is the result of building on past ideas—
and sometimes rejecting those ideas.

THE WORLD OF MONEY, FINANCE, AND MARKETS IS HIGHLY SUS-ceptible to misunderstanding by many people because of its emotional ties, our natural behavioral flaws, politics, and even corruption. When I was first getting involved in finance I read all sorts of books that implied that young people can afford to take more risk, but this was precisely the time in my career when I shouldn't have been taking too much risk because I was too ignorant to actually understand the risks I was taking. I fell for a classic financial myth that caused me unnecessary financial harm. Unfortunately, myths don't only hurt us when we're young, but often hurt us throughout our financial lives. But we don't have to fall for all the myths and misunderstandings out there. By approaching money, finance, and markets through a less-biased and apolitical perspective, we can, I hope, view the world through a more rational and reasonable lens. In this chapter I shed light on some myths that drive market perception and actions.

MYTH 1—YOU TOO CAN BECOME WARREN BUFFETT

Few myths in the world of finance are more pernicious than the many that surround the career of Warren Buffett. Buffett is the most glorified and respected investor of all time. After all, it's widely believed that he became the world's wealthiest man essentially by picking stocks. But Buffett is also remarkably misunderstood by the general public. I personally believe the myth of Warren Buffett is one of the greatest misconceptions in the financial world.

To most people Buffett is a folksy, frugal, regular old guy who just has a knack for picking stocks. He works hard at finding value stocks and then just let's them run forever, right? It's the old myth that you can buy what you know (say, Coca-Cola because you like Cherry Coke or American Express because you like its credit cards), go through the annual report, plop down a portion of your savings to buy common stock, and watch the money grow through the roof. Well, nothing could be further from the truth, and here we sit with an entire generation that believes the simplistic approaches of value investing or buy and hold are the best ways to accumulate wealth in the market. Contrary to popular mythology, Buffett is an exceedingly sophisticated businessman. In order for you to understand how dangerous the myth of the folksy Buffett is, I have to dive deep into Buffett's story.

To a large extent the myth of Warren Buffett has fed a stock market boom as a generation of Americans has aspired to become rich in the stock market. And who better to sell this idea than financial firms? After all, a quick allocation in a plain vanilla value fund will get you a near-replica of the Warren Buffett approach to value investing, right? Or, maybe better yet, reading six months of *Wall Street Journal* and reviewing the P/E ratios of your favorite local public companies will send you on your way to successful retirement.

By oversimplifying this glorified investor named Buffett the general public gets the false perception that portfolio management is so easy a caveman can do it. And so we see commercials with babies trading from their cribs and middle-aged men trading an account in their free time. And an army of Americans pour money and fees into brokerage firms trying to replicate something that cannot be replicated. Financial firms want us to believe the myth of Warren Buffett. In fact many of their business models rely on our believing the myth of Warren Buffett.

Let me begin by saying that I have nothing but the utmost respect for Warren Buffett. When I was a young market practitioner, I printed every single one of his annual letters and read every word. It was, and remains the single greatest market education I have ever received. I highly recommend it for anyone who hasn't done so. But in digging deeper I realized that Warren Buffett is so much more than the folksy picker of value stocks portrayed by the media. What he has built is far more complex than that.

In reality Buffett formed one of the original hedge funds in 1956 (Buffett Partnership Ltd.), and he charged fees similar to those he now condemns in modern hedge funds. Most important, though, is that Buffett was more an entrepreneur than a stock picker. Like most of the other people on the Forbes 400 list of wealthiest people, Buffett created wealth by creating his own company. He did not accumulate his wealth in anything that closely resembles what most of us do by opening brokerage accounts and allocating our savings into various assets. Make no mistake: Buffett is an entrepreneur, hedge fund manager, and highly sophisticated businessman.

The original Buffett Partnership fund is especially interesting because of Buffett's recent berating of hedge fund performance and fees. Ironically Buffett Partnership charged a fee of 25 percent of profits exceeding 6 percent in the fund. This is a big part of how Buffett grew his wealth so quickly. He was running a hedge fund no different than today's funds. And it wasn't just some value fund. Buffett often used leverage and at times had his entire fund invested in just a few stocks. One famous position was his purchase of Dempster Mill in which Buffett actually pulled one of the first-known activist hedge fund moves by installing his own management. Buffett, the activist hedge fund manager? That's right. He was one of the first. His purchase of Berkshire Hathaway was quite similar.

Berkshire Hathaway isn't just your average conglomerate. The brilliance behind Buffett's construction of Berkshire is astounding. He effectively used (and uses) Berkshire as the world's largest option-writing house. The premiums and cash flow from his insurance businesses created dividends that he could invest in other businesses. Berkshire essentially became a holding company through which he could run this insurance-writing business while using the cash flow to build a conglomerate. But Buffett wasn't buying just Coca-Cola and Geico. Buffett was engaging in real investment, in many cases by seeding capital and playing a much more active entrepreneurial role in the production process. He also was placing some complex bets (short term and long term) in derivatives markets, options markets, and bond markets, and he often used leverage in the process. The perception that Buffett is a pure stock picker, as many have come to believe, is a myth.

It's also interesting to note that the portfolio of stocks for which he has become famous is the equivalent of about 28 percent of Berkshire's enterprise value as of 2013. His most famous holdings (Coke, American Express, and Moody's Corporations) account for roughly 8 percent of the total market cap. Interestingly two of Buffett's most famous purchases weren't traditional value picks at all but distressed plays. His original purchases of American Express and Geico occurred when both companies were teetering on the edge of insolvency. These deals are more akin to what many modern-day distressed-debt hedge funds do, not what most of us think of as traditional value investing.

Make no mistake—Buffett has the killer instinct prominent in many successful business leaders. Just look at the deal he struck with Goldman Sachs and GE in 2008. He practically stepped on their throats when they needed to raise capital in the depths of the financial crisis, demanded a five-year warrant deal, and profited handsomely. Of course Buffett described the deal as a long-term value play. If a distressed-debt hedge fund (which is a role Berkshire often plays) had made the same move, reporters might have described the fund manager as a thief who was attacking two great American corporations while they were down.

Warren Buffett is a great American and a great business leader, but do your homework before buying into the myth that you will one day sit atop the throne of "world's richest person" by using a strategy that is, in fact, nothing remotely close to what Berkshire and Buffett actually do.

MYTH 2—YOU GET WHAT YOU PAY FOR AND HIGH FEES MEAN GOOD VALUE

There's an old saying: "You get what you pay for." I guess there's some truth to it. The problem is you might pay a certain amount for something that ends up providing far less value than you expect. This is true not only for financial assets but for goods and services as well. And that is oftentimes a problem on Wall Street. We often get far less value from money managers than we should because we're too misinformed to know any better.

Financial Firms Want to Sell You the Ferrari

A big part of the misunderstandings in the world of finance results from the way financial firms sell the concept of investing. They want you to think that you're an investor when you buy stocks or hedge funds, or whatever they're selling, because investing implies high return on capital. If they called it allocating your savings, like I do, it would sound boring. You can't sell boring. So they market it the way you market any lifestyle fantasy product—by referring to it as something that's usually better than it really is. And investing is sexy. But allocating your savings, which is what most of us are doing, is the furthest thing from sexy. It's boring. It's a process. It takes patience. But we live in a world of immediate gratification so financial firms cater to this demand.

It's true that many stocks, and investment vehicles like hedge funds, will generate high returns. Some actually do real investing, as I discussed earlier. But this sales pitch doesn't always communicate the fine print. Financial firms often want to sell you the fast, sleek, compact, unsafe, expensive vehicle. They want you to take your life's savings and your family, pile into the back of a Ferrari, and speed down the road of life at 100 mph. And when you crash or spend exorbitant fees on what often turns out to be a lemon, it will be too late. For most of us our Ferrari is our self. We determine our own performance by becoming an expert in something we're good at. And the income we generate from this expertise is then allocated in a manner in keeping with the more traditional concept of saving. That is, it should be allocated prudently, safely, and inexpensively. In other words most of us should allocate our savings to the safe, unsexy, comfortable, and slower Honda Accord, not the Ferrari.

Many people outsource their savings portfolio to professional money managers who supposedly perform better because, well, they're professionals. But the money management business is just like any other competitive business. Not everyone can be great at it, and often times the people you think are professionals are not really professionals at what they advertise. I spent a brief stint working at insurance firms and the best-known brokerage firm on Wall Street before I started my own firm. Many of you would probably be shocked if I told you that most of these professionals are much closer to car salesmen than financial experts. In fact that's largely what the business of money management is these days. Too often these managers or advisers are selling you something they simply cannot deliver or are not experts in delivering. And the odds are they're charging you far in excess of what it would cost you to make these same investments on your own or through a less expensive alternative.

Research shows that the vast majority of actively managed mutual funds underperform a correlating index.[1] The reality of investment management is that many professional money managers cannot generate high-risk adjusted returns and add little value compared with buying a simple index fund. Those extra fees you're paying are usually a sunk cost. Let's look deeper into the mutual fund industry for clarity on this point. The following is an example of one of the largest mutual funds in the world. This fund manages almost $150 billion (yep, that's *billion*). It's called a large cap growth fund, so the managers build a portfolio of large cap stocks (big companies) that are supposed to be growth companies (companies expected to generate above-average revenues and cash flows). If you compare this fund to a highly correlated index such as the Nasdaq 100 (which is also comprised of large cap growth stocks) you see a similar story, as Figure 4.1 shows.

They're essentially the same funds with the same performance. The kicker is that the growth fund is charging 0.7 percent for its services while you can buy the Nasdaq 100 Exchange Traded Fund for 0.2 percent. In other words, if you owned $100,000 worth of Mutual Fund X, you'd be paying $700 per year, whereas you could buy a similar product for only $200 somewhere else. In the financial business this is called closet indexing. *Closet indexing* is mimicking an index fund and charging a fee in excess of that charged by a correlated index, even though the fund is not adding any value. The growth in a fund like this is all in the size of the management company's fee structure.

This highlights another important point—headline performance, or the annual returns generally cited for a fund, can be deceiving. If, as I've just described, the fund cannot beat a highly correlated index, its headline performance is rather meaningless. If, however, a prospective investor can calculate the fund's quantifiable risk and analyze its unquantifiable risks for real value, the headline performance becomes much more relevant. A part of this can be achieved by understanding how to calculate risk-adjusted return metrics like the Sharpe Ratio or

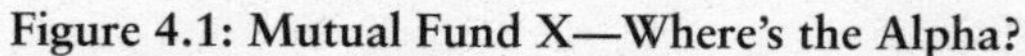

Figure 4.1: Mutual Fund X—Where's the Alpha?

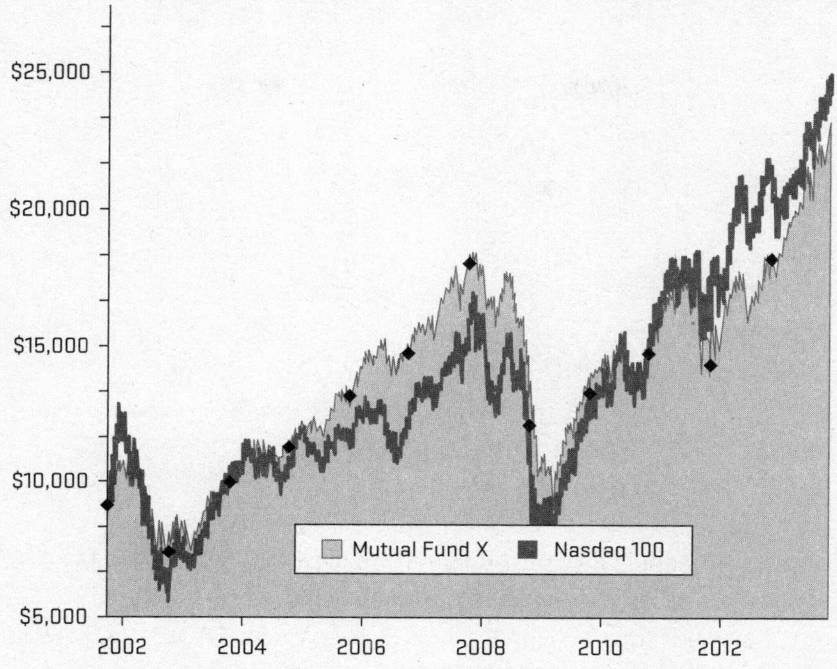

the Sortino Ratio, but even those metrics will fail to provide a comprehensive picture of what's occurring in a portfolio. To fully understand whether a portfolio's returns are contributing real value, you have to look under the hood and understand not only the process by which the returns are generated but also begin to understand how much risk was involved in achieving those returns. The headline performance says little about what a fund is really doing.

Unfortunately the fee structure in the example in Figure 4.1 is on the friendly side for the money management business. The average mutual fund charges 0.9 percent per year, according to *Morningstar Advisor.*[2] That's a whopping fee difference in a world in which the low-fee index fund has become so readily available. To put the fee effect in perspective, assume the S&P 500 generates a 7 percent annualized return for the next 30 years. If you purchased $100,000 of the average large cap fund that mimics the S&P 500 and paid 0.9 percent in fees each year for 30 years, you would end up with compound returns that were almost $150,000

Figure 4.2: The Adverse Fee Effect

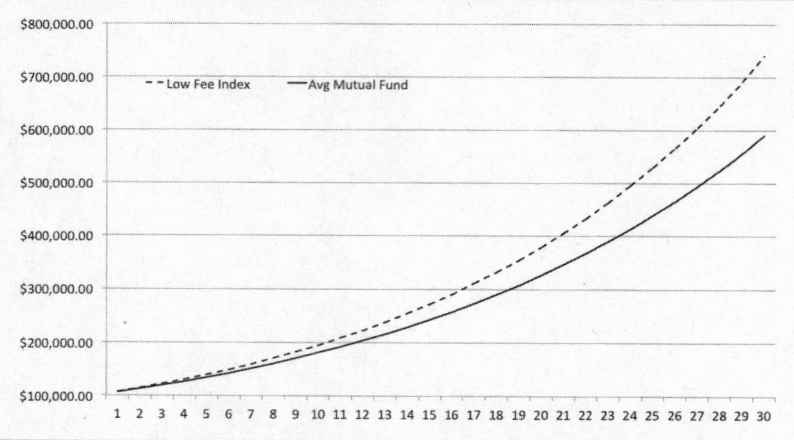

lower than owning exactly the same Vanguard 500 fund with a 0.1 percent expense ratio. In other words you would end up with $590,000 in the average large cap fund, whereas your Vanguard 500 fund ended up with $740,000. See Figure 4.2. Do you think a fund manager deserves 23 percent of your total gains ($150,000) just for copying an index fund? I don't.

Hedge funds are beginning to see similar trends with underperformance as the industry grows in size and more funds compete for excess returns. Most hedge funds once generated real value and could charge higher fees because they were truly providing something unique. But that's not true for the industry as a whole today. In addition to lackluster performance in recent years, the industry has also suffered from the same problem many mutual funds suffer from: they're simply closet indexers. The correlation between hedge funds and the S&P 500 has soared to almost 90 percent in recent years (see Figure 4.3). And while we can't be certain this will persist, it is likely to remain true for the majority of the industry as the number of funds continues to grow and competition for outperformance turns more and more strategies into a blend of something that looks pretty uniform across these funds.

When you look at the actual performance of hedge funds, you can see what has resulted from the increased competition and overlapping of strategies as more managers fight for the same alpha (excess return).

Figure 4.3: Correlation between Hedge Fund Performance and S&P 500

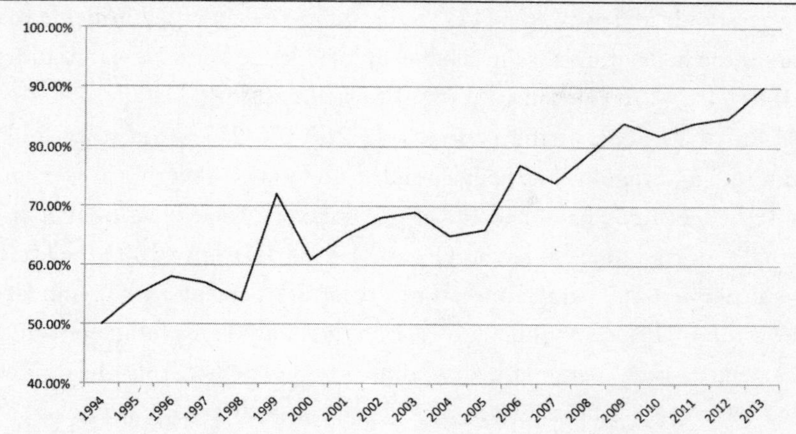

Source: Jacob Wolinsky, "Hedge Fund Alpha Is Negative," Valuewalk.com, July 11, 2013, http://www.valuewalk.com/2013/07/hedge-fund-alpha-negative/.

Figure 4.4: Growth of $10,000: Invested in Various Instruments, 1993–2013

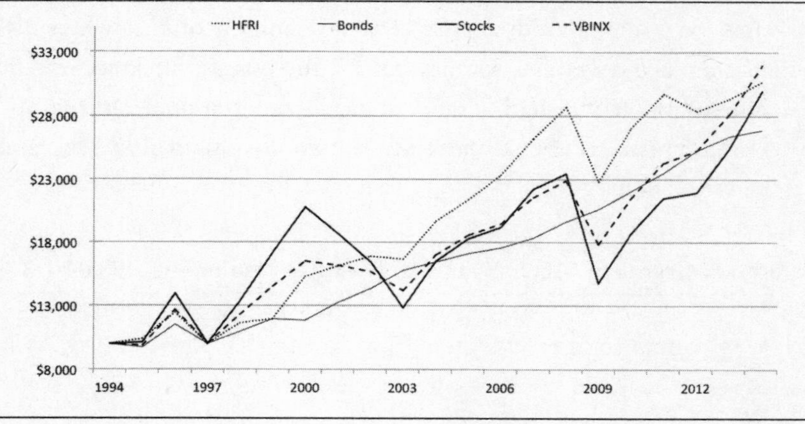

In hindsight hedge fund performance since 1994 looks quite favorable (see Figure 4.4). With a standard deviation (variance from the average) of just 10.5, hedge funds generated an average annualized return of 8.4 percent. The bond aggregate generated a return of 6 percent with a standard deviation of just 4.6. And equities generated a 10.4 percent return with a 19.17 standard deviation. The Vanguard Balanced Index (a 60–40 stock-bond fund) generated an average return of 8.57 percent with a standard deviation of 12. So this quick review of quantifiable risk makes the hedge funds, as measured by the Hedge Fund Research Index (HFRI), look pretty good on a risk-adjusted basis.

But if we look at the period from 2003 to 2013, the story looks quite a bit different. As hedge fund correlations have narrowed and more hedge funds have become closet indexers, their performance has actually started to lag substantially, see Figure 4.5. Since 2003 the HFRI has generated an average annual return of 6.2 percent with a standard deviation of 11. The bond aggregate has generated an average return of 4.9 percent with a standard deviation of 1.8. The S&P 500 has generated an average annual return of 9.7 percent with a standard deviation of 17.6. And the Vanguard Balanced Index has generated an 8.3 percent annual return with a standard deviation of 11.4. In other words, for just a bit more quantifiable risk, the Vanguard Balanced Index has generated a 2.1 percent greater annual return.

I should note that reviewing quantifiable risk is an extremely imprecise way to understand a fund's actual risks. For instance, Figures 4.4 and 4.5 are analyzed using a simple definition of risk where risk equals standard deviation. But does this really quantify risk accurately? Of course not. If you had a fund that generated annual returns of 5 percent, 25 percent, and 30 percent, and another fund that generated

Figure 4.5: Growth of $10,000: Invested in Various Instruments, 2003–2013

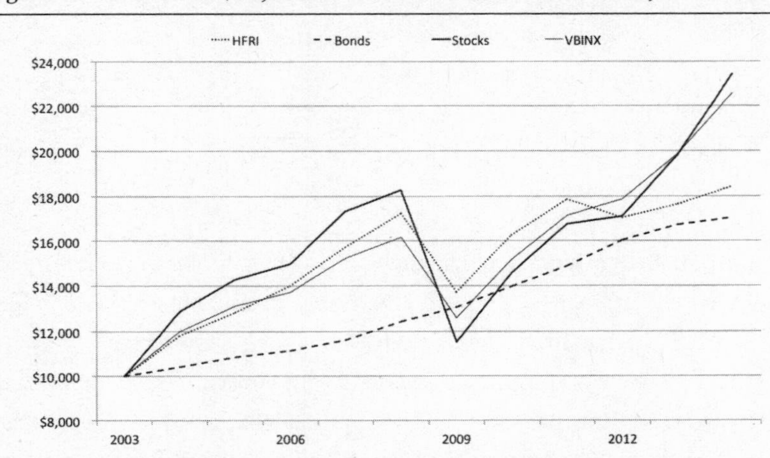

returns of 5 percent, –5 percent, and 5 percent, you might conclude that the first option is worse than the second option simply because standard deviation variance says so. But this ignores the actual risk that most real portfolios face—the risk of permanent loss. In fact the second portfolio exposes you to greater downside loss. This is just one of the flaws in relying on a measure like standard deviation for risk. There are risk-adjusted measures that correct for this (like the Sortino Ratio or the SDR Sharpe Ratio), but even these metrics can be flawed because they ultimately are on a fool's errand of overanalyzing past returns—and we must never forget the age-old rule that past performance is not indicative of future returns. But the point about quantifiable risk doesn't necessarily alter your conclusions about hedge fund performance because the real risks in hedge funds are often unquantifiable.

Unquantifiable Risks in Hedge Funds

In addition to the growing competition for performance between hedge funds, I think there are growing unquantifiable risks as well. These risks will become especially pervasive in the coming decades because hedge funds are now allowed to advertise to the general public. This highlights one major risk that no calculation can quantify—fraud. I think we're likely to see an increasing amount of hedge fund fraud in the coming decades.

Other risks in hedge funds are not always as prevalent in other investment vehicles. Those risks include:

1. *Leverage*—Most hedge funds use a fair amount of leverage, often disguised as a sort of hedging mechanism. But as Long-Term Capital Management proved in 1998, leverage is a beast that cannot always be corralled. This creates substantial risk for outlier events.
2. *Tail risk*—Hedge funds often engage in strategies that are rather opaque and undiversified, and expose the funds to excessive tail risk (tail risk is the risk of a 3 standard deviation event, or, more simply, the risk of an extreme outlier occurrence).
3. *Illiquidity*—Hedge funds generally require a lock-up period. You cannot necessarily access your funds on demand.

Additionally many hedge funds trade illiquid markets, reducing flexibility and stability in their asset holdings.

4. *Real, real return risk*—In addition to high fees, hedge funds are often extremely tax inefficient. This not only results in lower real, real returns but also creates a headache because of the many added filing requirements (real, real returns are your "in-pocket" returns, which include taxes, fees, and inflation).

Mutual funds and hedge funds once generated a fair amount of alpha, but as the asset management business has grown, good funds have become much more difficult to find. You have to be extremely careful about how you analyze a fund, an adviser, or a strategy before allocating your money there. I spend much of my time analyzing other managers and auditing their work. It's not easy to analyze a fund, but it's worth the effort. Real value adds are out there. Don't get me wrong. I am not saying that all portfolio managers or advisers are not adding value to your portfolio. But you have to do your homework and be wary of anyone who promises you something that sounds too good to be true.

MYTH 3—FOCUSING ON EITHER TECHNICALS OR FUNDAMENTALS IS THE OPTIMAL STRATEGY

There's a great deal of debate within portfolio management circles about the ideal way to go about constructing portfolios. The various approaches to portfolio construction tend to have two dominant themes—technical analysis and fundamental analysis. Technicians can be broken down into two different groups. The chartists use charts and graphical representations of the market to attempt to decipher future market performance. The pure technicians study data on past performance to attempt to decipher future market performance. On the other side of this debate sits the fundamentalists, or those who look at the underlying fundamentals of firms, entities, and assets to try to decipher future market performance. These strategists try to look at income statements, balance sheets, and corporate fundamentals in order to predict future price movements.

The reality of the market is that there is no holy grail. No single approach will necessarily help you outperform the market. Anyone who thinks it is possible to simply look at a chart of past security performance is likely suffering from an extreme case of recency bias, that is, they're just extrapolating the recent performance of an asset out into the future. After all, charts are just visual representations of an asset's past performance and may or may not tell you something about its future performance. Unfortunately simply trying to guess the future performance of corporate fundamentals doesn't leave us with a much better alternative. The debate about technicals versus fundamentals is essentially choosing between a rearview mirror and a crystal ball. And neither one will necessarily help us predict the future.

What this view ultimately comes down to is an inherent choice between two biases. Do you prefer to look at the past instead of the future? Are you using a rearview mirror approach or looking out the windshield into the future? The answer is a blend of the two. I believe that understanding the past is crucial to understanding how any nonlinear dynamic system performs and operates. The trick is to understand and learn from the past but not rely entirely on it. Additionally, as I started to discuss in Chapters 1 to 3, fundamentals help us understand why the monetary machine operates in a certain way. Understanding basic accounting and how to analyze a corporate financial statement can be an extremely valuable way of understanding the world. So portfolio construction isn't about choosing between the crystal ball or the rearview mirror. Portfolio construction is a process of understanding how to design a portfolio by understanding the operational role that different assets and instruments might play in a portfolio. That includes an understanding of the past as well as an understanding of operational realities and how certain instruments are likely to perform in the future.

The bottom line is that neither technicians nor fundamentalists have all the answers. But by studying both approaches you can acquire an understanding of the way the monetary machine operates and how you might build an approach to benefit from it. But be careful of falling into the dogmatic perspective that one of these groups has all the right answers. They probably don't.

MYTH 4—PASSIVE PORTFOLIO MANAGEMENT IS BETTER THAN ACTIVE PORTFOLIO MANAGEMENT

A never-ending debate rages in financial circles. The so-called passive managers and active managers are always trying to undermine each other's approach. Is it better to be an active trader or is it better to be more hands off with your portfolio? Is it better to be passive within a portfolio or is it better to be active?

Passive investing is traditionally understood as an approach to asset allocation that tries to avoid forecasting the market's future moves by aligning your asset composition with broad indexes in a low-fee environment with relatively limited ongoing portfolio interaction. *Active investing* is an attempt to forecast the future and benefit from those forecasts through ongoing trades and portfolio changes. I think the differentiation between active and passive is often a distinction without a difference, and this debate ends up causing a lot of unnecessary confusion.

The reality of the market is that we are all active to some degree. If you decide to allocate a lump sum in the markets in a buy-and-hold strategy, an element of timing is involved. If you dollar-cost average or reinvest dividends, you are essentially timing the market. If you rebalance your portfolio once a quarter or once a year, you are essentially timing the market. If you alter your portfolio approach as you age, you are essentially timing the market. And obviously if you are a trader, you are timing the market all the time. All these approaches have elements of active management in them. The thing is, some are less active than others, but they are simply a different breed of active management. I don't find the line in the sand between active and passive to be particularly helpful because it doesn't reflect the active reality of portfolio maintenance and the process we go through in the real world.

The reality is that we are all active managers to some degree. And the question boils down to, how active should we be to allocate our assets in the most efficient way? This gets to the crux of the debate, and I would argue that, in general, the fewer frictions (costs and churn) we can create in a portfolio, the better. After all, the sad math of the market is that, in the aggregate, we are all the market by definition. After taxes and fees the average less-active manager will outperform the average more-active manager. As a general rule of thumb you should always seek ways to reduce frictions and calculate your expenses meticulously. This doesn't mean more active approaches cannot ever add value, but in general we are better off allocating our savings in highly tax-efficient and fee-efficient ways in order to reduce the frictions that can contribute to portfolio degradation. More-active managers can and will add value to certain portfolios in many different ways. But in evaluating a portfolio or a manager it is necessary to dig deeper than simply claiming that an explicit distinction exists between active and passive management when there is a large gray area.

Perhaps most important, however, is the misconception that a passive approach doesn't involve any forecasting. I find this wildly misleading. The usual index fund participant is allocating assets in a low-fee manner into a buy and hold portfolio approach. That is, they're usually buying assets based on the idea that those assets are likely to appreciate if given enough time. As I've stressed, this is usually a pretty good bet. But don't confuse this with a forecast-free view of the world. Passive investing is what I call lazy macroeconomics. I don't use the word *lazy* in a pejorative sense. Rather, I am simply pointing out that the average passive investor is making an explicitly bullish macroeconomic forecast about future market growth and economic growth and is allocating assets in a low-fee and efficient manner in order to benefit from what has proved to be a reliable long-term trend. Most index funds are actually macroeconomic funds in a pure sense because they're broadly allocated aggregates designed around a (usually implicit) bullish macroeconomic forecast. But make no mistake—this is definitely a forecast, whether you think it through or are just betting on what appears to you to be common sense.

The view that you're either active or passive is an attempt to create a dividing line that doesn't really exist and leads to a dogmatic rejection of anything resembling the other side. The truth, as is often the case, lies in-between. A better understanding of active and passive investing reveals the flaws and errors in both and therefore leads to a more balanced perspective.

MYTH 5—THE STOCK MARKET WILL MAKE YOU RICH

Many people believe the stock market returns 10 to 12 percent per year and that they can outperform even this lofty figure. The reality is that the stock market returns about 8 percent per year after adjusting for inflation, and that's an index of the best companies in the world (for instance, the S&P 500 is arguably the 500 greatest companies in the world out of *millions*). If you tack on the average mutual fund fee of 0.9 percent and the long-term capital gains tax, your real, real return comes out to about 6 percent. That's *half* of what is widely reported in the mainstream media, but this is the actual return you're likely to see in your account (as opposed to the fictitious double-digit figure that is so often assumed). The point is that the stock market isn't likely to make you as fabulously rich as many of us assume.

But more important is that this mentality of becoming the next Warren Buffett puts the cart before the horse. A savings portfolio is what economists call a stock that flows from your income. In other words your income is the flow of funds, some portion of which you then allocate to a stock of assets such as equities, fixed income, and the like. Your primary source of income (your day job) is how most of us are likely to get rich. For most of us our portfolio is simply a repository that protects our financial wealth from the risk of permanent loss and loss of purchasing power. Thinking your portfolio is where you "get rich" is backward thinking. It's true that you *might* get rich by buying stocks, but the overwhelming majority of us are much more likely to get rich by focusing on our primary source of income.

What's important to understand, again, is the difference between your investment portfolio and your savings portfolio. The sum of these portfolios comprises your total portfolio, and you have to decide how you're going to allocate your assets to achieve your personal goals. It's true that you could get rich by investing in your education or starting your own company. You might even invest in private equity, thereby helping startups that make you rich as a result. Or you might buy restaurant franchises in the hope of increasing the production of the chain in the future. There are lots of ways you can invest in the hope of increasing your future wealth. But I think it's crucial to understand that your savings portfolio is designed to be there when you need it. Your savings portfolio is not where you get rich. It is where you protect against the risks of losing purchasing power and permanent loss of money. Most of us who allocate assets to the stock market are simply allocating our savings. But we often confuse our savings portfolio with our investment portfolio, a mistake that exposes us to risks that are often unnecessary or inappropriate.

When you think of the market and how you allocate assets, I want you to be precise about how you go about allocating these assets. Don't confuse your savings portfolio with your investment portfolio. And never, ever forget that the best investment you'll make is in yourself. Saving in the markets is important, but invest in yourself first. It will be your best return on investment.

MYTH 6—YOU HAVE TO BEAT THE MARKET

If you turn on financial TV or the evening news, commentators are likely to quote the daily action in the Dow Jones Industrial Average or the S&P 500 index. If you're a professional portfolio manager, you probably are benchmarked and compared to these indexes regularly. We're constantly being compared to these indexes and browbeaten with the idea that we have to beat the market. This has become the hurdle for almost anyone who purchases financial assets. But do we really have to beat the market, or is this just an insurmountable and unnecessary hurdle that the media have sold us?

The reality is that the S&P 500 is five hundred of the world's greatest corporations. Of the millions of corporations in the world, these are five hundred of the most powerful and dominant firms. It is, in many ways, an all-star team of corporations. Can you imagine telling your son or daughter that they're underperforming if they cannot perform better than the all-star team?

More important, most of us really don't need to beat the market. Most of us are just looking to maximize our primary source of income and allocate our savings in a way that helps us maintain our purchasing power while protecting us from permanent loss of capital. It would be nice if we could all generate returns in excess of 10 percent on our savings every year, but the reality is that you don't need to do that, and to achieve those kinds of returns you probably need to expose your savings to excessive risk. For most of us this is entirely inappropriate. Beating the market would be nice, but it's not necessary. And you're certainly not a loser if you underperform or perform in line with the S&P 500. In fact, if you know how to calculate your risk-adjusted returns, you might be doing extremely well despite underperforming the market in nominal terms.

Unfortunately this beat-the-market pursuit causes a great deal of unnecessary portfolio degradation. A 2011 research study, "The Behavior of Individual Investors," found the following:

- Individuals tend to underperform in relation to standard benchmarks.
- Individuals tend to sell winners and hold losers, which creates tax inefficiency.
- Individuals tend to misunderstand diversification.
- Individuals are unaware that their performance is poor on a relative basis.[3]

Trying to beat the market is actually more detrimental than we think. More important is that most of us are going through life trying to get from point A to point B in the most prudent way possible. We aren't looking to jam our kids in the backseat of a Ferrari and go speeding off at 120 mph while shelling out hundreds of thousands in fees as we go. We want safety, comfort, reasonable expenses, and something that will get us from point A to point B without exposing the whole family to huge amounts of risk. The reality is that you don't need to beat the market. In fact trying to do so could be bad for your wealth.

MYTH 7—THE NEXT BIG THING WILL MAKE YOU RICH

As market participants we're constantly barraged by the idea of catching the next big thing. We all dream of being among the first to buy shares in the next Microsoft or Apple and striking it rich. Even worse, we're sold the idea that there is some sort of strategy or approach that will provide us with market-beating returns, thereby leading us to riches. This search often is a risky and expensive one. And the sad reality of the market is that this holy grail simply does not exist, and the odds of your getting in on the ground floor are extremely low.

The market is made up of millions of corporations all issuing securities in the hope that they will maximize future production and be able to generate future profits. All the companies on a stock exchange these days have gone through a fantastic growth phase, from a handful of employees to meeting the strict listing requirements of a major market exchange. If you were among the founders or original investors in the firm, you've likely experienced substantial growth in your own personal net worth, and you've been rewarded for having created future production from little or nothing. By the time most of these companies go public and issue shares on large exchanges, where we can actually allocate our savings, the biggest gains have been made. And when they go public, it's often because the owners are cashing in their great personal investment. This doesn't mean the firm is no longer capable of generating higher future returns. It just means that you're buying what was really someone else's investment.

In addition we tend to see the next big thing only after it has become the next big thing. Because of our behavioral biases most of us tend not to see the next big opportunities in financial markets until they've become obvious. This is a major driving force in the psychology behind market bubbles—we fall victim to our biases and often engage in a market mania only after the market is in the most dangerous phase of its existence. This can actually increase risks in the assets we're involved in by adding to their price unrealistic expectations for the future. Chasing the next big thing can actually create more risk for our portfolio by exposing us to bloated prices based on an unrealistic future.

Secondary markets are developed markets where analysts have scoured companies, information is widely available and stock picking is increasingly competitive. The odds of finding a diamond in the rough are extremely low on a secondary market, so it's better to view secondary markets as the place where savings are allocated rather than the place where you'll find the next big thing. More likely, you'll find the next big thing investing in yourself or scouring primary markets where information is less readily available and competition is lower. Be wary of the idea that you're buying into the next big thing in a secondary market. There's a small chance you actually are, but the odds say you're not.

MYTH 8—STOCKS FOR THE LONG RUN IS THE BEST APPROACH

Many people think they can just put a portfolio of stocks on autopilot and never have to pay attention to it again. It's just not that easy, though. Portfolio management is a process that requires structure, periodic maintenance, attention, and some level of forecasting. This doesn't mean you need to trade your savings or rely on overly active managers, but there is a balance between maintaining a portfolio and simply letting it run on autopilot.

Since the mid-1980s it's become widely believed that the best way to construct a portfolio is through the buy-and-hold method, or the stocks-for-the-long-run approach. These are rather inactive approaches to portfolio management. But buy and hold doesn't really apply to most people in a strict sense. The problem with the buy-and-hold view is that most of us cannot realistically buy and hold a portfolio. Let me explain.

The problem with the stocks-for-the-long-run approach is that none of us can really adhere to such a simplistic view of the world. The reason is something I call the intertemporal conundrum. The *intertemporal conundrum* is the problem of time in a portfolio. A portfolio does not have a start date and end date, even though such approaches are usually sold using past performance data that stretch across many life spans. The problem is that our financial lives have lots of start dates and end dates. Most of us accumulate assets during the forty years between our midtwenties and our midsixties. During this period we are constantly encountering times when we must use substantial chunks of our savings for what we might call important life events. You might get married in your twenties. You buy a home in your early thirties. You have children around the same time. You buy the new car in your midthirties. You start planning for the kids' college payments in your forties. You plan for retirement in your fifties. You break a hip in your sixties. You see where I am going with this. Life doesn't start in your twenties and end at sixty-five. *Life happens all the time.* And constructing a portfolio is all about understanding and preparing for this. You have to balance a portfolio and allocate your savings in such a manner that you can create some certainty that it will be there for life's big events.

In addition, we have to recognize that we are indeed forecasting the future when we apply a stocks-for-the-long-run approach to our portfolio. We are making an explicit macroeconomic forecast about the future. That's fine, but we need to understand the potential risks in such a view and the biases that often lead us to believe that this view is always the most rational way to approach markets. In my view the stocks-for-the-long-run mentality tends to veer toward a dogmatic, and at times excessively optimistic, perspective on the future.

Unfortunately this didn't become obvious to many people until 2002 and 2008, when the cracks in the stocks-for-the-long-run mantra were exposed. If you just so happened to be the person sending kids to college in 2008, trying to retire, or planning to purchase a home, and you had your assets allocated along the lines of a simple buy-and-hold approach, you likely had to delay these important events. The point is that we encounter lots of different obstacles along the road of life. Portfolio construction isn't about assuming that we're involved in a marathon. We're actually involved in a series of sprints that comprise what looks like one long race. The concepts of buy and hold or stocks for the long-run sound great in theory, but in reality life just doesn't work out that way.

MYTH 9—COMMODITIES ARE INVESTMENTS

Commodities are raw materials that can be bought and sold for economic purposes. In recent years I've seen portfolio managers increasingly adopt the idea that commodities are forms of investments. I think this concept can be extremely misleading. As I've mentioned before, this depends on what you mean by investment. Are you using gold and other commodities in your end product in the hope of increasing future production? Or are you simply hoarding commodities in the hope that someone will buy them from you at a higher future price? In order to think about this realistically, consider how most commodities influence corporations and relate to prices. When a company uses a commodity such as steel to build a building, the cost of that steel is listed as part of the expense. If for some reason the cost of steel is higher than it was in the past (perhaps there was a supply constraint), the builder will have to increase the price of the end product in order to make a profit in excess of the cost of production. In other words the price of buildings will rise because the price of steel has risen (all else being equal). For this reason commodities tend to correlate closely with the rate of inflation as they represent a large portion of the costs that producers try to pass on to their end buyers. Or, in many cases the commodity is the end product (such as precious metals) so the cost of producing the commodity is simply marked up by the seller's trying to make a profit in excess of the cost of producing or mining that commodity.

Over extremely long periods of time commodities tend to generate low to negative inflation-adjusted returns because commodities are large components of the cost inputs in end products. In other words the commodity component of costs represents a substantial piece of the price

Figure 4.6: Commodity Prices Relative to Inflation (year over year % change)

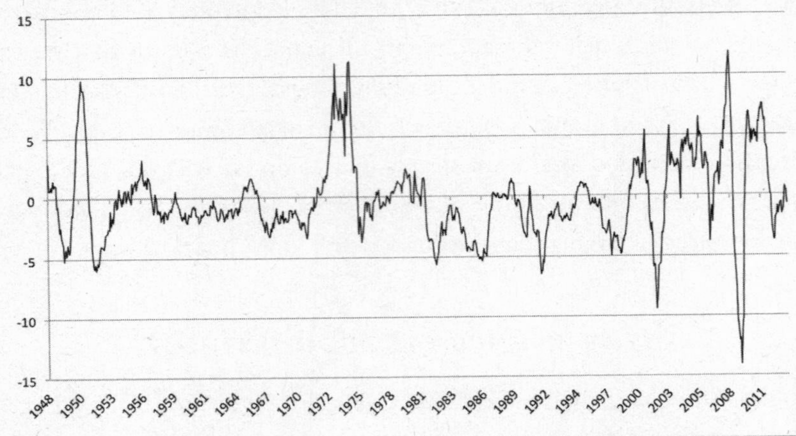

puzzle for most producers. A long-term chart of real commodity prices (Figure 4.6) shows that commodities spend about as much time in the red as they do in the black.

A good question to ask yourself when considering commodities in your portfolio is whether you want to own a barrel of oil or whether you want to own shares in a company that knows how to take that barrel of oil and turn it into something much more valuable. In other words are you someone who bets on innovation and progress or are you someone who bets purely on the supply and demand function of the raw materials we have on the planet? Perhaps you are the latter, but bear in mind that you're making an explicit bet against the innovators in this case. If you think the price of commodities in general will rise, you're making an explicit bet that human beings will not find ways to use commodities more efficiently or, better yet, that we won't find ways to circumvent the need for commodities in many things we use.

A more fundamental problem that has developed in commodities is largely the result of the use of commodities as an alternative allocation asset. Since the mid-1970s the percentage of commodity futures markets attributable to speculators has increased from 25 percent to 45 percent, according to asset management firm GMO.[4] As a result the term structure of commodities futures has led to a much more prevalent contango environment, which means that the contract must be rolled into the next month, thereby creating a negative roll return.[5] As more and more asset managers seek diversification in this asset class, this situation is likely to persist and further erode the return from what is already an asset class with a history of generating a flat real return.

This doesn't mean all commodities will always be a bad bet as there will almost certainly be commodities that rise in value because of sheer scarcity, but as a whole I think it's dangerous to think of commodities as investments because, as an asset class, they tend not to generate a real return over long periods of time. Commodities might provide hedging components in the near term, but I think commodities should not be core holdings in a portfolio.

MYTH 10—YOUR HOUSE IS A GREAT INVESTMENT

According to data from Thornburg Investments, housing returns are barely positive on a real, real return basis.[6] When I say "real, real" return, the calculation includes taxes, fees, and inflation. The real, real return is the return you actually see, not the fictitious textbook return that many use. Since about the mid-1980s housing in the United States has generated a real, real return of just 0.74 percent per year. That's substantially lower than US large cap stocks over the same period (5.79 percent) and long-term government bonds (3.38 percent). But is this really surprising? After all, most of us don't really calculate the true cost of owning a home because we don't actually tabulate all the recurring expenses that go into being a home owner. Unlike stock and bond owners, home owners have to pay huge fees for upkeep, maintenance, and other things, all of which can make home ownership expensive.

When thinking about all this, you might find it helpful to think of real estate as two distinctly different pieces. First, there is the land you own. Second, there is the actual house itself. The land value is likely to appreciate because available land is likely to become increasingly scarce (land is hard to come by, people who want it are not). The house itself, however, is a depreciating asset that is guaranteed to fall apart, just like your car will. A house is a lot like a car that comes with a piece of land. If it has any investment components, those are subjective and not necessarily financial (though I guess they *could* be, for instance, if you work from home).

If you're familiar with Robert Shiller of Yale and his work on real estate, you have likely seen Figure 4.7, which shows inflation-adjusted house prices since 1890. Since 1890 housing in the United States has averaged a 3.2 percent annualized return. It's been slightly better since 1960, at 4.2

Figure 4.7: Real House Prices (Case-Shiller adjusted CPI scaled to 100)

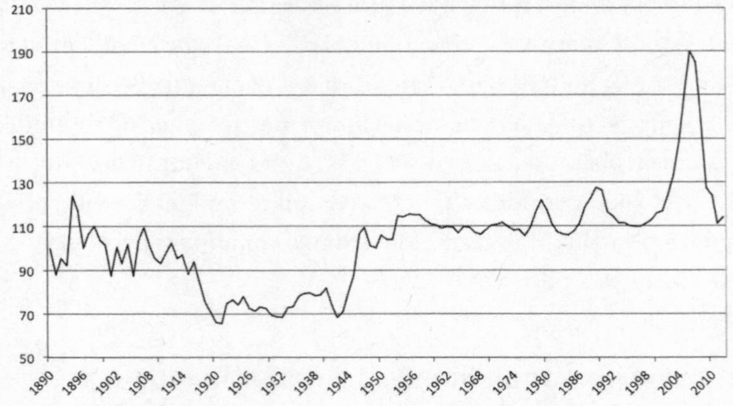

Source: St. Louis Federal Reserve FRED Economic Data, S&P Case Shiller 20 City Home Price Index, *August 2013, http://research.stlouisfed.org/fred2/series/SPCS20RSA.*

percent, a bit better than that since 1970 (4.8 percent), and more in line with the historical average since 1980 (3.8 percent). That might not sound so bad were it not for inflation. Inflation has historically averaged about 3.2 percent as well. Hence Figure 4.7 shows housing prices close to the inflation adjusted 100 level throughout their history. Said differently, real estate doesn't generate a high rate of return when accounting for inflation.

I should also note that there are always costs attached to purchasing various financial assets. Most of these fees are recurring to some degree and can range from reasonable (for example, ETFs—exchange-traded funds—or discount brokerage fees) to high (those for most hedge fund fees or annuities). Real estate is not immune to fees, and the associated costs arise in ways that are easily overlooked.

All purchases of financial assets guarantee that the purchaser will begin ownership in the red in the amount of the fees involved in purchasing the asset. Homes are an unusual financial asset in that they're extraordinarily expensive from the perspective of upfront costs. You have Realtor commissions, closing costs, inspection, appraisal, insurance, and a slew of other potential costs such as moving or maintenance. This is before you've even set foot in your investment and before you've started paying the real fees (like your mortgage, which will cost you, on average, almost 75 percent of the cost of the home during the 30-year mortgage—not to mention the maintenance).

For simplicity I'll use as an example of a home worth $200,000 and assume some relatively modest upfront costs. Like many American home owners, the new owners have a fixed-rate 30-year mortgage, at 5.5 percent. Assuming some fairly conservative estimates for commissions (split between buyer and seller), closing costs, and inspection—nothing too complex—the total comes to about 5.25 percent of the cost of the house. That's similar to the cost of buying an A-share mutual fund, which is generally a bad idea.

Home Price	$200,000
UPFRONT COSTS	
Commission	$6,000
Closing Costs	$4,000 (2 percent)
Inspection	$500

But these are only the beginning of the fees involved in this financial asset. Over the life of a home the owners will have to pay taxes, mortgage payments, property insurance, utilities, water, waste, and routine maintenance. These are all fixed costs; whether we rent or buy, we'll have to pay some of these fees no matter what. So forget utilities, water, and waste because we have to live somewhere. But when we own a home, we're still paying the mortgage, taxes, and property insurance, and we'll have to maintain the property.

According to the Census Bureau's 2009 American Housing Survey these costs come out to about 7 or 8 percent of the value of the home every year.[7] Here's the breakdown:

RECURRING COSTS	
Taxes	$2,100
Mortgage	$12,400
Property insurance	$775
Maintenance	$400

The mortgage cost includes principal payments so, using the average national mortgage rate according to the AHS, it's safe to assume that the 30-year mortgage will cost the home owners roughly $165,000 in interest alone over the life of the mortgage. According to a basic amortization schedule, the owners would be paying monthly interest payment of $800, or $9,600 per year. That brings their annual costs down to about 6.5 percent. They could also back out part of the taxes because of the mortgage interest deduction, so assume that the home costs them about $10,000 per year, or roughly 5 percent of the mortgage. Even in the best periods, when real estate returns 4.8 percent, the return is still negative. That's an expensive financial asset.

But none of this analysis means that buying a house is a bad idea. We have to live somewhere, and this analysis does not compare the specifics of renting versus the specifics of buying a house outright, buying a house with a mortgage or using the property as an income source (which could be viewed as investment and an alternative income source). The analysis is simply intended to put the total costs and real, real returns in the proper perspective for those of us who buy a house with a mortgage and live in that home (as most people do). I view buying a home as a less expensive way to live than the option of renting (you could make both arguments depending on where you live). Plus, numerous intangibles involved in owning a home make it a wise purchase. But we shouldn't always think about housing as if it's an amazing investment. Whether we rent or buy, we are experiencing an expense. The real costs of that expense will depend on your specific situation. But in both real returns and real, real returns (including taxes and fees), the returns are unlikely to be anything to boast about. And certainly not what I would refer to as a good financial investment.

Of course, you might time the market just right, and some speculators will always be able to time their use of financial assets better than others, but over an entire market cycle you have to consider the poor real, real returns of housing and the strong likelihood that you won't get rich by investing in a home.

MYTH 11—MODERN PORTFOLIO THEORY EXPLAINS PROPER PORTFOLIO CONSTRUCTION

Financial experts suffer from a wildly destructive case of science envy. We hate that we can't prove many of our views empirically. The problem is that the field of money and finance is largely a construct of the mind. Financial instruments are not real in the same sense that air and water are real. There's a variable in the financial world that makes many things hard to prove empirically—the human mind. Despite our personal beliefs and biases otherwise, we're rather inefficient creatures, and as a result we often respond to our uses of financial assets in inefficient ways. This stands in direct contrast to modern portfolio theory (MPT), the efficient market hypothesis (EMH), and the way many financial professionals have constructed their understanding of the financial world.

Modern portfolio theory assumes that we can calculate risk and create efficient portfolios by understanding this quantifiable variable. The efficient market hypothesis assumes that market participants are rational and incorporate all existing information in pricing assets, thereby making it virtually impossible to outperform the market. MPT and EMH suffer from what I believe are several flaws in the foundation of such thinking:

1. Beta, or risk, is not the same thing as volatility (which is how academics quantify risk).
2. Because modern portfolio theory assumes that risk equals volatility, the theory assumes that asset price returns are normally distributed.
3. Correlations are not static. Therefore returns can vary according to different macroeconomic environments.
4. Markets work with highly imperfect information obtained by highly imperfect participants, rendering their conclusions imperfect and at times completely wrong.

The efficient market hypothesis and modern portfolio theory assume that risk is something that can be quantified and measured. Risk is generally calculated as equivalent to volatility, or standard deviation. This makes it easy to calculate and works great in a textbook. But volatility is not equivalent to risk. Risk is much more than volatility. In fact volatility might even make a portfolio *less* risky. For most practical purposes *financial risk* is defined as the potential that we will not meet our financial goals. This is not the same thing as volatility, and perhaps investors should not rely entirely on such a narrow definition to steer the portfolio process.

The second point is an extension of the first point. Modern portfolio theory assumes that asset price returns are normally distributed because risk equals volatility. However, the actual returns of markets do not always validate this view. There are far too many outlier events within markets to validate such a view. Nassim Taleb refers to these events as "black swans." Black swans shouldn't exist in a world in which returns are expected to follow a normal distribution. This is in part why academic models failed for Long-Term Capital Management in 1998 and could not protect banks against the rare event of a 30 percent decline in housing prices (as they did during the housing bust). It's also why the academic models failed to recognize that the stock market is susceptible to crashes like those in 1987 and 2008.

The third point can be best understood by looking at the macroeconomic environment since the mid-1980s, a period in which bonds have largely performed in line with equities. Modern portfolio theory, using static correlations and a relatively small data set of past information, would never have predicted such a thing. Yet some of the greatest risk-adjusted returns since the mid-1980s (an entire portfolio time horizon for most people) came from simply holding one of the lowest-risk asset classes. The error in MPT was that the theory is based on expected future returns, variance, and risk that do not hold true through all portfolio periods. And if you just so happen to be living during one of those periods when the back-tested assumptions fail, then, as Harry Markowitz, the father of MPT, states: "*The point where the assumptions break down . . . lead[s] to distastrous consequences.*"

Additionally, MPT and EMH assume that market participants are rational. But numerous studies show that this is far from the truth. Most of us are highly irrational and, more important, working with information or an understanding that is often deficient or inaccurate. This means that the market price is always the market price, but that doesn't always mean the market price is the right price.

Proponents of such theories like to compare financial markets to such simple markets as a supermarket line—they claim that all of us cannot choose the fastest line during checkout. I'm sure you've encountered this scenario a million times in your life. But most financial markets are nothing like such a simplified market. Financial markets are extremely complex systems that are widely misunderstood and are being interpreted by highly deficient participants. This doesn't mean that outperforming the market is easy. In fact interpreting the irrational decisions of others is part of what makes it so difficult to outperform the market, but understanding that financial markets are often irrational and deficient is crucial to properly understanding how the monetary system and the financial world operates.

Another distinction here fits in well with the core understandings of primary markets and secondary markets. EMH is generally used to explain the price performance of various assets in a secondary market. The broader conclusion is that it's useless to try to outperform the market because the market is more efficient at digesting information than individuals are. But does this apply to primary markets as well? If it did, there would be no point in starting a new company because the market would have already digested any new information that could be introduced to allow you to succeed. In other words you'd be better off just working for someone else at all times because the market has already come up with the most efficient way to produce what a new market participant might produce. This is obviously wrong. Entrepreneurs essentially engage in a form of arbitrage in which they identify a market flaw and produce something superior to what exists or supply what doesn't exist. The secondary market is simply an extension of the primary market. And it is a much more public market—more information is readily available, and there is greater competition to arbitrage any price discrepancies that might occur. But that doesn't mean the secondary markets are perfectly efficient. It just means they're *more* efficient than the primary markets. Interestingly, much of the information that is available to any entrepreneur is available to anyone making a decision in a secondary market, so you should conclude that successful entrepreneurship should be impossible if you adhere to the strong form of the efficient market hypothesis. Again, that's obviously false. Entrepreneurship is not easy. And most companies don't succeed. But that doesn't mean it is impossible, and it certainly doesn't mean that the market is perfectly efficient.

Interestingly, I actually agree with many of the findings from EMH and MPT, but I disagree with the way adherents of these theories arrive at these findings. For instance, I generally agree that most of us should not engage in secondary markets by trying to beat the market or pay high fees, but that is not because I believe most market participants are rational agents making wise decisions. In fact I agree with the aforementioned point because most market participants are irrational agents making unwise decisions. Ultimately the market is the market. If you think the value of stock A is $100 and the market never confirms your belief, the value of stock A will never reach $100. Whether the market is right, rational, or properly digesting information is rather meaningless in the end. But we have to be careful about building our foundation of understanding from premises that assume markets are made up of rational agents or such notions as risk equals volatility. Doing so will likely lead you astray and likely into a narrow and dogmatic view of the financial world.

CHAPTER 5

HOW THE NEW MACROECONOMY IS CHANGING PORTFOLIO CONSTRUCTION

It's a macroeconomic world and we're just living in it.

THE FINANCIAL WORLD IS UNDERGOING A HUGE TRANSITION: local economies and individual companies are no longer the center of attention; instead indexes, asset classes, and global perspectives play an increasingly important role in portfolio construction. Macroeconomic trends are influencing markets like never before. This is changing the way we allocate our assets, understand the financial world, and engage in the global economy. Understanding the new macroeconomic world is all about understanding the relationship of the various components of the monetary system and designing a process that connects our goals and needs to the proper instruments that can help us achieve those goals.

Unfortunately, many of us are still playing the microeconomic game. We are too focused on analyzing specific firms, specific markets, and local economies. The following factors are changing the way we approach portfolio construction:

1. The hyperglobalization trends I discussed in Chapter 2 are only becoming more prevalent. As the world becomes increasingly globalized, we all have to adapt to it. The old playbook won't work in the future. Your approach to the markets and portfolio construction has to account for this.

2. Seventy-one percent of market movements are now the result of macroeconomic trends, while bottom-up company-specific trends account for just 29 percent of market movements.[1]
3. To survive and thrive in the new macroeconomic world, you can't set sail without understanding the direction of the current, where the big storms are, or which way the winds are blowing. The big picture matters more than ever.
4. Corporations are becoming increasingly global entities. 30 percent of the S&P 500's revenues come from abroad, up from 23 percent in 1990.[2] This trend is likely to increase in the coming decades. To understand the microeconomy we have to understand the macroeconomic trends driving corporate balance sheets and income statements.
5. Government policy is changing in the new macroeconomic world. As the world becomes more and more interconnected, central banks and governments are playing a more interventionist role than ever. This requires a vast understanding of the total landscape like never before.
6. Armies of analysts, researchers, insiders, and high-frequency computer algorithms are scouring stocks for arbitrage opportunities and ways to profit from the markets. Beating these analysts, arbitrageurs, and computers is a full-time job that few people are likely to succeed at. By the time a company is being listed on a public exchange, it has already experienced the majority of its most explosive growth and the owners are cashing out. This doesn't mean there is no value left in buying individual securities on a secondary market, but it does mean that the easy money has likely already been made by someone else. The stock analysis game has become highly competitive; unless you have a computer in your brain, you're likely to be excluded from the playing field over time.
7. Owning individual securities increases the overall risks of a portfolio. Various studies have shown that you need to own more than a hundred stocks to reduce diversifiable risk by 90 percent. In other words, to reduce company-specific risk sufficiently you must own a large number of securities, increasing portfolio fees, frictions, and other costs.[3]

8. Sufficient individual stock diversification generally results in closet indexing. By the time you're managing a portfolio that sufficiently neutralizes company-specific risk, you're essentially holding a portfolio that closely resembles that market itself. What is the point, other than creating a huge amount of hassle, tax inefficiency, and fees?

Many financial books these days tell fantastic stories about how to make a fortune picking stocks, get rich using opaque strategies, or how to follow a famous guru's path to riches. I hate to disappoint you, but this story is different. It's not that I don't think you can get rich by investing and allocating your savings. It's just that once you understand what I regard as investing and saving, you'll realize I have no get rich quick plan that you can implement. And when you combine this with a macroeconomic perspective, you will, I hope, have a better overall understanding of your role within the monetary system.

Macroeconomic portfolio construction is a process of understanding how macroeconomic factors affect your personal portfolio. When approaching portfolio construction, you need to understand what I referred to in Chapter 4 as the total portfolio. This means understanding the distinction between saving and investment. And this means viewing portfolios differently than we have been taught.

UNDERSTANDING THE TOTAL PORTFOLIO

It's most prudent and appropriate to view your portfolio of financial assets as one total portfolio. Within this total portfolio I want you to understand that you have a savings portfolio and an investment portfolio. Your investment portfolio is where you allocate funds for the purpose of future production. This means you should have assets dedicated to your area of expertise and other endeavors that might fall under the category of investment. Remember, investing is spending not consumed for future production. Things like education, job training, job certifications, side businesses, entrepreneurship, and the like all would fall under the category of investment. In general this should be money you can afford to lose. These are the assets you're using to hit your financial home run. In most cases they are a bet on yourself and your ability to maximize your primary source of income. Bear in mind, it could be that not all your investments will pan out. But you have dedicated these funds for a specific purpose in order to avoid conflating your savings portfolio and your investment portfolio.

In addition to this investment portfolio I want you to look at what we traditionally think of as our investment portfolio as a savings portfolio. These are the assets that we generally set aside for life's big expenditures—a house down payment, retirement, college tuition, emergencies, and so on. This savings portfolio is comprised of assets that need to grow but can't be exposed to huge amounts of risk of permanent loss. In other words they need to be there when we need them. *This doesn't mean they literally need to perform like a zero-risk savings account, but they should not be exposed to big risks.*

When we start to think of the total portfolio, it helps to think of ourselves as a cash flow generator. As Figure 5.1 shows, you generate an income, part of which is consumed and part of which flows into the total portfolio. From that total portfolio you have to decide how much you will invest and how much you will save (remember, this is not investment in the traditional sense).

If you earn an after-tax income of $5,000 per month and, like most people, save roughly 5 percent of disposable income, you have $250 per

Figure 5.1: The Flow of Funds Through the Total Portfolio

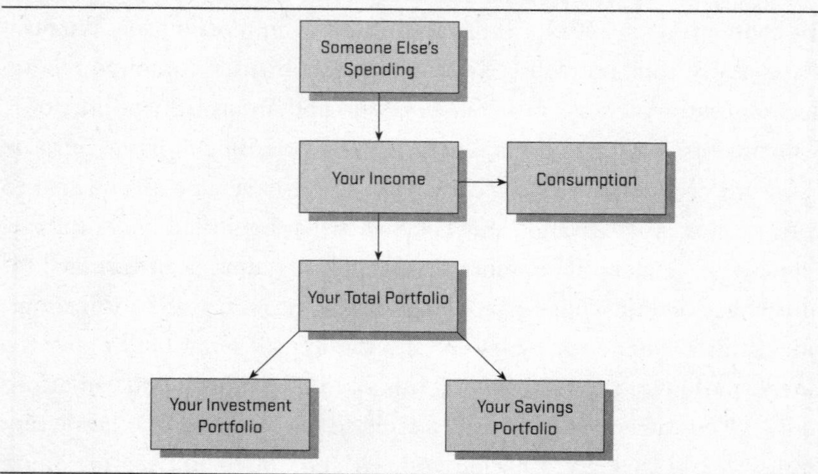

month to allocate. In a year you will have amassed $3,000 in total savings. What do you do with that? This is a personal question. Some readers might be willing to use this unconsumed income for the purpose of investment and trying to maximize future production. But the majority of this saving is likely to end up in our savings portfolio. These funds are placed aside to help us create a sense of confidence in planning for specific events or uncertainties in the future. To begin understanding how to construct a savings portfolio, it is necessary to first understand some of the building blocks of the financial markets.

In the next sections of this chapter I will discuss how to think about your savings portfolio. Remember, your investment portfolio is where you're likely to generate the vast majority of your financial wealth during your lifetime. I wish I could write a book about the holy grail for true investing, but only you can discover your talents that the rest of society will find value in. You won't discover this in any books. While I hope this book helps provide you with perspective, I hope you also realize that many of these answers ultimately lie with you. That said, let me explore the idea of the savings portfolio in greater detail because this is a portfolio I can help you learn to construct and understand.

RETHINKING THE EFFICIENT FRONTIER

In Chapter 4, I started to describe why the views espoused by many users of modern portfolio theory (MPT), the efficient market hypothesis (EMH), and ideas like stocks for the long run are flawed. The primary problem is that these views intermingle the idea of savings and investment in one portfolio that exists on secondary markets and then build a model for how to interpret asset movements using largely unrealistic assumptions.

No assumption is more pernicious than the idea that risk equals reward. This is a concept so universally accepted that you can't crack a finance textbook on this subject without having this hammered into your head. And the key flaw in this model of the world is the attempt to quantify risk by equating it with standard deviation. Standard deviation is variance from the average. If you look at the efficient frontier used by modern portfolio theorists, you'll find it generally looks like Figure 5.2.

Figure 5.2: The Efficient Frontier

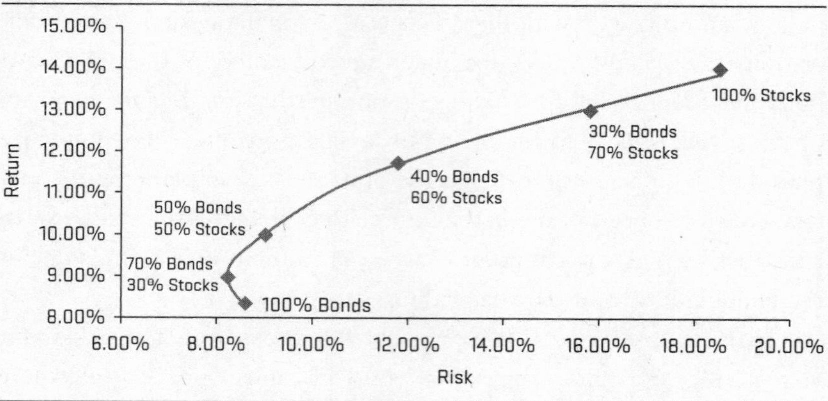

Most people approach the markets with the mentality that they want to maximize returns and the way to do that is simply by taking more risk. Given enough time, we're taught, this risk is worth the reward. This can be a highly dangerous and misleading view of the world. After all, if risk was simply volatility, or standard deviation, then high-risk assets like stocks could *always* be relied on to generate high returns over the long term. But these high returns do not always materialize across equities. In fact, if you look at primary markets, where the majority of businesses actually exist, you'll find that 30 percent of all small businesses fail in their first year, 50 percent fail within the first five years, and 70 percent fail within the first ten years.[4] Risk certainly does not always equal reward here.

With regard to secondary markets, the average real return on equities can be low or even negative for long periods of time, as shown in Figure 5.3.

The implicit assumption of this view of the world is that high-risk assets must generate a high return over the long term. But history does not always justify such optimism, and in fact risky assets can sustain long and painful periods of poor performance that could persist through much of one's entire portfolio time horizon.

Unfortunately false assumptions are only the first of many flaws in this approach. This view of stocks for the long run looks great in a

Figure 5.3: S&P 500 Average Ten-Year Real Returns

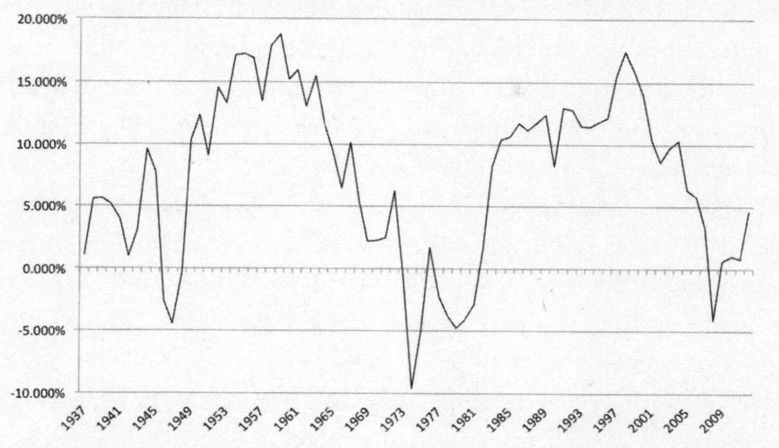

textbook or in a mathematical model, but when it's actually translated to the real world, it doesn't work out so cleanly. This is largely because of the problem of time within a person's savings portfolio—the aforementioned intertemporal conundrum.

UNDERSTANDING THE INTERTEMPORAL CONUNDRUM

An assumption embedded in the use of modern portfolio theory and the concept of stocks for the long run is that our lives are one nice clean line from the point where we begin to save to the point where we retire. The reality is that life does not start when we're 25 and end when we're 65. Life happens all along the way. This introduces the problem of time into our financial lives. Our financial needs are evolving and require a certain level of certainty in order for us to plan appropriately for the future.

The reason why we save assets along the way is so we can be prepared for life's big events. The perspective of stocks for the long run simply ignores this reality. In fact in the famous book by the same name, the author Jeremy Siegel states that a conservative risk tolerance with a 30-year time horizon should be 90 percent allocated in equities and that a risk-taking allocation with 30-year time horizon should actually leverage up to a 131 percent equity allocation.[5] Life happens all the time. And our portfolios can't be thrown 130 percent into this roller-coaster ride in the equity market based on the assumption that we can just ride it out. Few of us actually ride it out in the nice smooth manner that these academic rearview mirror models assume.

That's not all, though. This concept becomes even more flawed as we age. As we get older, the portfolio with stocks for the long run will likely grow larger, which will actually expose it to an even greater risk of permanent loss if we are allocated along the traditional lines of the efficient frontier and MPT. Yes, compounding interest is often used as evidence of how powerful high stock market returns can be, but as we grow older this concept can actually increase the risks in our overall portfolio by exposing us to greater equity market risks. And this is occurring precisely when we should be rebalancing our portfolios to account for the shorter portfolio duration. For instance, when you're 35 you really don't have a portfolio time horizon of 30 years, because once you're 45, you're going to be starting to rethink risk exposure along the lines of MPT. Therefore, if you're allocated in a high-risk 100 percent stock portfolio at 35, by the age of 45 you should be reallocating your portfolio to something more conservative, such as a 70–30 allocation mix—which means that 30 percent of your equity allocation was not actually exposed to a stocks-for-the-long-run mentality at all. It was exposed to a stocks-for-the-ten-year-run allocation. Given the variance in stock market returns in short periods of time, it's necessary to approach the world of portfolio construction with more realistic expectations, that is, in a way that actually reflects the way we really live our lives, not theoretical textbook models.

UNDERSTANDING RISK

Risk is an important concept to understand in the financial world because it is one of the key variables that goes into our decisions about allocating assets. We're often told that risk is a number. In textbooks and many financial models, risk is a specifically defined figure such as standard deviation. This is convenient for modeling because it can be concluded that risk fits into a nice neat equation. Therefore it can be modeled and predicted with some precision. The problem is that the word *risk,* as it pertains to financial markets, is much more than standard deviation or volatility. For instance, here are a few simple questions that shed serious doubts on this perspective: Were stocks risky in 2007 when volatility was very low? Were they less risky in 2009 after they had fallen 40 percent and the Volatility Index had soared tenfold? Are stocks more or less risky after they go down or up? Is a highly volatile appreciating asset more risky than a low volatility asset that depreciates in value? Does a stock that goes up dramatically deserve to be labeled as risky as a stock that goes down dramatically just because both are volatile? The answer: it depends.

As many know, we often think of risky environments as volatile environments. We tend to view 2009 as an environment that was more risky than 2007. Obviously this was the wrong way to view risk. Volatility itself is not necessarily a sign of risk and in many cases merely reflects the flawed way we perceive certain environments. Hyman Minsky's financial instability hypothesis states that a capitalist system will gravitate from stability to instability and that in fact its very stability can contribute to the instability.[6] In financial markets the riskiest periods are often those periods when it looks as though everything is stable. Why? Because this is when human beings become complacent and irrational. And this is when humans take their efficient market models and embed unrealistic future projections based on rearview mirror data and extrapolate out into the future. And then, when the model has found a perfectly low-risk way to produce profit, humans leverage the model up and count the dollars flowing in. This is essentially an oversimplified description of the global housing bubble and how stability created instability. When financial firms realized they could take an asset that supposedly never goes down (US housing prices had not experienced substantial negative year-over-year returns before the bubble burst), they embedded this unrealistic future projection into an asset that was viewed as being low risk (because it had low historical negative volatility), and they leveraged it up. And over several years this leverage was built up in what looked like a very benign environment. Until, of course, the illusion of stability led to instability. And in 2008 the credit-based monetary system started to crack, and as the defaults picked up momentum, the psychology shifted from complacency to panic, and the financial system eventually buckled.

Investment firms also interpret risk differently than their clients generally perceive it. For portfolio managers this usually leads to discussions about beta. *Beta* is a measure of relative volatility intended to help one decipher an instrument's sensitivity to market movements. By definition the beta of an overall market is 1.0 so an instrument with a beta of 2.0 means that the instrument will tend to move by twice the return of the market. In other words, if the market is up 5 percent, the instrument with a beta of 2.0 will tend to rise 10 percent.

In general beta is used to help understand a strategy's alpha. *Alpha* is the excess return that a fund or strategy generates compared to its benchmark on a risk-adjusted basis. In other words, if a fund has a beta of 2.0 and generates a return equivalent to 2.5, it has generated alpha because its actual performance has been better than its expected performance. This means the managers are adding value relative to their benchmark.

Benjamin Graham and David Dodd described the quantification of risk as something "entirely too indefinite":

> The relation between different kinds of investments and the risk of loss is entirely too indefinite, and too variable with changing conditions, to permit of sound mathematical formulations.[7]

These statistical calculations can be helpful in gauging the value of a particular manager or strategy, but they leave *much* to be desired. For instance, do we know that the manager who chose a hundred stocks in the S&P 500 was anything other than lucky by outperforming the other 400 stocks? Do we know if the fund used leverage? Do we know if the fund was exposed to outsized specific company risk? Will the strategy the manager used in the past generate the same returns in the future environment? Statistically we can come up with specifically quantifiable values that help us gauge the past value of a particular strategy, but they don't tell the full story about either the past or the future. This is, in large part, because that risk, or beta, is an extremely imprecise input.

This is a particularly large problem in the current climate of asset management because the idea of beta creates a benchmarking conflict: the managers of assets face increasing pressure to compete against a benchmark. The manager may overemphasize beating a benchmark, whereas the client is likely more worried about the risk of losing purchasing power and permanently losing money. If a year like 2008 occurs and the manager loses 30 percent relative to the benchmark, which lost 40 percent, the manager will claim victory. But was this a victory for the client? Of course not. The manager has failed to protect the client from the client's perception of risk.

The vast majority of assets are managed by people who perceive risk as something very different than the way their clients likely perceive it. And this is because of the failed attempt to define risk as a specific number. This enormous problem in investment management desperately requires an alternative approach.

What we're beginning to see is that financial risk is much more than volatility, standard deviation, or beta. Financial risk is a much more complex and abstract concept than the math behind many models makes it appear. *Instead of thinking of financial risk as a number, I want you to think of financial risk as the potential that you will not meet your financial goals.* Financial risk, in the most practical and realistic sense, is the likelihood that we won't have the money we need when we need it. This is the risk the average person confronts when allocating savings to a secondary market. And it should be the central risk you try to protect against when designing a savings portfolio.

SETTING REALISTIC GOALS

The first thing to understand about a savings portfolio is the primary goals it is serving. A savings portfolio is comprised of assets that must help create some level of future certainty. Let me be very clear, though—a savings portfolio is not a no-risk portfolio or no-growth portfolio. Remember, the term *saving* is simply unspent income. We can allocate that saving in many ways, and the term *saving* should not be used merely for something analogous to a zero-risk savings account. Indeed the term *saving* is as abused as the word *investment*.

Risk is the potential that we will not meet our financial goals. This can happen for several reasons and is not merely the result of potential losses. So our goals have to be broader than merely protecting against the risk of permanent losses. *Because a savings portfolio is made up of funds that need to meet specific and timely goals, we need these funds to primarily protect us from the potential*

Loss of purchasing power.
Permanent loss of money.

Because we reside in a credit-based monetary system, we have to understand the dangers of inflation. Inflation reduces the amount of goods and services that a dollar in 2014 can purchase in 2015. Inflation increases the number of labor hours it takes to acquire the same number of goods and services (assuming stagnant wages). In other words, when your $1 buys you a ten-minute massage in 2014, inflation of 1 percent will actually reduce your ten-minute massage to a 9.9-minute massage in 2015. Your dollars don't buy the same amount of massage. This is a decline in your financial living standard. If this situation were to persist for many decades, your living standard could deteriorate dramatically. One thing the financial markets provide us with is the opportunity to purchase assets that will protect us against the loss of purchasing power by helping our dollars perform better than or equal to the rate of inflation.

The problem with buying financial assets is that they expose us to the risks of the entities that issue them. This means there is substantial risk of permanent loss. Warren Buffett famously described his two rules of portfolio management as follows:

Rule No.1: Never lose money.
Rule No.2: Never forget rule No.1[8]

This is important to understand because of the unfortunate math behind market losses. As you can see in Figure 5.4, losses are enormously destructive to our future living standards because they are increasingly difficult to make up in the future. For instance, while a 10 percent loss on $100 requires just an 11.1 percent return to break even, a 50 percent loss requires a 100 percent return to break even. If we assume the real, real return on a pure equity portfolio is 6 percent per year, a 50 percent loss will require twelve years just to get back to your *original* living standard.

Figure 5.4: The Unfortunate Math Behind Market Losses

Initial Account Balance	% Loss	Balance After Loss	Return Required to Break Even
$100	-10%	$90	11.10%
$100	-20%	$80	25.00%
$100	-30%	$70	42.90%
$100	-40%	$60	66.70%
$100	-50%	$50	100.00%
$100	-60%	$40	150.00%
$100	-70%	$30	233.00%
$100	-80%	$20	400.00%
$100	-90%	$10	900.00%

In other words substantial portfolio declines can be enormously disruptive to your future living standards.

Buying common stock exposes you to the underlying performance of the specific corporation. Buying corporate debt exposes you to the credit risk of the specific corporation. Buying government debt exposes you to the risk of that government's fiscal and monetary actions. Remember, in a credit-based monetary system all assets and liabilities have two sides of the ledger. Someone's assets are another's liabilities. If those liabilities are issued by a weak entity, the asset holder is risking the permanent loss of capital. While we want to grow our assets (we hope in excess of the rate of inflation), we also do not want to do so in a manner that exposes these assets to excess risk of permanent loss.

HAVING REALISTIC EXPECTATIONS

When we confront the allocation of our savings, we must begin by setting realistic expectations. Unfortunately we have been conditioned to think that our portfolios will crank out recurring returns of 10 to 12 percent or better. At least that's what the stocks-for-the-long-run mantra claims. As a result we often use our assets to chase stock market returns. By setting the bar so high we are setting ourselves up for disappointment before we even begin.

I mentioned real, real returns in Chapter 4 and earlier in this chapter. This is the return you can expect to actually put in your pocket, the return that actually matters to your financial life. This means we have to net out inflation, taxes, and expenses when looking at returns. Since the mid-1930s the S&P 500 has generated a real (inflation-adjusted) return of just under 8 percent. After accounting for taxes and expenses, that return dips to just over 6 percent. So the real, real return on ownership in the S&P 500 has been about 6 percent per year. Not bad but almost half of what many of us expect to earn in the stock market based on widely cited statistics.

The US government bond market provides a less cheery picture. The real return on US government bonds (inflation adjusted) has been about 2.25 percent since the mid-1930s. If you adjust this for taxes and fees, you're looking at something closer to 1 percent. That's keeping your head above water, but it's not exactly going to make you fabulously wealthy.

If we look back even further into the history of bonds and stocks, the numbers are even more sobering. According to the *Fundamental Index Newsletter,* stocks have generated a nominal return of about 8 percent since 1802, and bonds have generated a 5 percent return.[9] In this context our real, real returns are likely to be somewhere in the low to mid single digits in the two major asset classes. Of course a two-century perspective doesn't mesh perfectly with the modern-day financial world, but the overarching point is that real, real returns are generally much lower than most of us expect.

If we look at the broader household balance sheet, the story gets even *more* sobering. As I showed in Chapter 4, real estate tends to perform roughly in line with the rate of inflation and will likely generate a negative real, real return when you calculate all your expenses. In short, the real-life returns on all these asset classes are much lower than most of us probably assumed. And these are the assets that make up the vast majority of the private sector's balance sheet. In other words our expectations are often wildly out of whack with reality.

My goal is not to depress you or make asset allocation appear like a fruitless endeavor. But we have to be realistic about our prospects for the future so we can properly approach our savings portfolios. The idea that you're likely to get wealthy picking assets on a secondary market is not entirely a myth, but you have to keep things in the right perspective before embarking on something that is likely to be counterproductive.

PROPER PORTFOLIO CONSTRUCTION IS ABOUT PROCESS

This book is about a way of viewing the monetary world and understanding basic principles that will, I hope, provide you with a general framework for understanding the world of money. Portfolio construction is central to this framework as it is ultimately our portfolio of financial assets that we are accumulating, spending, and protecting. We've been trained to think of portfolio construction in these rigid terms by assuming that risk equals reward or that portfolio allocation is all about understanding how different assets fit into a cookie cutter approach. I hope by now you're beginning to question some of these assumptions.

Instead of thinking about portfolio construction in these rigid terms, I want you to begin thinking about portfolio construction from the perspective of the capital structure by understanding how certain assets fit into the monetary machine and why they provide certain benefits to the holders of those assets. Thus portfolio construction is all about process and methodology based on understanding the roles assets play in the monetary system. More important, we can get away from the many false assumptions about expected returns, immeasurable risk, and the other variables that make many of the mainstream models unrealistic.

RISK OPTIMIZATION IN A PORTFOLIO

When we construct a savings portfolio, we're really trying to balance our risks. That is, we're trying to increase the odds that we will meet our financial goals. Since the two biggest threats to meeting our financial goals are purchasing power loss and permanent loss of capital, we can begin to think of strategic and tactical ways to optimize risk in our portfolio. The key tools to achieving risk optimization are

1. *Methodology*—maintaining a process and plan that helps you structure a portfolio for achieving your financial goals.
2. *Strategic diversification*—structuring a fixed core portfolio with many different cash-flow streams to help achieve a balanced and stable return.

3. *Tactical diversification*—the tactical execution of a portfolio process and plan that helps reduce exposure to uncertainty and tail risk.

UNDERSTANDING TRUE DIVERSIFICATION

Diversification is traditionally thought of as allocating assets across non-correlated assets or low correlated assets in order to create positive off-setting asset returns with reduced unsystematic risk (company-specific risk). One traditional way of viewing diversification is by looking at sectors within the equity market. It's often believed that there are such things as defensive stocks that are not highly correlated with the business cycle. For instance, it's widely thought that utility stocks are defensive because most people always pay their utility bills in good times or bad. This makes these stocks defensive because their profits are better shielded from business cycle risks. But history does not show this actually exists, and as the new macroeconomic world has emerged, this concept of defensive stocks has deteriorated. In fact, if you were fully invested in utility stocks in 2008, your portfolio declined by more than 45 percent.

More recently the correlations between all industries have been extremely high, as Figure 5.5 shows.

You just don't get as much diversification *within* the equity market as you might think. Whether you owned defensive stocks or growth stocks in a year like 2008 was rather inconsequential. You still lost a lot of money. That's not diversification. A rising tide lifts all boats, but a falling tide also grounds all boats. It doesn't matter if you're in a sailboat or a speed boat. If we look at Figure 5.6, we can see a snapshot of the ten-year asset class correlations for many of the major asset classes.

In order to provide some level of true diversification you have to go well outside the equity markets. Diversification is really about structuring a portfolio so that you're optimizing different cash-flow streams to create a more stable and balanced return. One asset class alone is not going to achieve this.

There are several ways you can implement a diversified approach:

Figure 5.5: Correlation between the Industry and the S&P 500 (3 years)

Energy	0.82
Consumer Discretionary	0.99
Consumer Staples	0.95
Financials	0.92
Health Care	0.98
Industrials	0.97
Materials	0.74
Technology	0.97
Utilities	0.8

Source: Select Sector SPDRs, Correlation Tracker, http://www.sectorspdr.com/sectorspdr/tools/correlation-tracker.

Figure 5.6: 10-Year Asset Class Correlations

	Large Cap Stocks	Small Cap Stocks	MSCI EAFE	Emerging Market	Corporate Bonds	High Yield Bonds	EM Debt	Commodities	REITs	Hedge Funds	Equity Market Neutral
Large Cap Stocks	1.00	0.95	0.90	0.80	-0.26	0.70	0.60	0.52	0.79	0.81	0.58
Small Cap Stocks		1.00	0.86	0.74	-0.31	0.73	0.54	0.45	0.83	0.75	0.54
MSCI EAFE			1.00	0.90	-0.17	0.77	0.66	0.60	0.71	0.87	0.71
Emerging Market				1.00	-0.05	0.82	0.79	0.66	0.62	0.90	0.60
Corporate Bonds					1.00	-0.03	0.34	-0.18	0.02	-0.21	-0.10
High Yield Bonds						1.00	0.85	0.56	0.72	0.78	0.43
EM Debt							1.00	0.48	0.65	0.66	0.39
Commodities								1.00	0.39	0.72	0.49
REITs									1.00	0.56	0.49
Hedge Funds										1.00	0.58
Equity Market Neutral											1.00

1. Strategic diversification, which involves a fixed set of core assets that are inactively managed.
2. Tactical diversification, which would involve the use of more active allocation (such as hedging) in an effort to reduce portfolio uncertainty and tail risk.
3. Some combination of the two.

True diversification is about understanding the broad array of asset classes and how those asset classes generate cash flows that can help create a more stable and reliable portfolio return. Implementing a diversified approach requires an understanding of how to create a portfolio methodology and plan.

UNDERSTANDING THE DIFFERENT ASSET CLASSES

When we begin to look at various assets, it helps to understand the purpose they serve in the economy and why they exist in the first place. I'll briefly review some of the asset classes available to us:

Equities—Equity, or common stock, as it is more commonly referred to, represents ownership in a firm. It is issued in order to raise capital and to specify ownership. Common stock is subordinate to preferred stock, bondholders, and other debtors in the capital structure, which means that in the event of bankruptcy the common stockholders are last in line. The success of corporate equity is tied directly to the underlying performance of the company. As profits rise the claim that owners have to those profits will rise as well. Stock is unique in that it is the instrument that gives us a pure claim on the underlying output of a corporation. Corporations are the key to output expansion, innovation, and future growth so this instrument plays a unique role in any portfolio.

Preferred stock—Preferred stock is similar to common stock but has a higher claim on assets and earnings than the common stock does. It will also generally be issued with a dividend, thereby generating a more consistent and secure cash-flow stream.

Corporate bonds—Corporate bonds are a debt security sold to investors to raise capital. Corporate bonds are usually issued with a fixed interest rate that pays the owner a fixed rate of return. When the bond reaches maturity, the owners will be paid back their initial loan and they will have earned their interest payments over the life of the bond. Like common stock, corporate bonds rely on the performance of the underlying corporation. If a corporation cannot meet its financial obligations, the bonds may be defaulted on; however, debtors are always paid before equity holders, so the structure of this product (with a fixed interest rate and higher claim on assets) gives bonds a certain margin of safety that is not embedded in the equity issue. Corporate bonds are rated by various ratings agencies and can vary from investment grade (high quality) to junk bonds (low quality).

Government bonds—Government bonds are issued by a government in order to raise money for the purpose of government spending. When a government runs a budget deficit (taxing less than it spends), it will issue bonds to cover the difference. The taxing authority of a government makes government bonds particularly safe. That is, unlike most other entities, the government has a highly certain stream of income that can be used to meet its debt obligations. This makes the potential for insolvency comparatively low compared to most private entities. Governments sell varying durations of bonds that expose the owner to different levels of principal risk. In the United States the common debt types are Treasury bills (less than one year), Treasury notes (one to ten years) and Treasury bonds (more than ten years). In addition the government may issue inflation-protected securities, which are indexed to the rate of inflation and pay a fixed interest rate.

Cash and deposits—The safest assets we hold are cash and deposits. Cash is issued by the US government while deposits are issued by the banking system as liabilities of the banks and assets of the owners.

CONNECTING THE DOTS ON THE CAPITAL STRUCTURE AND CORPORATE PROFITS

To understand how we use various assets to achieve our financial goals, it helps to understand precisely why certain assets achieve the cash flows they do. In order to achieve this, it helps to understand where corporate profits come from, which requires a macroeconomic understanding of the world. When we buy claims against firms, we are essentially buying a claim on a portion of their cash flow. Equities, for instance, provide the owner with a claim on profits. Corporate debt provides the owner with access to a fixed percentage of interest plus principal at maturity. These instruments are just claims on the firm's cash flows. But where do these cash flows come from? Remember, the monetary system is just the sum of all the transactions that occur within it. So we know that profits come from a specific flow of funds. According to the Jerome Levy Forecasting Center we can derive profits from a simple equation:

Profits = Investment–Household Savings–Government Savings–Foreign Savings + Dividends

In short, profits come from business spending, household spending, government spending, and foreign spending.[10] This equation is expressed visually as a percentage of gross domestic product since 1960 in Figure 5.7.

Figure 5.7 shows, as a percentage of GDP, the contributions to corporate profits from the government deficit, net investment, dividends paid (business is dividends plus net investment), personal saving, and the foreign sector. US households generally net save, and the foreign sector has been in current account deficit for most of the last fifty years, so corporate profits have been driven mainly by net investment, dividends, and the government deficit.

The savings portfolio, to a large degree, is simply an extension of this cash flow from profits. As you can see in Figure 5.8, US firms generally

Figure 5.7: Corporate Profits Breakdown (Percentage of GDP)

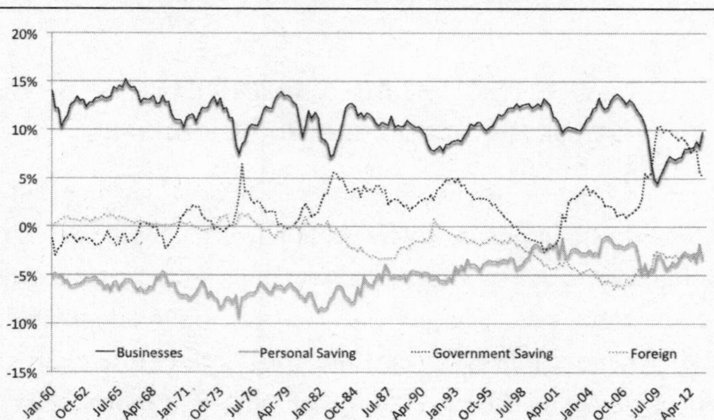

Figure 5.8: After Tax Corporate Profits (millions)

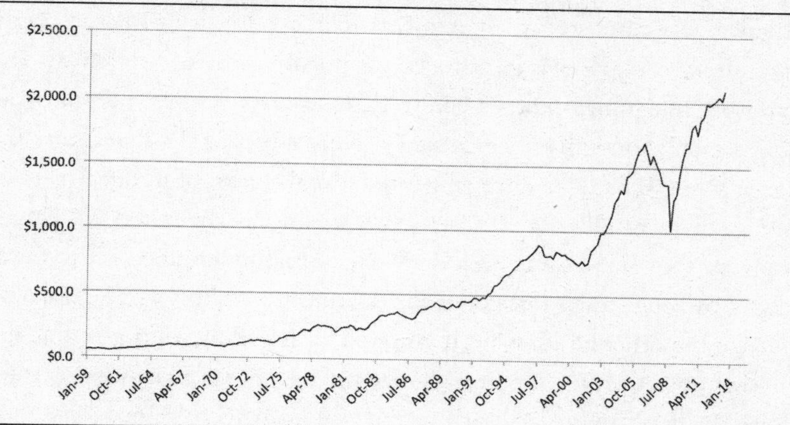

increase corporate profits over time, which means that the cash flows to shareholders and debtors are increasing. This is just a more microeconomic version of the economy's overall output.

The problem, from an asset allocation perspective, is that corporate profits are extremely cyclical. Figure 5.9 shows the year-over-year percentage change in profits. It looks a little like an EKG, right? And if your savings was 100 percent correlated with that profit stream, your portfolio would most likely resemble that EKG as well. That's enough to give you a heart attack.

Figure 5.9: Percentage Change in Corporate Profits (Year over Year)

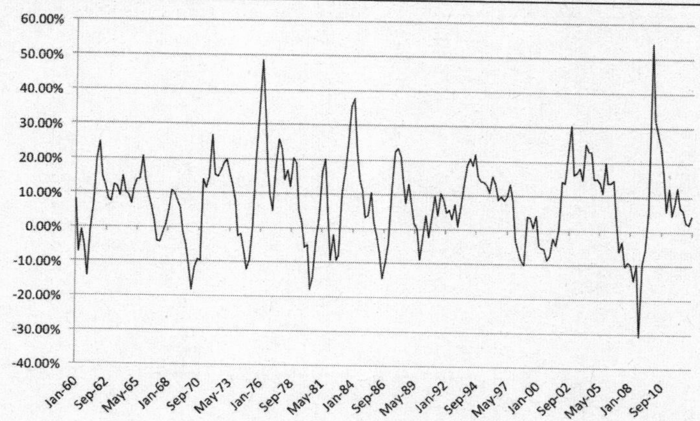

So what we really need to do is build a portfolio that creates more balance. We can't be overly exposed to the pure profit picture or we create unnecessary risk in our savings portfolio. Said differently, overexposure to equities exposes you to excessive risk of permanent loss. US government bonds have generated a real return of 2.25 percent since 1928, while US stocks have generated a real return of about 8 percent. A very plain vanilla 60–40 stock-bond blend has generated a 6 percent real return over the same period. When compounded since 1928, the effect of owning stocks over bonds is enormous, as shown in Figure 5.10.

On the other hand, what if you had been willing to forgo some purchasing power protection in exchange for greater permanent loss protection? Wouldn't that be closer to achieving your true financial goals? By layering different types of cash flows and assets into our portfolio, we can create a portfolio that more closely meets the goals of reducing loss of purchasing power and permanent loss of capital.

Figure 5.11 shows how the contribution of bonds to a portfolio can reduce the potential for tail risk in a portfolio. The more balanced portfolio reduces the risk that you will encounter a year like 2008, when more than 40 percent of capital was wiped out, confronting people with the daunting premise of requiring returns of greater than 66 percent just to break even. Often the pursuit of upside returns requires the pursuit of reduced potential for downside returns.

Figure 5.10: Growth of $10,000 in Bonds, Stocks, and Blended

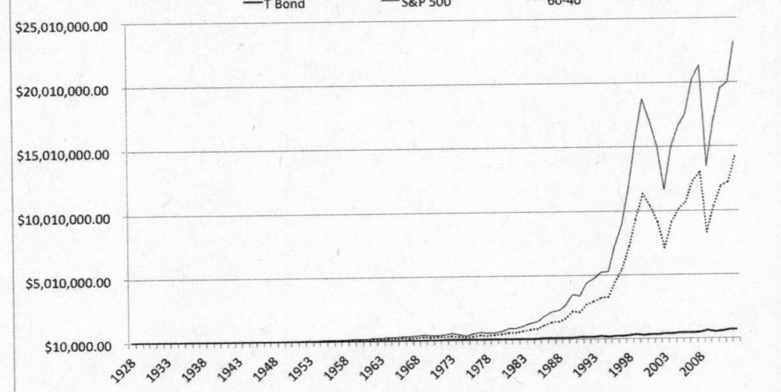

Figure 5.11: Percentage Change in Stocks and Blended Portfolio (Year Over Year)

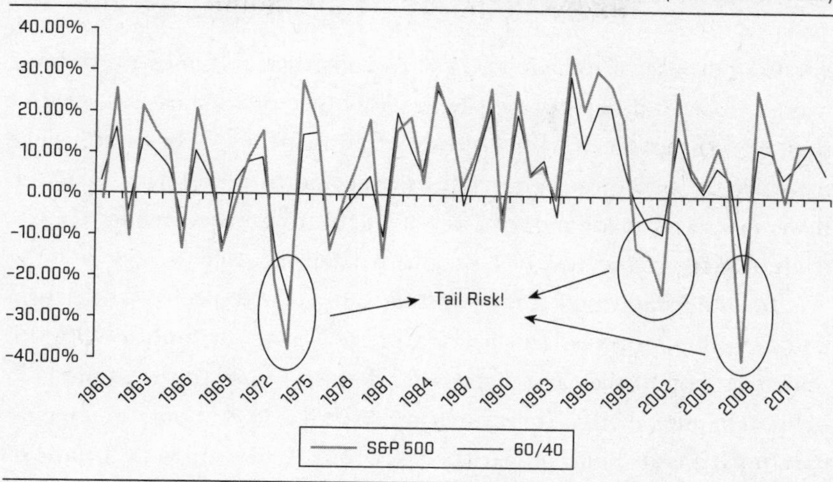

When I refer to the concept of *true diversification* it's crucial to think of the full spectrum of available assets and how they fit into an asset allocation plan. Equities should be an integral piece of any asset allocation plan because they are the asset which connects us directly to productivity and output thereby providing us with protection against purchasing power loss. But we must also consider how other assets can be used in conjunction with the equity component to help us achieve our goals. In particular, fixed income plays a key role in helping balance the risk of permanent loss. To emphasize this point, I want to highlight the nature of a bear market in fixed income. While many of the current fears in fixed income portfolios are valid, a bear market in bonds is nothing like a bear market in stocks. For instance, since 1928 the ten-year Treasury note has been negative in just 14 calendar years. And those negative years have averaged just –4.2 percent. On the other hand, US stocks have been negative in 24 calendar years since 1928 with an average decline of –13.6 percent. The worst calendar year decline in stocks was –43 percent, while the worst calendar year decline in Treasury notes was –11 percent. The data is even less bearish for the aggregate bond market where the worst calendar year return was just –2.9 percent. Let's talk about true diversification in more detail.

THE FINANCIAL GOALS SPECTRUM

For the purpose of explaining how to construct a savings portfolio, I want to look at different assets to see how they provide us with protection against purchasing power loss and permanent loss of capital since these are the two primary risks our savings portfolio is trying to avoid. If we look at a broad range of assets available to us, we can build a spectrum of assets to see how well they help achieve our goals.

To understand how certain assets should be expected to perform and how much protection they can provide in a portfolio requires an understanding of the capital structure. Let me return to the example in earlier chapters of the capital structure of a basic economy in which a corporation issued corporate debt and equity. Professor Marc Lavoie of the University of Ottawa likes to say, "Everything comes from somewhere and goes somewhere."[11] What he means by that is that all the instruments we use in the financial world are issued by specific entities and held by someone who purchased them. So, in order to understand the user of an asset, you must also understand the issuer of that asset. When we study the capital structure of any economic participant, we must keep this in mind at all times. For instance, the common stock you own in your brokerage account did not just magically appear there; it was issued by a firm. The bank deposit you hold in your bank account did not just magically appear there; it was issued by a bank.

This very basic understanding of the capital structure and different asset options allows us to begin to formalize how different assets serve different roles in a portfolio. With that in mind, we can then begin to construct assets on a spectrum to visualize how certain assets protect us from purchasing power loss and permanent loss. Figure 5.12 is what I call the financial goals spectrum, which portrays our different asset class options on a spectrum that shows how well they protect us from permanent loss and purchasing power loss.

Tier 1 Assets—Emerging Market Equities and Developed Market Small Cap Equities

Tier 1 assets are our high-octane assets. These are the assets that have the highest potential for protecting purchasing power because they are the market share invaders. These are somewhat established firms that

Figure 5.12: The Financial Goals Spectrum

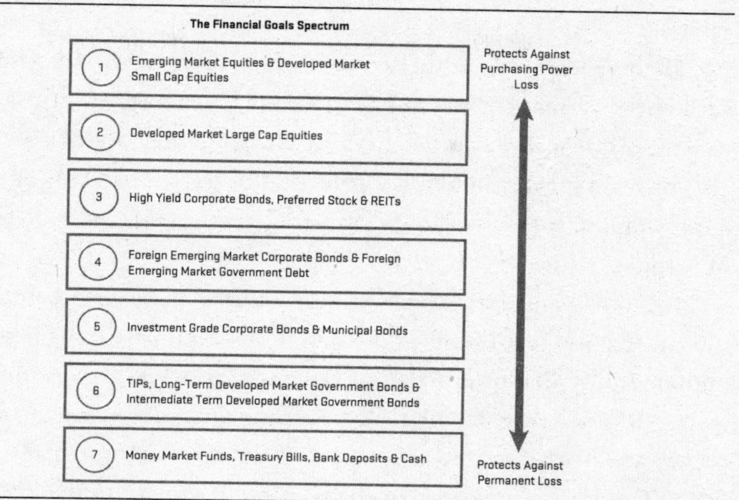

are seeking to take market share from their more developed brethren. These assets will expose you to substantial risk of permanent loss as well as substantial protection from loss of purchasing power.

Tier 2 Assets—Developed Market Large Cap Equities

Tier 2 assets are near the top of the spectrum because they provide us with substantial potential protection against loss of purchasing power. These are the assets that, over long periods of time, can be most relied on to provide purchasing power protection because they are the asset most closely correlated with broader output. In other words, if we assume that our economy will expand over time, we should assume that profits and large corporations will also expand. While tier 2 assets provide substantial potential purchasing power protection, they also expose us to substantial risk of permanent loss, though the risk here is lower than it is for less established firms.

Tier 3 Assets—High-Yield Corporate Bonds, Preferred Stock, and REITs

Tier 3 assets provide the owner with varying levels of protection against both purchasing power loss and permanent loss but generally provide a lower level of purchasing power protection than both tier 1 and tier 2 assets.

High-yield bonds, also known as junk bonds, will expose you to substantial permanent loss risk because they are issued by firms that tend to have a less secure capital structure. Because they are less secure they also provide greater potential protection of purchasing power. As their name implies, these instruments generally pay a high yield or fixed rate of income.

REITs (real estate investment trusts) are a hybrid fixed income–equity–real estate asset that provide you with a fixed income and an equity-like return that is generated from underlying real estate assets. REITs generate their income by providing you with access to real estate investment income, usually from large commercial real estate firms. This gives the asset class many attractive qualities that can protect you from permanent loss as well as purchasing power loss.

Preferred stock is another hybrid debt-equity instrument that usually provides the owner with a fixed dividend as well as equity-like exposure to capital appreciation. Like REITs and high-yields bonds, they can provide substantial exposure to both purchasing power protection and permanent loss risk.

Tier 4 Assets—Emerging Market Corporate Bonds and Emerging Market Government Bonds

Tier 4 assets include emerging market bonds of all types. These are high-risk fixed-income assets that provide less protection of purchasing power than tier 1–3 assets and expose the holder to substantial risk of permanent loss.

Tier 5 Assets—Investment-Grade Corporate Bonds and Municipal Bonds

Tier 5 assets are high-grade fixed-income assets issued by high-quality corporations and municipalities. They are generally stable, providing some steady level of purchasing power protection but still exposing the owner to some risk of permanent loss.

Tier 6 Assets—TIPs, Long-Term Developed-Market Government Bonds and Intermediate-Term Developed-Market Government Bonds

Tier 6 assets are high-quality developed-market government-issued instruments that provide a stable and steady income and generally modest purchasing power protection. In general these assets are nearly risk free in that they are likely to mature at par (100 cents on the dollar); however, they will expose the owner to some risk of permanent loss during the life of the instrument because of principal fluctuations.

TIPS are Treasury inflation-protected securities. These are government-issued bonds designed to cover the purchaser's exposure to the rate of inflation during the life of the bond. As designed these assets protect against the risk of losing purchasing power and also provide some protection against permanent loss.

Tier 7 Assets—Money Market Funds, Treasury Bills, Bank Deposits, and Cash

Tier 7 assets are comprised of the safest assets available. They provide an extremely high level of protection against the risk of permanent loss but provide virtually no protection against loss of purchasing power. Tier 7 assets—money market funds, Treasury bill, bank deposits, and cash—are unique in that they not only include the medium of exchange (money) but also provide flexibility. Remember to think of tier 7 assets as a call option with no expiration. This means that the accumulation of cash and equivalents serves a specific purpose within a portfolio that not only protects against permanent loss but also can be used as an asset that you can exercise within your portfolio. This is a unique asset in that it provides flexibility and options.

In addition to the broad well-known assets are several that don't fit into the spectrum for different reasons. A closer look at these instruments should help you better understand how they fit into this perspective of the world.

Derivatives—Derivatives are instruments whose price is based on some underlying asset. Some derivatives can be used in much the same way as the instruments in the financial goals spectrum but are also more traditionally used as hedging instruments. They don't have a specific place on the spectrum because their uses vary widely according to the type of derivative. The most common types of derivatives include equity futures, commodity futures, options, and foreign exchange futures.

Commodities, collectibles, and real estate—Diversification works best by using assets that balance one another in contributing to the two primary goals of protection against permanent loss of capital and loss of purchasing power. In other words, diversification within your savings portfolio is really about understanding the capital structure of different entities and how the cash flows and asset performance can be combined to generate a balanced return consistent with your overall goals. In recent decades portfolio managers have started to include in their models many different asset classes that have not traditionally been thought of as an essential part of the average portfolio. Specifically they are increasingly using commodities, collectibles, and real estate to diversify portfolios. But none of these instruments will generally provide consistent protection against purchasing power loss or permanent loss of capital, your two primary goals.

As I discussed in Chapter 4, the real, real returns from both real estate (as a place you'll live, not an investment property such as commercial real estate or a REIT) and commodities tend to be poor over long periods of time. Therefore these assets generally don't help provide purchasing power protection or protection from permanent loss. Housing should be thought of as an expense when viewed through real, real returns, while commodities are also generally an expense in the capital structure. Like derivatives commodities can be used as a hedging instrument but will not always provide consistent protection against permanent loss. Many collectibles are thinly traded or poorly tracked, and recent studies have shown that art in particular does not generate the high returns that are widely believed.[12] Broadly collectibles are niche items that cannot be regarded as reliable assets that help us consistently achieve our primary goals. As a whole this means commodities, collectibles, and real estate are potential hedging or speculative instruments but not reliable as core portfolio holdings because they cannot be relied upon to achieve our two primary goals.

Gold and silver—Gold and silver are unique assets because they are not only commodities but a form of money. Gold and silver are a few of the closest things we have to a global medium of exchange. In addition we're still just a few decades removed from the time when gold was considered the purest form of global money. This makes these assets unique in the way they are *perceived*.

I think we ultimately have to view gold and silver more like commodities and less like money. The probable future of modern money does not lie in physical money but in electronic money. That is, money is increasingly becoming a record of account that exists in computer systems and on accounting statements. Money is being used less and less as a physical item. Therefore owning gold in the belief that it is a form of money requires a particularly high level of faith (or distrust in the fiat monetary system) and historical mysticism. This is what I would call a faith put. In other words embedded in the price of gold and silver is a premium above and beyond their actual productive value as a real resource.

An asset that has no cash-flow stream but whose users view it as valuable because it is money derives its value largely from mere perception, not from its actual economic utility. This makes gold and silver potentially dangerous assets to own because their value as purchasing loss protection assets lies primarily in the belief that they are valuable rather than any actual productive use. This means they expose you to substantial permanent loss risk with relatively unreliable purchasing power protection. This creates sizable permanent loss risk in these assets if society were to view them merely as commodities and not as forms of money. And, as I've noted previously, commodities don't tend to generate positive real terms. Therefore gold and silver should be viewed as hedging vehicles, not essential pieces of the financial goals spectrum.

THE PURPOSE OF THE FINANCIAL GOALS SPECTRUM

Once you understand the general premise of the financial goals spectrum, you need to understand where your priorities lie so you can apply this understanding to an actual portfolio. Are you more concerned about purchasing power protection or are you more concerned about permanent loss protection? The savings portfolio scale in Figure 5.13 provides a visual representation of how to apply the spectrum to the savings portfolio concept. The savings portfolio scale shows how financial goals relate to asset allocation. As you can see, the saver who allocates 100 percent of their assets to stocks will have less protection against permanent loss, while the saver who allocates 100 percent of their assets to cash will have less protection against the risk of purchasing power loss. Once again balance provides the answer.

As a general rule I think it's safe to assume that the vast majority of savers should have some balance between these goals with an emphasis on purchasing power protection if you're in the asset accumulation phase of your life and an emphasis on permanent loss protection if you're in the asset protection phase of your life. The savings portfolio scale provides a general framework for allocating assets in three broad periods of our lives.

Productive Asset Gathering—Younger people who are in the most productive asset gathering phase of their life need balance in their total portfolio so as to maximize their personal investment portfolio. But these asset gatherers also need to plan for the future by constructing a savings portfolio. So thirty-year-olds in the asset accumulation phase of their life will generally need more balance in their savings portfolio than seventy-year-olds. The thirty-year-old productive asset gatherer will be more inclined to implement something along the lines of a balanced 70–30 stock-bond portfolio with the goal of achieving balanced protection

Figure 5.13: The Savings Portfolio Scale

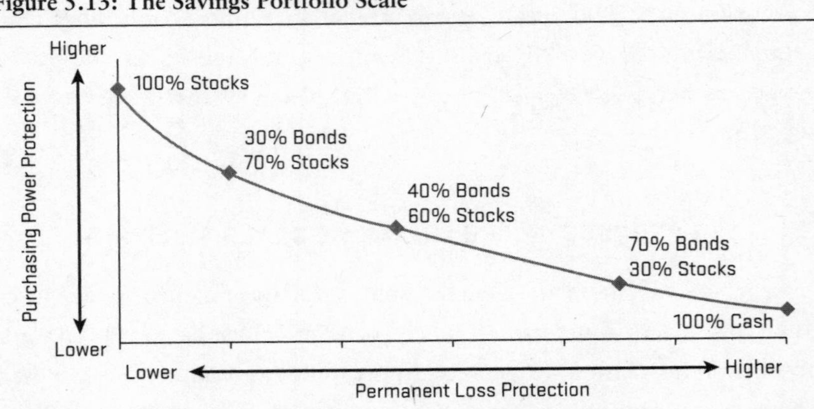

against purchasing power loss and permanent loss risk, with an emphasis on purchasing power loss protection.

Productive Asset Protection—Middle-aged people are in the prime of their earning years but are also transitioning into a time when they must be more cognizant of protecting their assets. Therefore they are focused on enhancing their investment portfolio and are increasingly concerned about the risk of permanent loss within their savings portfolio. The productive asset protector is therefore more inclined to seek balance in a portfolio with something like a 60–40 stock-bond blend.

Asset Protection—Asset protectors are generally older workers or retirees who have developed a fairly substantial asset base that must keep pace with inflation but need not outperform inflation to the degree that younger people require. The asset protector is moving into a phase in which stability is more important than ever and permanent loss risk becomes less important. This person is looking for something more consistent with a 30–70 stock-bond split or perhaps heavier allocation to bonds or cash.

Of course this is a general guideline, and the real details of implementation depend entirely on your personal needs and goals. The more sophisticated macroeconomic market participant might be inclined to implement tactical strategies that I will discuss in a bit more detail later.

WHY REINVENT THE WHEEL?

Some people will look at this asset allocation approach and wisely ask: Why do we need to reinvent the wheel here? Why can't we just understand asset allocation along the same lines as the efficient frontier and modern portfolio theory? The purpose is not to reinvent the wheel but to improve it by clearly defining what our financial goals are and applying more realistic solutions to achieving those financial goals. The purpose of this perspective is to get away from the dangerous idea that risk equals return and the concept that we can ride out risk if we have a long enough time horizon.

Perhaps most important, this approach doesn't require that you predict the future by using vague mathematical inputs, erroneous assumptions, and historical back-testing. Instead you're using a set of simple understandings to formulate a rational and objective approach to portfolio construction. You're understanding assets as they actually exist in the capital structure and the role they play. You're understanding the intertemporal conundrum and how this creates the need for greater portfolio stability. You're understanding the financial goals spectrum and how specific assets help us achieve our goals. And you're using the savings portfolio scale to more properly visualize risk management in your portfolio. These concepts render many of the MPT concepts flawed. And it shows that the idea of stocks for the long run is largely inapplicable. The total portfolio approach provides a much more realistic approach to portfolio construction.

PUTTING IT ALL TOGETHER

These building blocks provide a general framework for approaching the markets and understanding how to construct a portfolio. Here are some general guidelines you may find helpful in structuring a savings portfolio:

- Set realistic goals and expectations. Are you primarily an investor or saver? And what type of saver are you? Use the savings portfolio scale to determine what your goals are and how they apply to a general asset allocation approach.
- Establish whether you will outsource your portfolio to an asset manager or whether you will manage it yourself. If you outsource it or choose more active asset managers, you need to properly review and audit those managers.
- Settle on a methodology and how you're going to go about specifically implementing a portfolio. If you manage your own assets or choose a manager to manage the portfolio for you, you must decide whether to implement a methodology including strategic diversification, tactical diversification, or both.

1. Establishing a Methodology

Putting together a portfolio is useless if you don't have a plan for executing the portfolio process and maintaining it over time. Nothing is more important than sticking to the plan you create for your total portfolio.

For most of us it's easy to get caught up in other things in life and forget about maintaining our portfolios. This is where having an adviser, while not necessary for everyone, can be beneficial for many people. Managing your own assets is not as hard as most people think, but when you're a professional in another field, it helps to have someone looking over your shoulder at times. Whether you use an adviser, manage your own assets, or allocate assets to managed funds, you must base your portfolio on a defined methodology.

Establishing a methodology, or finding an adviser or manager with a methodology, is the most crucial element of the portfolio construction process. This ensures that you'll have structure within your portfolio and will help you stay on track. Portfolio construction is all about process, so establish your plan, dollar cost average, rebalance to maintain your allocations, review your holdings periodically, and reinvest in your plan whenever possible. This means you need to define your specific approach and implement specific rules and guidelines for maintaining that approach throughout your life. If you can automate your plan, you don't even need to invest a significant amount of time in it. Modern technology makes it increasingly easy to transfer funds, automate periodic purchases, and create structure within a portfolio. But you have to be willing to create a methodology and a plan for managing your own assets. Otherwise, your savings portfolio will be neglected, and the risk of failing to meet your financial goals will increase. If you can't establish a plan or maintain a plan, use an adviser to help ensure you stay on track.

2. Using Strategic Diversification to Establish a Core Portfolio

Strategic diversification involves structuring a portfolio with many different cash-flow streams to help achieve a balanced and stable return. For most firms or individuals this is the primary allocation of a savings portfolio and could even comprise the entire portfolio. At the very least the different cash-flow streams should comprise the core, or foundational component, of your savings portfolio.

At its most basic level macroeconomic portfolio construction is about using a top-down big-picture perspective of the world to develop a way to benefit from specific macroeconomic cycles, trends, and events. The simplest form of strategic diversification is what I call lazy macroeconomics, or what most people refer to as passive index fund investing. Although most passive investors might not know it, they're implementing a specific type of macroeconomic strategy based on a specific macroeconomic forecast.

A passive index fund approach is usually based on an explicitly bullish macroeconomic forecast. As you may recall from the discussion of Figure 2.2, Gross World Product, the global economy tends to expand over long periods of time. A lazy macroeconomic portfolio is essentially an inactive way of betting on this trend. Using this macroeconomic forecast, you then devise a specific portfolio that benefits from this bullish macroeconomic forecast by creating a diverse, simple to manage, and fee-efficient portfolio comprised of low-fee ETFs (exchange-traded funds) or index funds. A lazy macroeconomic portfolio is not concerned with business-cycle trends, specific short-term asset class trends, or tactical macroeconomic changes. These portfolios are designed around a bet on long-term growth. While this is generally a safe bet over the long term, it could expose portfolios to excessive risks in the short term as there is no global growth guarantee for brief periods.[13]

3. Using Tactical Diversification to Protect Yourself Against Uncertainty and Tail Risk

Tactical diversification is the tactical execution of a portfolio process and plan that helps reduce exposure to uncertainty and tail risk. This can be helpful because a traditional asset allocation approach does not necessarily diversify risk away due to the high correlations between available asset classes. One advantage of taking a tactical global macroeconomic view of the world is that it is a license for flexibility and opportunity. This often involves hedging, the use of options, long or short approaches, or other tactical processes that help reduce portfolio risks. A tactical approach is not always necessary or appropriate for all portfolios and plays a far less important role than strategic diversification for most of us. It is most commonly used by firms and more sophisticated portfolio managers trying to reduce exposure to specific business risks. For instance, an airline might buy crude oil futures contracts to reduce its exposure to price swings in the oil markets, thereby creating stability in its business planning. A tactical approach often involves the use of derivatives to pare risks or neutralizing risks in a portfolio through approaches like shorting and hedging.

A global macroeconomic tactical portfolio does not just assume the world or economy is going to benefit over the long term. Rather, the global macroeconomic tactical approach accounts for the negative correlation of many markets and macroeconomic trends that will often be negative as well as positive. An opportunity always exists somewhere because every market cycle is different and provides different opportunities. A tactical global macroeconomic approach studies different markets, data, and broad economic trends to decipher certain asset class directionality. These strategies often involve accessing larger and more liquid markets using derivatives, indexes, interest rates, currencies, and broad asset classes. These strategies, while ranging from quite simple to opaque and difficult to implement, have proved to be a useful portfolio addition since the new century began. Since BarclayHedge began its Barclay Global Macro Index, the index has handily outperformed the S&P 500, Vanguard Balanced Index, and the HFRI on both a nominal and risk-adjusted basis, as Figure 5.14 shows.

This approach has proved particularly useful in protecting against tail risk. In 2008 the Barclay Global Macro Index posted a –0.65 percent return versus the S&P 500's return of –37 percent. In 1999, 2000, 2001,

Figure 5.14: Barclay Global Macro Index Relative Performance

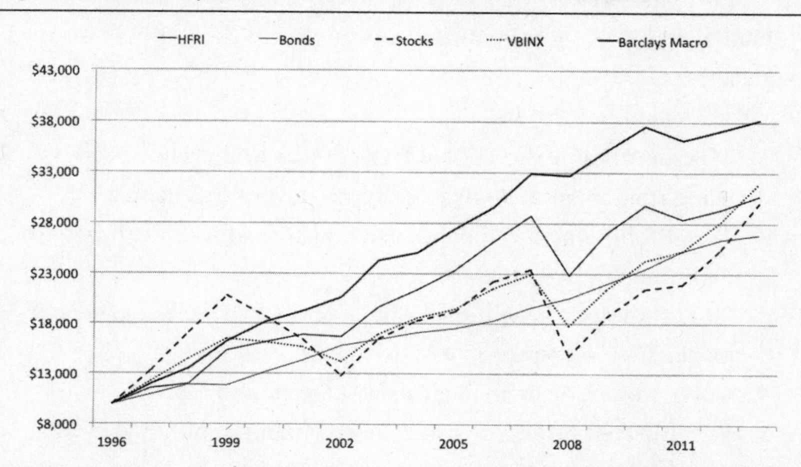

and 2002 the Barclay index posted returns of 20.18 percent, 11.86 percent, 6.31 percent, and 7.07 percent, while the S&P 500 posted returns of 21 percent, –9.1 percent, –11.89 percent, and –22.1 percent.[14] Of course past performance should not be relied upon for understanding future returns, but the diversification and flexibility of the global macroeconomic approach is something that everyone should consider, regardless of their approach.

IMPLEMENTING A TACTICAL APPROACH

Tactical macroeconomic approaches are generally based on understanding broader macroeconomic trends in an attempt to create flexibility through a free-rein style of management in search of absolute returns. This means the manager is generally trying to achieve an absolute positive return by having the flexibility to trade any market the manager deems appropriate. Global macroeconomics is, in many ways, the ultimate in flexible strategies because it provides a portfolio with nearly universal options for potential asset classes and approaches. This approach requires a sophisticated understanding of how the monetary system operates and the factors that could influence future trends. A tactical macroeconomic portfolio manager implements a strategy by using approaches that hedge for potential uncertainty in the business cycle or seek to benefit from macroeconomic trends. A tactical global macroeconomic approach is a license to use cash as a call option for any opportunity that arises.

Global macroeconomic approaches generally fall into these main categories:

1. Macroeconomic directional trend trades and cyclical trends using fundamental analysis of future price movements.
2. Trend-following approaches using historical technical data to determine future prices.
3. Pairs trades, or benefiting from price discrepancies in similarly or negatively correlated assets.
4. Carry trades, or financing one asset with another.
5. Event-driven trades, or using specific themes, political events, or market events for profit.

The most obvious macroeconomic directional trend is the one discussed in the lazy macroeconomics or long-term bullish approach, however, a tactical approach will generally be implemented by someone who recognizes that the business cycle is likely to vary during this longer-term bullish trend. A tactical view might be implemented upon recognizing a potential for sustained long-term negative trends in the macroeconomy. Examples of this include many of the peripheral European countries since 2004 and Japan's deflationary battle of the 1990s and 2000s. Few passive index fund heroes emerged triumphant from the view that these markets were ripe for a stocks-for-the-long-run approach to portfolio building.

A classic tactical approach based on understanding the business cycle is Harry Browne's permanent portfolio. Browne devised an all-weather strategy that is also implemented by Ray Dalio of Bridgewater Associates. This strategy is designed to withstand all the environments to which changes in the business cycle might give rise. Specifically this strategy is designed to benefit from inflation, deflation, recession, and expansion. To achieve this the manager will allocate assets tactically (usually in 25 percent allocations) across four different components: stocks—expansion exposure; bonds—deflation protection; cash—recession protection; gold or other precious metals—inflation protection. This is a relatively inactive cyclically based macroeconomic approach.

A more active tactical approach to the macroeconomic environment generally involves an understanding of the credit cycle and the business cycle and how these cycles influence the market cycle. You will better understand this concept after reading Chapters 6 and 7, which discuss the monetary system and the behavioral component of the markets, but it's helpful to begin thinking of the macroeconomic environment as cyclical. Within this cycle the manager is generally trying to gauge market direction or trend by understanding geopolitical trends, corporate trends, broader economic trends, demographic trends, and other events that produce themes that are potentially profitable. For instance, a manager might understand that China's central bank is buying government bonds that will boost returns while also understanding that such a policy has the potential to put downward pressure on the exchange rate relative to the US dollar. A manager might benefit from such a trend by making a bullish bet on the bond while shorting the currency relative to the dollar. Global macroeconomic tactical approaches are generally agnostic in relation to specific bull markets or bear markets as these approaches view markets as being multifaceted and search markets that have the potential for both upside and downside in prices. As a result many global macroeconomic managers are using long and/or short strategies or long-biased approaches with offsetting hedges in place. This gives these funds the potential to embed significant tail risk protection or protection from extreme risk of permanent loss.

In terms of gauging the business cycle, keeping a close eye on cyclical indicators is crucial. Some key indicators of the business cycle and its relationship to the market cycle include

- The Conference Board Leading Economic Index (http://www.conference-board.org/data/bcicountry.cfm?cid=1).
- Initial jobless claims—one of the best real-time cyclical indicators (see the St. Louis Fed FRED database for many of this and many of the other indicators—http://research.stlouisfed.org/fred2/).
- GDP, Markit PMI global indexes, German ZEW, and EuroCoin Index—broad indicators of global growth, prices, and employment.
- Corporate profits, corporate revenues, earnings—specific corporate indicators.
- Rail traffic—one of the best real-time economic indicators.
- Credit indexes (Merrill Lynch High Yield Bond Index, St. Louis Fed Financial Stress Index, Fed Funds Curve, debt-income ratios, ten-year break-even)—indicators of bond market health and future interest rates.
- Private investment, durable goods orders, industrial production—broader corporate sector indicators.
- Purchasing power parity—an indication of the relative value of differing foreign exchange rates.
- Z.1 Financial Accounts of the United States—one of the most comprehensive data sets for the American economy. This will provide you with everything you need to understand the sectoral balances and the health of the different sectors in the economy.

WHERE DO ACTIVE MANAGERS FIT IN?

Portfolios, whether managed by you or by someone else, by means of index funds or stock picking, are really just varying degrees of active management. Even the most passive approach requires upkeep, maintenance, rebalancing, and reinvestment; has elements of timing; and makes a specific macroeconomic forecast about the future. Therefore it's better to think of all of us as active to some degree.

This debate about active versus passive also creates a blurred distinction and often misleading portrayal of what an active manager does. Studies show that managers who are highly correlated with the S&P 500 often underperform because of closet indexing, but these studies often fail to account for the involvement of many active managers in markets that often go well beyond the scope of the various mutual funds that closet index the S&P 500. These studies also rarely properly account for risk-adjusted returns using any proper measurement of what risk is. In other words the studies are almost always narrow in scope, based on false inputs, and extremely vague in their conclusions. As for closet indexing, it's relatively easy to quantify when a manager doesn't add value and doesn't outperform, but be careful about claims that all active portfolio-management styles are therefore negative.

Additionally this idea that there is such a thing as a passive portfolio management style leads many people to think that they don't need to maintain their portfolios, when maintaining your process and plan over time is one of the most important things you will need to do. Portfolio construction is all about process, and that process does indeed require some active elements during the portfolio's life.

Even worse, the idea of a passive portfolio implies that the portfolio involves no forecasting at all. This couldn't be further from the truth. A passive index fund approach is a specific bet on a bullish future outcome in markets. Most people don't think they're making a forecast because most people assume stocks usually rise or economies always expand, but they are indeed making a specific macroeconomic forecast. Granted, this tends to be a pretty good bet in most cases, but we shouldn't confuse that with being a nonforecast.

The bottom line is it doesn't actually help to be dogmatic and draw a line in the sand between active and passive portfolio management to understand what can hurt a portfolio's performance. The real key to viewing the world of active management is to know when you're doing something that might be beneficial and when you might be doing something that is detrimental to achieving your financial goals.

That said, there's a simple arithmetic truth that every saver has to come to grips with when allocating assets on secondary markets—the market is ultimately the market. And since all of us, in the aggregate, represent the market (active participants of all different varieties), it is undeniable that the average participant with low frictions will generate a higher return than the average participant with high frictions. As Eugene Fama and Kenneth French have stated:

> Passive investors earn the return on the market minus their fees and expenses. In aggregate, active investors also hold the market portfolio, so they also earn the market return minus their fees and expenses. If the fees and expenses of active investors are higher than those of passive investors, active investors must in aggregate lose to passive investors. This is the unavoidable arithmetic of equilibrium accounting.[15]

Therefore we have to be extremely cognizant of portfolio frictions such as fees, taxes, and other inefficiencies that can reduce potential real, real returns.

I think active managers prove their worth by how efficiently they can provide differentiated cash-flow streams relative to what could otherwise be done in a simple correlated index. An active manager provides value in two primary ways:

Strategic Value—Strategic value is when a manager has access to tools, instruments, or a methodology that might not otherwise be replicable through an index. The odds are, if there's a highly correlated index for a specific strategy, that manager is unlikely to add significant value over a highly correlated low-fee index. There are times, however, when a manager provides strategic value by giving you access to instruments or strategies that are not widely available in current inactive index funds or ETFs. This is most valuable when a methodology is difficult for the average retail client to implement. An example of this might involve a hedge fund that can give you access to private equity or other alternative assets that are often difficult to acquire in a retail brokerage account.

Procedural Value—Procedural value is added when a manager helps provide structure to your portfolio by helping you stay on track or implementing the plan for you. Many people don't want to manage their own assets or don't have the time, understanding, or discipline to do so. Managing your own assets can be time consuming, difficult, and intimidating. Finding someone who has a high level of integrity, competence, understanding, and process can be extremely valuable for people who are too busy or overwhelmed to handle their own assets. An active manager with a low-fee structure can be appropriate for many people in this situation.

Valuable active managers and advisers are not always easy to find in today's world where closet indexing is so rampant, but that doesn't mean they don't exist. You just need to know what you're looking for and whether an active manager is really adding value to your overall approach. What follows is a simple guideline for picking active managers.

GUIDELINES FOR PICKING ACTIVE MANAGERS

When you analyze the performance of a more active manager, you have to be careful to understand how they conduct their business to ensure that the manager is not closet indexing or adding unnecessary frictions. This makes reviewing a manager an important part of the fund selection process. Some requirements I would expect from an active manager include

1. Transparency—Unfortunately we live in the age of Bernie Madoff. With the huge technological advancements and expansion of access to the financial world comes the increasing ease of fraud and scams. There have been corrupt users of money as long as money has existed, and it's never been easier to execute such corruption. Transparency of your assets is paramount. If you can't log in to your personal account and see your assets on a daily basis, you should feel uncomfortable about allocating assets to a manager at that firm. There's simply no need for this type of secrecy in the modern technological asset-management age.

2. Mutual goals—Make sure the interests of the manager are aligned with yours. I prefer to know that a manager has a substantial asset allocation in the portfolio you're allocating savings to. If the manager is confident enough to run a particular strategy for their clients, they should have no problem having skin in the game. If the manager won't put their money where their mouth is, why should you put your money there?
3. Liquidity—Illiquidity is a dangerous strategic approach for an asset manager, and it impedes the client's ability to access funds. Funds should be liquid so as to give the client easy access to assets and greater flexibility. Lockup arrangements are generally unnecessary and unfair to the client. If you can't access your funds on demand, look elsewhere. Consider an exception in the case of some primary market investments.
4. Low fees—We live in a low-fee world. As a general rule, if a manager charges more than 0.5 percent, you can probably build a similar portfolio for less. Sometimes a slightly higher fee might be acceptable, but that requires substantial strategic and procedural value by the manager.
5. Minimal frictions—Fees aren't the only friction in a portfolio. Ensure that the manager isn't causing adverse tax effects or passing on to you hidden frictions in the portfolio.
6. Process—Portfolio management is all about process and methodology. If your manager doesn't have a clear, concise, and differentiated methodology, they're not adding value.
7. Strategic diversification—Concentration is a killer in the portfolio management world. Excessive exposure to certain asset classes or individual securities is a red flag. Always look for managers with diversified strategies but avoid closet indexers.
8. Big-picture understanding—We don't live in a world where managers can simply understand niche markets and expect to succeed. So many macroeconomic currents are converging that managers need to diversify their portfolios as well as their knowledge. Ignorance of the new macroeconomic world is a red flag that should always make you question whether a manager is lucky or good.

A WORD ON HEDGE FUNDS

Hedge funds are the new hot thing in the world of finance, and I expect the industry to grow substantially in the coming decades. Hedge funds can be valuable for several reasons. The primary reason is that they have a great deal more flexibility in executing their strategy than most traditional asset managers. For most retail clients there is rarely reasonably priced access to derivatives, commodities, and some of the other products and strategies offered through hedge-fund approaches. This gives hedge funds a great deal of potential strategic diversification value. Hedge funds also provide a good deal of procedural value as most of these funds are run under strict strategies that have a highly specialized methodology.

On the other hand hedge funds have a number of drawbacks, including illiquidity, high fees, lack of regulation, use of leverage, and lack of transparency. Most of us simply have no need to allocate assets to hedge funds. This doesn't mean they are all useless; however, unless you are extremely sophisticated in analyzing the funds and establishing whether they are adding value to your portfolio, it's probably unnecessary to allocate capital to such funds. When considering a hedge fund always consider a third-party opinion or audit.

REVIEWING SOME KEY CONCEPTS

You can apply the principles in this chapter to your portfolio in many different ways, and depending on your needs, you can layer various tactical approaches or even different strategic approaches throughout your entire portfolio. For most of us the basic rule of "keep it simple, stupid" is probably the most appropriate. Understanding high-level macroeconomics and tactical approaches is not entirely necessary for building a rather basic savings portfolio. This is particularly true if you choose to manage your own assets. Simplifying your process will increase the odds that you will actually invest the time to properly manage your own portfolio.

That said, let me recap some basic concepts.

As you construct your total portfolio, you need to understand where to make real investments and where to allocate savings. Your investment portfolio will be where you invest in increasing your future production (primarily through your primary source of income and area of expertise) and will help generate the cash flow that builds your total portfolio. Your savings portfolio, on the other hand, should be comprised of assets that need to be there for specific future needs or uncertainties.

Once you have maximized your investment portfolio, you have to figure out how to construct a savings portfolio with a specific methodology. Remember, you have two simple goals for such assets: to protect against loss of purchasing power and permanent loss of capital. From there you must decipher which goal is more important to you without forgetting that balance should be your baseline. Are you trying to achieve both goals or are you less concerned about protecting your purchasing power and more concerned about simply keeping what you already have? How will you execute your methodology or will you pay someone else to execute your methodology for you?

In reviewing the different instruments available to achieve these goals, you can begin to estimate some reasonably safe ways to diversify your assets across these instruments to meet your personal goals. Apply the financial goals spectrum to the savings portfolio scale to build a balanced portfolio that helps you meet your personal goals. For most of you a low-fee, diversified, and inactive portfolio will be adequate.

Maintain a specific methodology. Remember, portfolio construction is about process. And a process requires a plan, maintenance, and upkeep. There's no point creating a plan if you're not going to stick with it over the years.

Consider tactical diversification as a way to protect the portfolio further against uncertainty and tail risk. Although this isn't always necessary, it can be appropriate if applied using the right active manager or methodology.

Those are the core understandings for constructing a portfolio. in addition, it's also helpful to remember some of the key rules that should drive your specific portfolio construction process:

1. Fees are your enemy. As I showed in Chapter 4, the average 0.9 percent fee structure can have catastrophic effects on the portfolio over the long term. As a general rule I would be hesitant to ever pay a management fee of more than 0.5 percent, and the odds are that you can construct a perfectly appropriate portfolio for even less than that. If you feel more

comfortable outsourcing your portfolio to an adviser or manager, adhere to the same basic rule. Few managers can justify a high fee structure these days.

2. Don't chase returns, benchmarks, or play the beat-the-market game. Most of us have simple goals—we are trying to generate a moderately high risk-adjusted return while protecting our portfolios from permanent loss and purchasing power loss. You don't need to beat the market in your savings portfolio. At the same time you need to understand benchmarks so you can avoid more active strategies that are closet indexing.
3. Don't play the microeconomic game. It's a macroeconomic world, and your portfolio should properly reflect that. The microeconomic game is a loser's game for most of us. You can't compete with computers designed to take your money, PhDs writing algorithms that search for value, or the army of investment bankers specializing in what you're trying to do in your spare time. Also don't forget that the markets are dominated by macroeconomic trends now. The microeconomic approach is a far less important market driver in the new macroeconomic world.
4. Set realistic expectations and goals. Your savings portfolio is not your get-rich-quick portfolio. Further, most financial assets probably generate a lower return than you've come to believe; keep an eye on the return that goes into your pocket—the real, real return.
5. Create a process and methodology you can track. Portfolio construction is about process. This requires strict structures within the portfolio design process. If you aren't comfortable managing your own assets, make sure that your manager has a strict methodology and adheres to the same principles you would expect if you were managing the assets on your own.
6. Automate your plan when possible. Your behavioral biases will be your worst enemy. Take yourself out of the game where possible, but don't eliminate yourself from the game entirely.
7. Always contribute to your plan. Remember, your savings portfolio is the repository of savings that flow from your primary source of income. Maximize and invest in your primary

source of income so you can always contribute to your savings portfolio. Think of cash as a call option with no expiration date that you can exercise whenever you want. This also means you should emphasize dollar cost averaging, rebalancing, and reinvesting in your plan.

8. Keep it simple, stupid! A simple plan is an easy plan to execute. The biggest risk to your savings portfolio is that you won't execute it and maintain it. When in doubt, simplify, simplify, simplify.
9. More active portfolio approaches can add value, but double-check your managers. There is real value in having an adviser or manager if you can find strategic and procedural value without the high fees.
10. Never, ever forget that your total portfolio is something that is part of your life, but it is not your whole life. You don't live to accumulate money. You accumulate money so you can live.

CHAPTER 6

THE IMPORTANCE OF UNDERSTANDING BEHAVIORAL FINANCE

The battle to understand money is won in your own mind.

BOBBY JONES, THE WORLD FAMOUS GOLFER, ONCE SAID THAT the game of golf is played primarily on the five-inch course between your ears. Golf, however, is won not only with your mind but with your physical abilities. The world of money, on the other hand, is something that exists almost entirely in our minds and is used as a way to represent the physical world in order to give us access to it. Money is really nothing more than something we created in our heads. And understanding its many uses, the macroeconomic system, and the financial system is largely about understanding how we think and react to the uses of money.

The field of behavioral finance is the study of understanding the economy through the psychologically driven actions of its participants. If we know that our economy is little more than the sum of the transactions that occur within that system, then understanding the behavior that drives those transactions is paramount in understanding how the system operates. Sun Tzu says in *The Art of War,* "If you know neither yourself nor your enemy, you will always endanger yourself."[1] Understanding behavioral finance isn't only about becoming smarter and better informed about the world around you; it's also about understanding yourself and the way others think so you can be better prepared to engage in this system. This matters for politics, markets, and everyday life.

YOU ARE PROBABLY YOUR OWN WORST ENEMY

The uniqueness of the human mind is what separates people from the rest of the animal kingdom. We are exceedingly intelligent, calculating, and emotional. While these emotions are some of our greatest benefits in everyday life, in the financial world they are often our worst enemy. The unfortunate reality is that human minds aren't particularly well designed to handle the many problems that arise when interacting with money. Money complicates a seemingly simple existence by introducing a highly complex variable into our lives. While it's intended to simplify things, money can actually create a huge amount of stress in our lives because it is something we all need, few understand, and we are all ill equipped to handle. Understanding money is largely about understanding how we are poorly designed to handle modern money. By understanding our own natural weaknesses, we can better prepare ourselves to deal with the problems our own actions will inevitably produce.

PROSPECT THEORY, INHERENT RISK AVERSION, AND EXPECTED VALUE

In 2011 Dr. Andrew Lo wrote a superb research paper, "Fear, Greed, and Financial Crises: A Cognitive Neurosciences Perspective."[2] Lo used a variant of prospect theory, developed by Daniel Kahneman and Amos Tversky to describe how we tend to value gains and losses differently.[3] Lo's paper asks us to consider two investment opportunities. In the first you're guaranteed a $240,000 profit. In the second you're offered a $1 million lottery ticket with a 25 percent chance of winning the money and a 75 percent chance of winning nothing. The first opportunity has an expected value lower than the second one, but most people will choose the first option because of the guarantee. They are naturally more risk averse. But Lo then asks us to consider a different scenario. In this case option 1 guarantees a loss of $750,000 and option 2 is a lottery ticket with a 75 percent chance of a $1 million loss and a 25 percent chance of $0 loss. In this case Lo found that most people gamble and take the riskier option, even though the expected value is exactly same as in the first example. Lo notes that the payoffs for the two most popular decisions have a lower overall probability of gain than the two options people tend not to choose. We tend to become more irrational when confronted with the potential for losses. In other words our natural instinct leads us to make inefficient decisions.

This point also highlights our inability to think in terms of expected value. Our inherent risk aversion leads us to fail in calculating which option will give us the most efficient outcome. At the 1989 annual meeting of Berkshire Hathaway Warren Buffett was asked about the way he thinks of his aggregate decision-making process. He said: "Take the probability of loss times the amount of possible loss from the probability of gain times the amount of possible gain. That is what we're trying to do. It's imperfect, but that's what it's all about."[4] This perspective is a lot like understanding the way a good blackjack player bets. Casino games are always bad ways to make money because they're designed for you to lose, but certain players can increase their odds of winning by knowing when the odds favor them. Card counters are the classic example of gamblers who take a pure gamble and turn it into a more calculated bet. They're essentially calculating the expected value of particular hands and then figuring out when it makes the most sense to make big bets. Buffett is the stereotypical patient portfolio manager who places tactical bets when he thinks the odds favor him. He uses his cash like it's an option he can exercise at any time, and he uses expected values to know when to exercise. And perhaps most important, Buffett adheres to his own mantra of "be greedy when others are fearful and be fearful when others are greedy." In other words Buffett is a master at feeding off the emotional miscalculations of others.

A MONKEY ECONOMY AS IRRATIONAL AS OURS

Although human beings are far removed from the rest of the animal kingdom, we are still animals at our core. And we suffer from many of the same strengths and weaknesses that the rest of the animal kingdom does. At the core of this is a basic survival need. In 1915 the Harvard physiologist Walter Cannon discovered the fight-or-flight response. This is an innate and primitive reaction that occurs in animals under duress. Interestingly what happens to people in such a situation is a near-transformation of our thinking. Our thinking changes from a broad focus to a narrow focus. Fear takes over our mind. Everything is a potential threat to our survival. We are quick to respond and often inefficient to respond. And more often than not, it is easier to flee than fight. That's what we're designed to do. And when dealing with money and markets, the mentality of survival at any cost can be highly destructive. It drives us to respond rapidly, inefficiently, and irrationally. Markets and money often take away the one thing that gives us so much power over our surroundings—a sense of calculated control. While we are extremely attached to our need for money, money doesn't care about us at all.

When confronted with complex decisions, we make mistakes, we panic, we turn to our animal instincts, which scream, "Survive at any cost." And despite our evolutionary progress, our survival instincts remain quite primitive. Don't worry, though. We aren't unique in this regard. Despite our evolutionary leaps and bounds, we are not so far removed from our animal brethren when it comes to how our survival instincts interfere with our ability to interact with money.

In an excellent TED video from 2010, Laurie Santos, a professor of psychology at Yale, describes how she examined the workings of a simple economy using monkeys and found that we are far less sophisticated than we think.[5] In fact her findings were eerily similar to those of Andrew Lo's. Santos began her experiment by teaching monkeys how to use a currency to trade for food. She went on to create a monkey marketplace where the monkeys could exchange coins for food. What did she find? She found that the monkeys don't like to save. They often steal from one another and from the market salesperson. They display greedy tendencies. Sound familiar?

She then performed a simple experiment that shows just how irrational humans can be and how our natural instincts can drive us to make irrational decisions when confronted with a complex situation that affects survival. Pretend you have $1,000. You have two options. In option 1 you can you flip a coin: heads, you win $1,000 more, tails, you win nothing. In option 2 you are given a risk-free $500—a 50 percent risk-free return. According to Santos, most people will choose option 2.

In the second experiment she gave a human $2,000 and offered the person two ways to *lose* that money. Option 1 was again a flip of a coin.

Heads means a risk of losing $1,000. Tails means the person loses nothing. In option 2 the person can play it safe and lose $500 with certainty. Most people choose to flip the coin, taking more risk.

In game 1 you max out your gains at $2,000 if you flip the coin but risk gaining nothing. The risk-free decision leaves you with $1,500. In the second game you max out your gains at $2,000 if you flip the coin but take the risk of losing 50 percent of your capital. If you choose the risk free path in game 2 you again end up with $1,500 just as you did in game 1. So the risk-free result is the same no matter what; however, when it comes to the option of potentially losing money, most people decide to take excessive risk by flipping the coin in game 2. That's precisely what Lo found in his similar experiment. Santos found that monkeys do the exact same thing. Their survival instinct is to avoid losing something they already have, but in doing so they're irrationally willing to take excessive risk.

So what's going on here? Why are we making a poor risk management decision here? Santos says this is the result of two biases. The first is our instinct to think in relative terms. We have a difficult time thinking in absolute terms. We always compare our current position to something else—a benchmark, our neighbors, our coworkers. The second bias is loss aversion. Humans hate losing anything of value they have obtained. So in a misguided attempt to save money, we actually take more risk at times. Sound familiar? Ever held on to a stock just hoping to break even? Ever been in the red in Las Vegas, taking money out of the ATM and telling yourself you will just get back to even? It's exactly the same thing.

Santos concludes that many of our biases that result in poor decisions are no different than the irrational survival-related instincts that drive other animals' decision-making processes. Therefore many of these biases are inherent and difficult to overcome. But the most important takeaway here is her conclusion. Santos concluded that the best way to overcome our limitations is the simple act of recognizing them. Accept that you know less than you think you do. Accept that you can and will be wrong. Accept that you will make mistakes, learn from them, and only then can you actually overcome them. Humans are irrational, therefore markets are irrational; however, that doesn't mean you have to be the one constantly making irrational decisions.

THE ANIMAL SPIRITS THAT DRIVE ASSET PRICES

At the most basic level transactions are driven by human decisions. And the price at which those transactions occur is largely the result of the behavior of market participants. It's important to always think of the complete picture (macro view) in this multidimensional manner. You are not the only one involved in the transactions you make. This is important to understand because many people use a microeconomic understanding to describe a more macroeconomic concept. For instance, when you sell a stock in your brokerage account, you see your stock disappear and your cash balance increase. It sort of looks like the stock just disappears and the cash appears from nowhere. But that's not really what happens. Someone was on the other side of this trade. The other person decided they wanted to own more stock, and you decided you wanted to own more cash. When you agreed on a price, the trade was executed. It was a simple exchange, just as the name of the New York Stock Exchange suggests.

What's interesting to note is that the value of the stock can fluctuate relative to the amount of cash in the market. The price you arrive at in the course of this market exchange will depend largely on the eagerness of the buyer and seller during the transaction. If you're extremely fearful and you just want to get out of a position, you might be willing to sell at a price lower than you would if you were more patient. Likewise, if the buyer is patient they might be willing to enter a purchase price that is below what you want to sell the asset for. This dynamic is most relevant in illiquid markets.

During my career I've traded thin (illiquid, low-volume) markets substantially. There's no better way to learn market price dynamics than trading in a thin market. For instance, I'll never forget being awake at 4 a.m. California time in a position that was worth several hundred thousand dollars. I was engaged in an event-driven trade based on an earnings report, and the news was bad all around. But the market for the stock was illiquid to begin with, and at 4 a.m. there were literally no buyers. You could see the market wake up as the morning wore on as potential buyers would put in bids 20 percent below yesterday's close, then 19 percent below, then 18 percent. And that's where they stopped. The news was so bad that no one was willing to put in an order above an 18 percent loss from the day before. And there I was, holding the bag on a stock that I now knew was worth at least 18 percent less than the day before. Unfortunately I was eager to sell and no one was eager to buy so I walked away that morning with a bruised ego, a much smaller bank account, and an expensive lesson in market dynamics.

Markets are just much bigger versions of millions of these transactions. And because these transactions occur around the business cycle, they tend to move in a highly cyclical fashion. Figure 6.1 shows the roller coaster of emotions we tend to experience as the business cycle or market cycle expands and contracts. This cycle ranges from the phase of hope, when it looks like things are getting better, to pure delusion, when everyone thinks nothing can ever go wrong, to denial when no one believes things are deteriorating, to despair when we throw in the towel and think it can only get worse.

UNDERSTANDING MARKET BUBBLES AND ASSET PRICE COMPRESSION

Have you ever been to the theater when everyone started clapping at the end of a performance and you just joined in for no rational reason?

Figure 6.1: The Cyclicality of Market Behavior

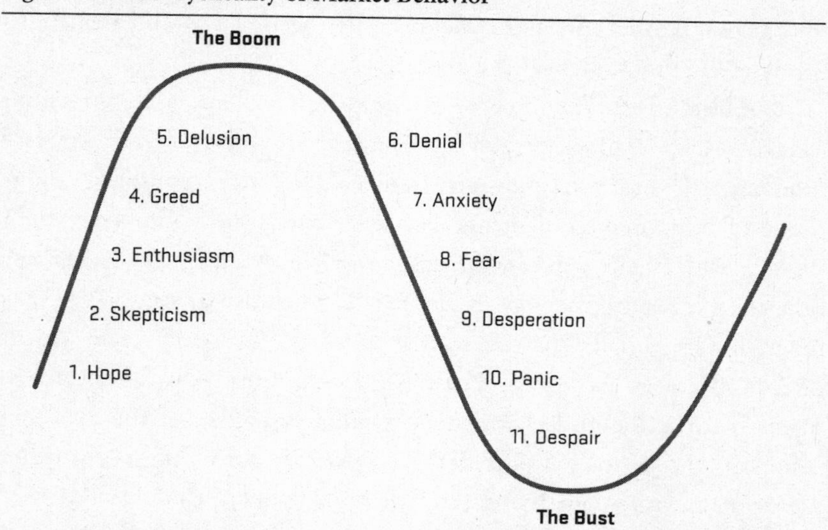

Have you ever seen a few of those clappers then stand up as you think to yourself: "Does this mean I need to stand up? I don't want to stand up." But you find yourself standing up just moments later for fear of being the only person who isn't standing up and clapping in perfect rhythm with a group of total strangers. Most of us have probably experienced something like this. If you think about it, it actually doesn't make a lot of sense. There's no way every single person in the theater enjoyed the show equally, and some people certainly didn't think it deserved a standing ovation. Then why did everyone feel the need to clap in perfect unison? You didn't necessarily want to clap, you didn't necessarily want to stand up, and there was no reason for everyone to clap in unison. But that's the common result. Why? Humans are pack animals. And pack animals herd. And animals travel in herds because they feel safer traveling in herds. No one wants to be the outcast. This is one of the most powerful dynamics that drive irrational markets.

Friedrich Nietzsche once said: "Madness is a rare thing in individuals—but in groups . . . it is the rule."[6] We've all had our fair share of experiences with market bubbles since the mid-1980s. We know prices can react irrationally, but why do they do this? Why do prices tend to deviate from their fundamentals to such an extreme degree that they become unstable? Why do bubbles form? Before we can even answer that, we should ask what a bubble is. A *bubble* is an environment in which the market price of an asset has deviated from its underlying fundamentals to the point that its current market price has become unstable relative to the asset's ability to deliver the expected result.

Bubbles are the extreme result of what I call price compression. Market prices are ultimately a function of the way we perceive corporate fundamentals, past price movements, macroeconomic trends, and a multitude of other market elements. Perhaps none is more important than the way we actually perceive the actions of others. At times this perception will exacerbate the way market participants drive asset prices. Our inherently irrational responses will at times price in many years' worth of data in a very short period of time. This creates a disequilibrium in prices because the underlying asset is unlikely to deliver the expected results in the period of time that its price currently reflects. In other words many years' worth of asset price performance is bid into the price of the asset, creating the potential for a disequilibrium. One of the most famous examples of this is the Nasdaq Bubble in the 1990s when the potential astronomical long-term growth was priced into many present asset prices. Of course, many of these firms never met the expectations that the markets had priced into their shares and when this realization came to fruition the price compression turned into a market crash.

Figure 6.2 illustrates this dynamic. Both charts show the asset reaching the same final price in the same period of time. But the lower price chart shows a compression occurring as market participants price in the final result in a very brief period. This is the disequilibrium and resulting increase of risk that often occurs inside a market bubble or an asset price mania.

Said differently, because market participants have priced in such high expectations, if the underlying asset does not deliver the returns expected by its owners, the asset is susceptible to substantial downside risk as a repricing occurs to adjust for the price compression. The owners have essentially borrowed future returns for less probable current returns. The boom leads to the bust. Understanding price compression is

Figure 6.2: Price Compression

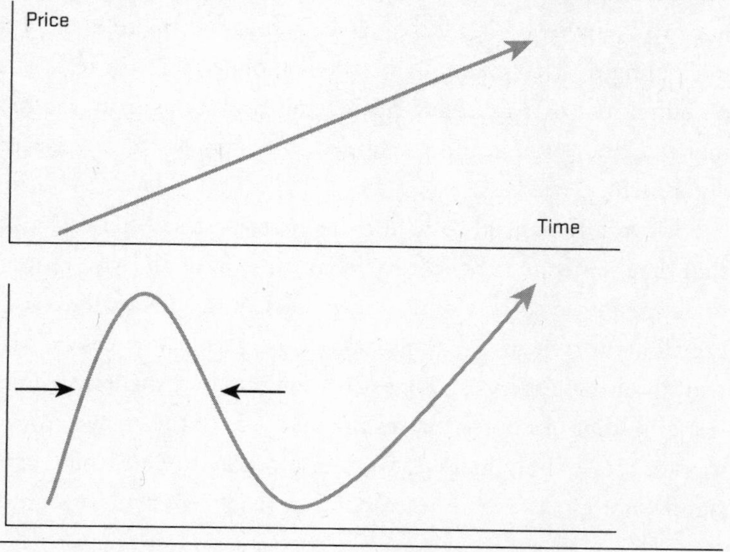

ultimately about being able to recognize risk in the market price of assets so as to be able to determine when the expected value of an asset is lower than the market perceives it to be.

THE PSYCHOLOGY BEHIND A RISING MARKET

What really causes the market to behave irrationally? To a large degree it is the general disdain for rising market prices. Why would this be? Because, the odds are, you aren't participating in all the gains. There's some sad math behind the reality of financial asset price increases, and that math says we all can't benefit from the market's rises. You see, all securities issued are always held by *someone*. The market, in the aggregate, is the market. And we don't all have all our chips in rising financial assets, because, by definition, we can't. When I buy stocks, someone else sells their stocks. Again, all securities issued are always held by someone. And someone's ownership of stocks means someone else doesn't own stocks. Someone is now sitting on cash, potentially regretting having sold to me, as I am now benefiting from rising prices.

When financial asset prices go up, there's an inevitable sense of opportunity loss (by someone). You feel like you're missing out on gains you could have been a part of. You probably feel like you're falling behind. This is a perfectly common reaction, but it's also totally unreasonable and almost certainly misguided. Why? Because we don't really have to be involved in all the markets gains all the time. As I discussed in Chapter 5, what we really need our money to do for us is outperform potential loss of purchasing power and protect us from the risk of permanent loss of capital in a manner consistent with our risk tolerances and portfolio needs.

It's totally natural to hate rising asset prices. After all, it's a certain sign that someone is benefiting from something and you're not. But the worst response to this opportunity cost is to believe that you need to position yourself in a manner that could result in excessive risk on the way to chasing returns. That's just classic herd mentality, and it's this response that ultimately drives the madness of the crowd from a benign market to a bubbly market. So, yes, it's okay to hate rising asset prices. But it's not okay for you to respond to rising asset prices irrationally.

THE MARKET IS A HEARTLESS BEAST

When you consider the reality that someone is always going to hate rising stock prices (as a result of being left out), we must also realize that the market doesn't care at all about the way we feel. The market doesn't have emotions or feelings. As Adam Smith succinctly put it:

> A stock is, for all practical purposes, a piece of paper that sits in a bank vault. Most likely you will never see it. It may or may not have an Intrinsic Value; what it is worth on any given day depends on the confluence of buyers and sellers that day. The most important thing to realize is simplistic: the stock doesn't know you own it. All those marvelous things, or those terrible things, that you feel about a stock, or a list of stocks, or an amount of money represented by a list of stocks, all of those things are unreciprocated by the stock or the group of stocks. You can be in love if you want to, but that piece of paper doesn't love you, and unreciprocated love can turn into masochism, narcissism, or, even worse, market losses and unreciprocated hate.[7]

Markets do not care about you. They don't care about your family or your feelings, and they particularly don't care about your wallet. The market is a heartless beast that has no feelings. When you approach these markets, you have to always remember that the less emotionally involved you get, the better off you'll be. Don't fall in love with a financial asset. Fall in love with a process. By having a process you'll avoid the heartache involved in often thinking that the market cares about you.

HOPE IS NOT A STRATEGY

It was October 2007 and the bull market in Asia was rip-snorting mad. I was having a spectacular year, sitting on gains in excess of 25 percent in my personal portfolio and probably letting my hubris get the best of me. I had begun to dabble in overseas trading that year as I expanded my strategies and tried to add another weapon to the arsenal. My ignorance and overconfidence were about to treat me to a front-row lesson in market bubbles.

I have always been a bit of a contrarian, but I have also always tried to wait for fat pitches. China's bull market in 2007 was the contrarian fat pitch that just kept getting fatter. In the middle of October 2007 I took a cut. I shorted (bet against) a number of Hong Kong–traded stocks. Primarily large cap stocks traded in Hong Kong *and* Shanghai. It just so happened that I had shorted the market to the very day of the peak in Shanghai. I had nailed it. But a funny thing was going on in Hong Kong. Regulators were talking about a way to reduce the price discrepancy between the Hong Kong market and the Shanghai market.

In case you don't know, China has three large stock exchanges—Shanghai, Hong Kong, and Shenzhen. Many of the same Chinese companies trade on multiple exchanges. But the exchanges have different rules. For instance, only citizens of mainland China can own the Shanghai A shares. In Hong Kong, however, foreigners can purchase stocks (as I was doing). The problem with this format is that you can have the same company trading on two exchanges at very different prices. Many experts say that the rules in Shanghai create liquidity restraints and make for a less efficient market. They say this is why the Hong Kong shares often trade at more reasonable valuations. There's nothing rational or efficient about all this, but it is what it is.

The Shanghai market began to tank immediately after I sold the Hong Kong shares short. I had top-ticked the market—I was going to make a fortune, right? No. See, traders in Hong Kong were buying Hong Kong shares while shorting shares in Shanghai. It was an arbitrage opportunity for those who understood the regulatory changes. Being right had never felt so wrong. As someone who had never traded Hong Kong stocks before, I didn't understand what was going on. During the next three weeks the Hong Kong shares I was short rallied 20 percent on average. I spent three sleepless weeks staring at the computer screens, trying to understand the mistake I had made. I was too smart and too good at trading to make such an error, right? Wrong. I spent those three weeks endlessly learning and stressing about the mounting losses as the stupidity of my error became evident.

I thought I was right. I thought the market was about to roll over hard, but I hadn't understood the intricacies of the market before I placed the trade. In a stress-induced frenzy I added to the position. Mind you, it was a fairly small portion of my portfolio (less than 25 percent), but for me that was too much volatility in one portion. I had let my emotions get the best of me. I was unraveling. I experienced a drawdown of more than 10 percent on my entire portfolio that *month*. This was the largest intramonth loss I had ever experienced. I was floating in the market's wind like a feather as opposed to hedging and controlling price through a process as I had grown accustomed to. I felt as though all my years of hard work were suddenly flawed. Then it all reversed.

The first fifteen days of November 2007 were nothing short of spectacular. The Hang Seng folded like a lawn chair. I made another classic psychological error and cut out at my break-even point. The stress had been too much. This was not exactly what I had in mind when I placed the trades just a few weeks earlier. My macroeconomic thesis at the time had been right, but the market had proved me wrong. I made not one penny on the trade and probably aged a few years. But the education would have been worth even a 20 percent loss. Among the lessons I learned:

Never let emotions drive your decision-making process.
Never participate in what you don't understand.
Making mistakes is going to happen.
Always learn from your mistakes.
Hope is not a strategy.

A macroeconomic approach is all about process and methodology. If you don't have the process, you aren't prepared to endure the inevitable behavioral battles you will confront.

THE MOST DESTRUCTIVE EMOTION—FEAR

Winston Churchill once said, "I am an optimist. It does not seem too much use being anything else." Truer words were never spoken. While reading this book you might have gotten the feeling at times that I have an inherent optimism about certain things. I might be biased, of course, but I tend to view the world through an optimistic lens. That is, I tend to believe that human beings will make progress over the long run because there are more of us waking up every day trying to do good things than those of us waking up deciding to do bad things. That's an oversimplified view of humanity, but you get the gist. Betting against humanity has proved to be a very bad bet for tens of thousands of years.

Unfortunately there's big money in the business of fear. We're easily scared and always susceptible to falling victim to our emotions. And there are people looking to prey on those emotions so you'll buy into their sales pitch. It will be right at times. If you scream "Fire!" in a crowded theater for a hundred years straight, you might end up being right eventually. And then everyone will hail you as a hero so long as they ignore your having been wrong for a long time. The business of fear benefits a small slice of the population and hurts most those who fall prey to it. The world of money is filled with people hoping you will buy their fear in exchange for your money.

Humanity has encountered an enormous number of hurdles in our short existence. But we have persevered. Our story is basically one huge story of overcoming hurdles. In financial circles we often say that "stocks climb a wall of worry." In other words the skepticism about our future progress often fuels its success. Figure 6.3 shows some of the regular crises that cause the stock market to panic from time to time.

Since 1855 the US economy has been in recession a full 30 percent of the time. Since 1945 the US economy has been in recession 16.2 percent

Figure 6.3: Stocks Climb a "Wall of Worry"

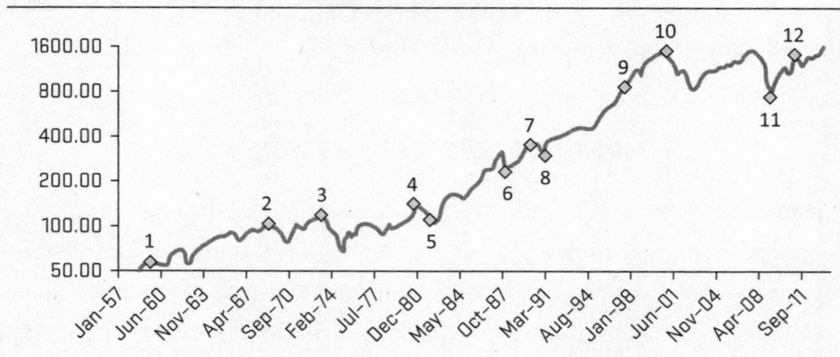

1 - Recession of 1958
2 - Recession of 1969
3 - OPEC Oil Crisis
4 - Recession of 1992
5 - LatAm Debt Crisis
6 - Crash of 1987
7 - Japan Asset Crash
8 - Savings and Loan Crisis
9 - Asia Financial Crisis
10 - Nasdaq Bubble
11 - Great Recession
12 - Euro Crisis

of the time. Since 1980 we have been in recession 14.6 percent of the time. Since 2000 we have been in recession 18.3 percent of the time. The flip side of course is that the economy has been in expansion 83.8 percent of the time since 1945, 85.4 percent of the time since 1980, and 81.7 percent since 2000.[8] Those are big numbers. And anyone who bets on perpetual doom and gloom must realize the poor odds they have to overcome.

This bad bet against humanity hasn't stopped the fear machine from rolling forward. As I said, there's big money in fear. I keep hammering on the point that you will make your own financial success by investing in your own personal development. And in order to do that you have to have a certain level of confidence that you have something positive to contribute to the world. In other words you have to be willing to take a certain amount of risk in order to benefit from this. You have to be willing to thrust yourself out into the world to prove to everyone that they need what you have to offer. That takes courage. Living in fear and being frozen by your own emotions will always hold you back.

Now, this doesn't mean you should be reckless. I say be a measured optimist. Be an optimist who views the world with skepticism and questions their surroundings. Don't be only a risk taker but be a risk manager as well. Question conventional wisdom and challenge those around you. That doesn't mean you are working against humanity. It simply means you are challenging the boundaries at which we seem to always constrain ourselves. But never forget that those selling fear probably are not out to serve your best interests in the long run. They are most likely serving their own inherently negative biases and self-interests in the hope that you will buy into their agenda.

Be wary of those selling fear, and be particularly wary of letting your own fear hold you back. Of course this doesn't mean you should be recklessly optimistic. The US economy and the global economy have and will encounter substantial turbulence in the future. But don't let your emotions paralyze your potential production.

TEN BIASES THAT INHIBIT OUR UNDERSTANDING OF MONEY, FINANCE, AND ECONOMICS

As emotional and often irrational animals we all suffer inherent biases. They're extremely difficult to overcome, but once we identify them we can train our minds to recognize environments in which we are prone to being biased. Many of the common biases we suffer from include

- The better-than-average effect—*The better-than-average effect* is the illusion that we are better at certain things than we actually are. A 1999 study by Justin Kruger and David Dunning found that the bottom 12 percent of workers ranked themselves in the top 62 percent of workers.[9] We tend to think the same with most things. We want to believe we're better than average drivers, lovers, and a whole slew of other things that more than 50 percent of humans can't be better than average at. But we all think it. Maybe you are better than average. But don't overestimate your actual skills. Overconfidence with markets and money is like thinking you've found the holy grail in your own head.
- Recency bias and the gambler's fallacy—*Recency bias* is the tendency to overemphasize the recent past. If stocks are rising, we tend to think they'll continue rising. We're inherently narrow microeconomic thinkers. A similar effect is the gambler's fallacy. We tend to think that a random event is more or less likely to occur following a series of similar events. I had a college friend who swore that he had figured out how to win at roulette. Falling for the *gambler's fallacy,* he claimed that we just needed to wait for a series of same spins to occur and then we would bet against that outcome because the odds would then favor us. What he was missing was that each spin in roulette is a unique environment with exactly the same odds and no connection to the last one spin or the last one million spins. We didn't use his strategy, thankfully. Markets and money aren't perfectly analogous, but each business cycle and market cycle is going to have a unique flavor. The past may rhyme but doesn't necessarily repeat. John Templeton once said that the four most dangerous words in markets are *it's different this time.* I disagree; each cycle is always different because each cycle has a unique environment, catalysts, participants, and variables driving it.
- The disposition effect—The *disposition effect* describes the tendency to sell shares that have increased in value and hold

onto shares that have decreased in value. This is similar to loss aversion in that we hate taking losses and hope we can always break even on our bad decisions. We hate admitting we were wrong. But the disposition effect shows the corollary. We aren't just bad sellers of losing financial assets. We are bad sellers of winning financial assets in that we tend to be more comfortable taking a small gain than taking the risk of letting it ride. Add these two emotional biases together and you have a tendency to sell your winners too early and hold on to your losers too long, thereby creating a portfolio nightmare.

- The sunk cost-fallacy—The *sunk-cost fallacy* hurts many facets of our financial lives. After we've paid for something, we tend to justify an irrational response to it by rationalizing that we've already paid for the item or invested so much in it. This is our failure to think in absolute terms. During our lives and financial interactions we often will confront losing causes that shouldn't be pursued further. But again we hang on to losing positions by rationalizing what we've already put into something. Classic examples of the *sunk-cost fallacy* include finishing a meal when you're full just because you paid for it or remaining in a bad relationship because you've invested so much in it already. Sometimes you need to know when to cut your losses.
- Past price fixation—*Past price fixation* is similar to the sunk-cost fallacy but applies specifically to financial markets. Have you ever held a losing position and told yourself you'll sell when the price gets back to your cost basis? If so, you've fallen for past price fixation. In financial markets it's best to understand the past, but when making decisions about financial assets you have to also realize that your purchase price shouldn't be the driving force behind your future decision to buy or sell.
- The bandwagon effect, herding, and confirmation bias—The *bandwagon effect*, *herding*, and *confirmation bias* are all related to the human bias of safety in numbers. If everyone else is doing something, we not only believe that our decisions are being confirmed by the actions of others, but we also feel a sense of false safety because others are doing it. In other words, if you're wrong you can always say everyone else was wrong also.

That might make your relative position better compared to the crowd's, but it won't necessarily make your absolute position better. Be careful of always feeling better while traveling with the herd. At times they're running toward the cliff and you won't see it until you've gone over the edge.

- Fallacy of composition—A *fallacy of composition* occurs when we think that what's true for part of a group is necessarily true for the group as a whole. This is extremely common in macroeconomics and financial markets. For instance, the idea that you can rotate out of existing stocks to add more cash on the sidelines for later use is a fallacy of composition. For you to move out of stocks and into cash, someone else must move out of cash and into stocks. When you think of money, it's always best to think in a macroeconomic way so as to avoid this sort of narrow and misleading perspective on the world.
- Political bias—*Political bias* can be extremely dangerous in markets and money. This is the tendency to intermingle your personal political beliefs with markets and monetary decisions. Of course politics and money will always be intermingled, but that doesn't mean you have to let your political biases drive your every monetary decision. The classic example of *political bias* was the 2008 financial crisis when the US government implemented the massive federal spending plan. Many people assumed this plan wouldn't work, but those who understood the Kalecki profits equation and that deficits contribute to corporate profits recognized that the government's spending program would likely add to corporate profits and drive the S&P 500 higher. While the politically biased railed against the efficacy of the spending program, the S&P 500, in its always apolitical fashion, just chugged higher and higher as profits surged to record highs.
- Entertainment bias—The financial markets can be a form of entertainment for some, but for most of us we are simply trying to find a place to allocate our assets so that they protect us against purchasing power loss and the risk of permanent loss. The financial markets are not a game, an entertainment show, or something that you should fool around with. Anyone who

tells you the financial markets are for entertainment purposes is probably in the business of selling you financial entertainment for their own personal gain.

- Negativity bias—Fear and bad news sell. We are prone to focus on bad news because we inherently think bad news is more important than good news. Bad news sparks our survival and problem-solving instincts. Unfortunately an excessive focus on the fear machine will also cause you to miss the reality that there's usually a lot more good going on in the world than bad.

THINK LIKE A CHESS PLAYER

The chess master Levon Aronian once said: "As a chess player one has to be able to control one's feelings, one has to be as cold as a machine." There's a reason machines are starting to take over financial markets—the machines operate more rationally than we do. In the financial markets half of winning often involves taking your own emotions out of the equation. But to really think like a machine you have to think like a chess player. You have to approach the markets with a simple understanding that the market is not the economy. In fact the market isn't even the underlying corporations that comprise that market. The market is the future expectation of the underlying asset's future performance. This explains why there tends to be little correlation between economic growth and stock market growth. Stock market participants aren't trying to guess what yesterday's or today's prices will be. They're trying to guess what tomorrow's prices will be, and they're estimating current microeconomic, macroeconomic, and other factors to make this projection. In other words the market cycle will tend to always lead the macroeconomic cycle as market participants try to anticipate future potential performance. See Figure 6.4.

To understand the markets you have to learn to think like a chess player, that is, several moves ahead. This is a form of what's called second-level thinking. The average person will solve a problem by thinking one level ahead. If you're going to be involved in the markets, you have to learn to think several levels ahead and consider how current decisions and future decisions will impact future prices.

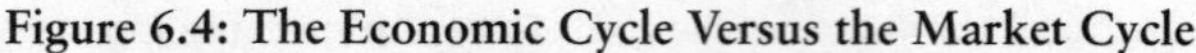

Figure 6.4: The Economic Cycle Versus the Market Cycle

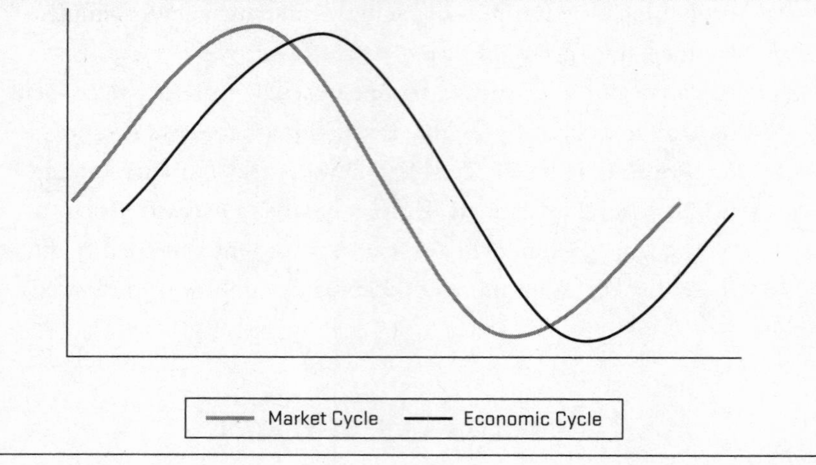

BEAUTY CONTESTS AND BEHAVIOR

Thinking like a chess player means not only learning to think like a machine but also to anticipate the moves of others. In Chapter 12 of the *General Theory of Employment, Interest, and Money* John Maynard Keynes, discusses how the market closely resembles a beauty contest:

> Professional investment may be likened to those newspaper competitions in which the competitors have to pick out the six prettiest faces from a hundred photographs, the price being awarded to the competitor whose choice most nearly corresponds to the average preference of the competitors as a whole; so that each competitor has to pick, not those faces which he himself finds prettiest, but those which he thinks likeliest to catch the fancy of the other competitors, all of whom are looking at the problem from the same point of view. It is not a case of choosing those which, to the best of one's judgment, are really prettiest, nor even those which average opinion genuinely thinks the prettiest. We have reached the third degree where we devote our intelligences to anticipating what average opinion expects the average opinion to be. And there are some, I believe, who practice the fourth, fifth and higher degrees.[10]

Thinking in a macroeconomic sense isn't just about understanding the big picture but also about understanding how to think about the way those around you are thinking. Thinking of the markets like they're a beauty contest means you have to understand that you're trying to understand the markets from your own interpretation while also being forced to respect the interpretation of those around you. If you believe a $100 stock is worth $200 and the market never agrees with your findings, you've lost the beauty contest.

IN BEING WRONG WE CAN LEARN TO BE RIGHT

If there's only one lesson you take away from this chapter, I hope it is that the world of money is extremely complex and will result in your making many mistakes as you navigate that world. But as you sail through it, you can understand it better so you reduce the number of mistakes you make. In a lot of ways navigating this world of money is not so much about getting everything right but about minimizing your mistakes.

That said, I want you to ask yourself a simple question: What is the last thing you were wrong about? If you can't remember or have to think hard, don't worry. That's perfectly normal. Humans are conditioned to avoid being wrong. And even when we are wrong, we will often work hard to convince ourselves that we are right. It's a natural defense mechanism. Our minds have always been our greatest tools. Unfortunately they can also be our most difficult obstacle. We fight being wrong because we see being wrong as a weakness. A person who is often wrong is viewed as having an inferior intellect. And an inferior intellect means your survival skills are inferior. And who wants to mate with someone who can't survive? You see how the evolutionary chain works here. And therein lies our greatest weakness. Our rather primitive "survive first" minds cannot accept being wrong. But in being wrong we can learn to be right. After all, it is in making mistakes and discovering our errors that we can find many of our greatest lessons. This is how we progress and move forward.

CHAPTER 7

UNDERSTANDING THE MODERN MONETARY SYSTEM

To understand money we must understand the system in which it exists.

UNDERSTANDING THE BIG PICTURE IS ALL ABOUT UNDERSTAND-ing the broad scope of the monetary system. If you want to understand the microeconomy you need to have a sound understanding of the macroeconomy. This is important for understanding not only how one will allocate assets or approach the world of investing. It is also crucial for more practical purposes like understanding what money means to you or why certain political policies do or don't make sense. Understanding the monetary system and the financial world around us has become a crucial element of modern human life. In this chapter I seek to provide a sound understanding of the modern monetary system from a global, big-picture perspective. And that is what macroeconomics is all about.

I have to warn you—of all the chapters in this book, this is the one that is the most technical and likely to be the most difficult to digest. It is also one of the more important chapters because it will give you a much better sense of the institutional design of the monetary system at its operational level. Take your time with it and let the material soak in slowly. This is a big topic and few people get it on the first go-around, so don't be discouraged.

INTRODUCTION TO MONETARY REALISM

My principal aim in this chapter is to objectively describe the operational realities of the modern fiat monetary system in the United States by using the understandings of what I refer to as monetary realism, or MR. This is an approach to understanding the modern monetary system by focusing on the institutional design and operational realities of the system. Although I will often use US-based examples in this chapter, this approach can be applied to many other nations throughout the world whose systems are similar or vary to some degree.

Before I begin I want to outline nine general understandings that will serve as the foundation for more detailed sections:

1. The primary role of money is to serve as a means of payment. Money can take many forms, but in the modern monetary system the final means of payment comes primarily from within the private banking system in the form of bank deposits. In other words the most important form of money in the modern monetary system is issued almost entirely by the private banking system.
2. The monetary system exists primarily for private purposes in order to have a means for the efficient exchange of goods and services. The private sector plays the leading role in helping to advance the well-being of the society in which money is used. The private sector drives the economic machine. While government assists in the economic process, the private sector ultimately is the primary driver of innovation, productivity, and economic growth. The private sector is what primarily propels increases in living standards; its activities are the most important factor in giving value and viability to fiat money.
3. In market-based systems such as the United States, UK, and the European Monetary Union, the money supply is essentially privatized and controlled by private banks that compete to create loans, which create deposits (money). Contrary to popular opinion, governments in such a system do not directly control the money supply or create most of the money.

4. Because the money supply is mostly privatized and is created by banks in the form of loans (debt), it is crucial to understand the central role that banking plays in the money system and how the stability of the private banking system is central to achieving economic stability and prosperity.
5. The public sector (the government) plays a facilitating role in helping to regulate and manage the infrastructure within which the money system operates. If properly used, the government can be an extremely powerful tool in helping to stabilize and create efficiencies within the monetary system.
6. Where governments are autonomous currency issuers, the central bank (the Federal Reserve in the United States) and the government have a symbiotic relationship and together are issuers of the currency to the monetary system. Currency, or what MR refers to as outside money (because it comes from outside the private sector), includes bank reserves, cash notes, and coins. In addition to the Federal Reserve, which issues bank reserves, the US Treasury issues outside money in the form of cash and coins. Households, businesses, and state governments are users of public sector–supplied currency and also private bank–issued monies (i.e., bank deposits are also known as inside money, because this money comes from inside the private sector).
7. The private banking sector issues bank deposits (inside money) and the public sector issues coins, paper cash, and bank reserves (outside money). Nowadays most means of payment involving private agents are transacted in bank deposits; as such, inside money is vital to understanding how the modern monetary system functions. While the private sector component of the monetary system takes center stage in the daily business of market exchanges and economic progress, the public sector also plays an important role through the use of outside money.
8. As an autonomous issuer of currency, the government has no solvency constraint as there might be for a household or business. In this regard we must be careful about comparing the federal government to a household because the federal

government can't run out of money it has the power to create. Households, on the other hand, have a real solvency constraint as they can quite literally run out of money.

9. The federal government's true constraint is not solvency but inflation. The government must manage its policies so as to avoid imposing undue harm on the populace through mismanagement of the money supply or inefficient use of government taxing and spending.

THE DISMAL SCIENCE AND GETTING BACK TO A DA VINCI METHODOLOGY

The primary goal behind the formulation of monetary realism was to come up with a better understanding of the monetary system at its operational level without emphasizing the role of policy. MR is simply a set of understandings that help us think about the way the actual monetary system functions at an operational level. Therefore one key element of MR is its political agnosticism. The purpose of MR is not to offer a political or policy bias but rather to describe the operational realities of a fiat monetary system in an attempt to help you gain a better understanding of how this system can be used and optimized to make your own informed decisions.

Economics is a social science that analyzes the process in which goods and services are produced, consumed, sold, and bought. Although scientific in many ways, economics has always tended to veer toward the ideological and political spectrum because of its direct connection to public policy. As a result one of the biggest problems with the profession of economics is that there is no firm foundation of understanding from which analysts can build their policy prescriptions. Further, the different schools of economics tend to be based heavily on normative rather than positive thinking, prescriptive rather than descriptive.

The MR approach is modeled on Leonardo da Vinci's approach to medicine and human anatomy. He viewed the human body as a machine, and as one of the first anatomists he provided the world with a better understanding of how that machine functions (e.g., how its pieces work together). To da Vinci it was all about finding out what is, not what can be. Only through rigorous analysis of how the machine worked were he and others able to offer advice about medicine and surgery. This superior understanding of the human body's operational realities provided the information that led to better medical approaches to solving problems with the human machine. I take a similar approach with economics by first trying to understand basic principles of how the machine works.

UNDERSTANDING FIAT MONEY

Money, as it exists in a modern monetary system, is a social construct that serves primarily as a medium of exchange (means of payment). Money also serves other purposes, but I will focus primarily on its most basic and common function. As a social species we exchange goods and services by using this tool. Throughout history many things have served as money and still do serve as money. Different assets can be thought of as having a higher "moneyness" than other forms of money within a particular society. In general that which is most readily accepted as a means of final payment can be thought of as having the highest level of moneyness. This is the item that serves as the most widely accepted medium of exchange.

Before I move on, let me provide a few basic definitions for common terminology used in discussing this system:

Fiat money: A form of money that is widely accepted because a government has designated it as legal tender.

Unit of account: A standard monetary unit for measuring the value of goods, services, and financial assets. In the United States the unit of account is the US dollar, in the UK it is the pound sterling, and in Europe it is the euro.

Medium of exchange: A widely accepted intermediary instrument that facilitates the sale, purchase, or trade of goods and services.

The most prominent form of modern money is fiat money. That is, money that exists by legal mandate. All fiat money is a specific legally mandated unit of account. These forms of money have no intrinsic value. That is, this money is not necessarily a physical thing. In the

United States, the dollar is the legally mandated form of money that we use as a medium of exchange and unit of account.[1]

The US government has designated the dollar as the denomination of money in the United States and oversees the regulation of the use of dollars within the US payments system. The actual money in this system can take many forms with varying levels of moneyness, but only the denomination of US dollar applies to the specific US monetary system as the unit of account.

It might help to think of the banking system like a soccer game. For instance, in the World Cup teams must use the official ball designated by FIFA, the international soccer federation. Teams cannot use their own ball. The monetary system is similar. FIFA has determined what the ball is in the system and regulates the use of that ball and how it is used. If you want to play ball in the economy, you have to use the ball that gives you access to that specific payments system. And just like the World Cup, the maker of these balls is outsourced to a private entity. Adidas AG is the current producer of the official World Cup soccer ball. In the monetary system the means of payment is generally outsourced to private entities called banks. These banks create money in the form of bank deposits when they make new loans. The government serves primarily as a regulatory agent to oversee the smooth functioning of this system in much the same way that employees of FIFA oversee World Cup matches as referees.

It is best to think of money as the social tool with which we primarily exchange goods and services. Money has its highest level of moneyness when it is widely accepted as a final means of payment for goods and services. Of course money is more than merely a medium of exchange, but its primary purpose and most prominent use is in exchanges for goods and services. Throughout history many things have served this purpose, and in modern transactions many different instruments can be classified as money.

If we consider something that serves as a means of payment as money, money can be different things to different people. For instance, in your local pawn shop gold might be considered a form of money since it might be one of the few things that the shop owner will accept as a medium of exchange. If you buy a sandwich from a shop that does not accept credit cards, the owner does not consider bank deposits to be money but instead accepts only cash bills or coin. Most businesses will accept not only credit cards but also cash. In other words they consider both forms of money to have a high level of moneyness. What most businesses do not consider to be money are things like physical gold, stocks, bonds, or physical commodities. Therefore the level of moneyness for these items can be thought of as relatively low.

UNDERSTANDING INSIDE MONEY AND OUTSIDE MONEY

In most modern monetary systems money is primarily distributed through the private competitive banking process. Banks compete for the demand of loans in a market-based system. The primary form of money in existence today resides in bank accounts as bank deposits within the local payments system. This mechanism to distribute money is essentially a privatization of the money supply to the private banking system. That is, the primary form of money we all use on a daily basis is controlled almost entirely by private banks.

As in the World Cup soccer analogy, it can be helpful to think of the monetary system as mainly existing on one playing field within the payments system. The payments system is a primarily electronic system regulated by the government and primarily maintained by the private banking system. That is, the government helps oversee the use of this system, but private banks maintain the daily processing of transactions that occur within this system. If you want to engage in that system, you need to become a user of bank deposits in some manner by opening a bank account in order to gain access.

Bank money is what MR calls inside money. Inside money is created *inside* the private sector. You might hear money referred to as *endogenous money* at times. This means that we all have a version of money we can create within the financial world, but the trouble with money, as Hyman Minsky, a renowned American economist, once noted, is in getting others to accept it. For instance, I can create CR notes, but it's unlikely anyone would find them valuable.

In the modern monetary system, inside money primarily includes bank deposits that exist as a result of the loan creation process (loans create deposits). This means our money supply is elastic—it can respond and flex with the changes in the economy and the needs of its users.

When the economy is healthy and banks are lending, the money supply can expand or contract to meet the economy's needs.

Inside money is the dominant form of money in the modern economy, and as the economy has become increasingly electronic as computers have taken on a more prominent role in transacting business. Money is no longer just a physical thing, a cash note or a gold bar. Its most common form is now numbers in a computer system. Increasingly money is a record of accounting that exists on spread sheets. It is a construct of the mind and applied to our lives through accounting relationships.

In today's modern electronic monetary system just 26 percent of all transactions occur with cash notes while electronic payments dominate the means of payment.[2] As I will show, the idea that cash is a more dominant form of modern money is false because cash serves primarily as a facilitating feature to inside money. Like all forms of outside money in the modern system, cash is facilitating money to the central form of money in the system (inside money). In other words, outside money like cash and coins exist for the users of inside money (bank deposits) to transact more conveniently or efficiently.

- Inside money, like bank deposits, is the dominant form of money in the modern monetary system because it serves as the primary means of payment at the point of sale.
- Outside money, like bank reserves, cash, and coins, is a facilitating form of money that supports the use of the inside money system.[3]

Inside money (money created by banks *inside* the private sector) can be inherently unstable because the entities that issue this money are inherently unstable. The nineteenth century and early twentieth century, for instance, experienced substantial volatility in banking as an inherent conflict of interest developed. Banks, as private profit-seeking entities, are inclined to maximize profits at all times. As Hyman Minsky once noted, stability creates instability.[4] This is particularly true in banking as economic stability tends to result in banks' relaxing their lending standards to maximize loan creation and profit potential. But this stability is often a mirage that results in future instability and, often, banking crisis. Government money can serve an important facilitating feature in stabilizing the inside money system. As I will detail later, this is essentially what the Federal Reserve System and other central banks achieve. Through its operations as a national payment clearinghouse, the central bank's main role is to help stabilize the inside money system.

This brings me to the other dominant form of money in our monetary system—outside money. Outside money is money created *outside* the private sector. This includes cash notes, coins, and bank reserves. Cash and coins are created by the Treasury while bank reserves are created by the central bank (reserves can be thought of as deposits held on reserve by the central bank). Although cash and coins are becoming obsolete in some money systems, they remain prevalent forms of money in most economies. This form of money primarily serves as a convenience that allows us to draw down a bank account of inside money (by using an ATM, for instance) to make transactions in physical currency. In other words cash and coins are used primarily by those who have an account that contains inside money for the purpose of conveniently transacting business in physical form.

In the United States the most important form of outside money is bank reserves or deposits held on reserve at Federal Reserve banks. These deposits are held for two purposes: to settle payments in the interbank market, and to meet reserve requirements. Bank reserves are used only by banks and the central bank in the interbank market and do not reside in the nonbank private sector. It is best to think of reserves as deposits held in accounts at the various Fed banks to settle payments within the banking system. It might be useful to think of bank deposits as the money that nonbanks use to access the payments system while bank reserves are deposits used by banks to access the interbank market. In other words deposits are the money most economic agents use to transact with one another, while reserves are the money banks use to transact with one another. For example, if you have a bank account at JP Morgan and you use your bank deposits to purchase a sandwich from someone who banks at Bank of America (and who subsequently deposits the funds at Bank of America), the banks will settle this payment by transferring reserves in the interbank market. This interbank system creates a market in which the Federal Reserve can help streamline settlement of payments and ensure stability and liquidity within the payments system.

What's crucial to understand here is that outside money serves primarily to facilitate the existence of inside money. That is, the creation of outside money is almost entirely a facilitating feature to influence or stabilize inside money. Through its vast powers the government can serve as an important stabilizing force in a system that is designed primarily around inherently unstable private competitive banking.

In understanding inside money and outside money, it is important to also understand that banks rule the monetary roost, so to speak. That is, banks issue almost all the money in circulation today in the form of loans, and the government supports this privatized money creation source. Contrary to popular belief, the government does not issue or print money (except in the most literal sense, that is, the US Treasury prints cash notes to meet demand for use by Federal Reserve banks to meet demand by bank customers who have accounts in inside money). The government is only the issuer of outside money, which is designed to facilitate and support the use of inside money.

UNDERSTANDING MONEYNESS

Modern forms of money are largely endogenous (created within the private banking system) but are organized according to law. The specific unit of account in any nation dictates how money will be denominated. The government therefore decides the unit of account and can restrict or allow certain media of exchange. The unit of account in the United States is the dollar. Organizing money as legal tender increases a particular form of money's credibility for the purpose of transaction as laws create protection for the users of the money. As a trust-based creation, money is likely to be unstable without proper oversight by its users. The government also helps oversee the viability of the payments system and can decide what can be used within that payment system as a means of settlement. In the United States the primary means of settlement are bank deposits and bank reserves. Therefore these forms of money serve as the most widely accepted forms of payment within the money system.

Different forms of money exist within any society, and they have varying forms of importance and moneyness. Moneyness can be thought of as a form of money's utility in meeting the primary purpose of money, which is as a medium of exchange. The thing with the highest level of moneyness also trades at par. This means that one dollar is one dollar in nominal terms. You don't generally have to worry that your bank deposits or dollar bill are not worth a dollar in nominal terms except in rare situations.

In the United States the money supply has been privatized and is dominated by private banks that issue money as debt. The US government and state governments grant banks charters to maintain the payments system in a market-based system. If the banks within this system do not meet the regulatory requirements outlined by the government, they are stripped of their charter.

Banking is essentially a business that revolves around helping customers settle payments. So it's helpful to think of banks as the institutions that run the payments system and distribute the money within which that system operates. As I have mentioned, outside money plays an important role in helping facilitate the use of the payments system but plays primarily a supporting role to inside money.

In a capitalist economy inside money exists primarily to disperse the power of money creation away from the government and toward a market-based system in which banks compete to create money. This system is by no means perfect, but it is right to think of it as a blend of a purely bank-owned system (as existed in the nineteenth century) and a nationalized system (similar to what you might see in China). It is primarily market based but has important government support mechanisms embedded within it.

It is helpful to think of money as existing on a scale of moneyness along which particular forms of money vary in degrees of utility (see Figure 7.1). As Minsky once said, anyone can create money, the trouble is in getting others to accept it. Getting others to accept money as a means of payment is the ultimate use of money. And while many things can serve as money, they do not all serve as a final means of payment.

The primary forms of money within the monetary system include cash, coins, reserves, bank deposits, financial assets (such as stocks and bonds), commodity money (such as gold), foreign currencies (such as the yen and euro), and other rare media of exchange (such as BitCoins or other alternative forms of money). Understanding the level of moneyness in each of these forms of money is crucial to understanding the modern monetary system.

Figure 7.1: The Scale of Moneyness

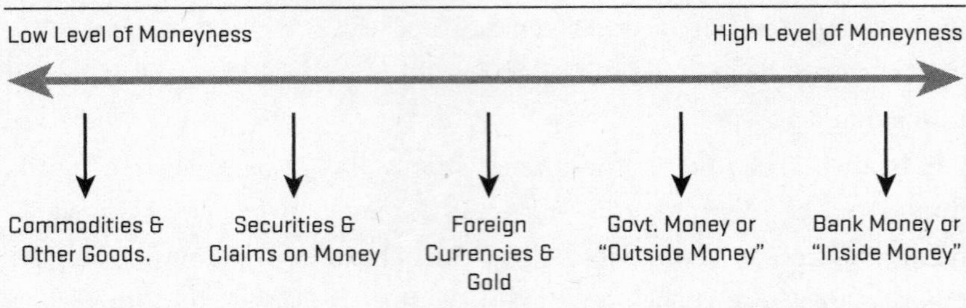

Bank deposits have the highest level of moneyness within the modern monetary system because they are the primary means of settling payments. As users of the modern electronic payment system, we are all users of the payments system, which requires us to transact in bank-issued deposits. The electronic payment system is, by a wide margin, the most widely used means of payment in developed countries.

Cash, coins, and bank reserves are also important forms of money in the modern monetary system but serve primarily as facilitating forms of money to the inside money system. Cash is a convenient form of money, but because it facilitates the use of an inside money account (by allowing the owner to draw down this account), it has a lower level of moneyness. Reserves are a crucial element of the interbank system of payment settlement but again serve mainly to facilitate the system of inside money by allowing banks to more conveniently settle interbank payments. So while reserves play an important role in the settlement process, their existence as a facilitating form of money for interbank settlement renders them a lower level of moneyness.

Since foreign currencies are fungible on a foreign exchange market, most foreign currencies have a moderately high level of moneyness. For instance, a euro is not good in most stores in the United States (because the unit of account in the United States is the dollar) but can be easily exchanged for US dollars of various forms. Gold, which is broadly viewed as universal medium of exchange, can be viewed similarly, though it varies in degrees of convenience for obvious reasons. Gold, for instance, is widely viewed as money but is not widely accepted as a means of final payment.

Most financial assets like stocks and bonds are money-like instruments but do not meet the demands of money users in terms of being acceptable as media of exchange. These financial assets are easily convertible into instruments with higher moneyness but are not widely accepted as a final means of payment.

Last, most commodities and goods are low on the scale of moneyness since they are unlikely to be accepted by most economic agents as a means of final payment.

WHAT GIVES FIAT MONEY ITS VALUE?

What gives this fiat money value if it has no intrinsic value? What backs the notes or electronic records of account that a society creates? What gives these pieces of paper, coins, and inputs value? It's helpful to break the demand for fiat money down into two components—acceptance value and quantity value.

Acceptance value represents the public's willingness to accept something as the nation's unit of account and medium of exchange. This is achieved mainly through the legal process. That is, the government and the people deem a specific thing (such as the US dollar) the accepted unit of account and medium of exchange. The government also regulates the monetary system within which that unit of account is used. But the government cannot force currency acceptance upon its users merely by stating what is usable as the nation's unit of account.

Quantity value describes the medium of exchange's value in terms of purchasing power, inflation, exchange rates, production value, and so on. This is the utility of the money as a store of value. While acceptance value is generally stable and enforceable by law, quantity value can be quite unstable and result in monetary collapse in a worst-case scenario. Quantity value is more important than acceptance value as it can actually cause acceptance value to decline in instances such as a hyperinflation.

Ultimately these pieces of paper or electronic records of account represent some amount of output and production that can be purchased. After all, we don't use money merely to collect money. We use money as a means to an end. If it cannot serve that purpose sufficiently, it has no utility. Notes or cash, for instance, in and of themselves have no intrinsic value but serve as a medium of exchange that allows consumers to exchange various goods and services of a particular value. The willingness of the consumers in the economy to use these notes is largely dependent on the underlying value of the output and/or productivity, the government's ability to be a good steward of the currency, and the banking system's distribution of credit and the ability to regulate its usage. I like to think of this as a bond that connects these various forces. If any link in the bond is broken, the nation's monetary system is at risk of collapse.

Production sits at the top of this hierarchy (see Figure 7.2). After all, if a nation has nothing to produce, the formation of a monetary system serves little purpose. Further, a system that does not evolve by means of production can expect to become increasingly unstable over time as living standards stagnate.

The value of any form of fiat money is ultimately derived from the three key linkages shown in Figure 7.2: output and productivity; money supply management; and laws and regulation.

Output and productivity are vital in giving money its value. The goods and services that are produced by owners and workers in the economy and the value that consumers are willing to pay for these goods and services is what ultimately makes any fiat money viable. Therefore government has an incentive to promote productive output and maintain sound stewardship of the money supply. A government that implements

Figure 7.2: The Fiat Monetary System's Linkages

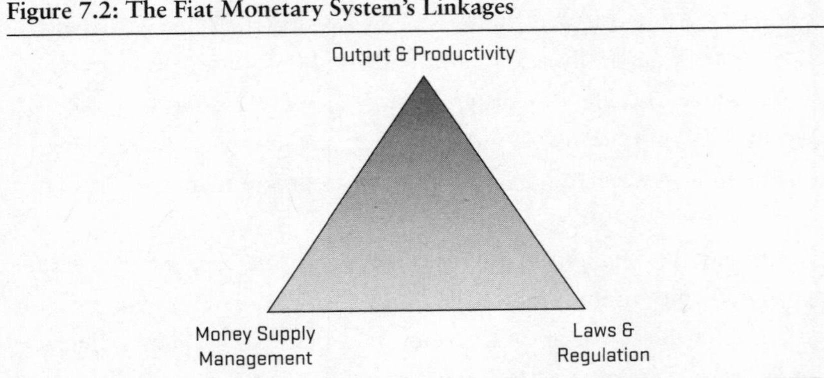

poor policy, disincentivizes productive output, and abuses the money supply threatens the stability of the monetary system. A money system whose institutions and government are corrupted will likely become corrupted as a whole.

While the government plays an important role in setting the acceptance value of money, money is not necessarily valuable only because the state says it is money. The value of money involves the other linkages. Keynes once compared money to a theater ticket, saying:

> Money is the measure of value, but to regard it as having value itself is a relic of the view that the value of money is regulated by the value of the substance of which it is made, and is like confusing a theatre ticket with the performance.[5]

This is a good way to think of money in a modern fiat monetary system. Fiat money, in and of itself, has no intrinsic value. Similarly a theater ticket has no value aside from the paper it is printed on; however, if they value the performance, theatergoers will be eager to attribute a certain value to these tickets because the theater has made them the tool of entry to the show. If the theater mismanages the number of tickets in circulation, the ticket will be devalued. In much the same way the government deems a dollar to be the ticket with which we can see (and interact in) the economy. If the show is good (output and productivity are high), the number of outstanding tickets is not mismanaged (the banking system prudently manages the money supply), and the tickets are sustained as the viable forms of entry to the show (the tax and legal system sustains itself), this money remains a viable medium of exchange. But ultimately the value of the tickets is dependent primarily on the quality of the show, which is determined by the quality of the nation's productive output.

MONEY IS NOT TRUE WEALTH

It's important to understand that money is not necessarily true wealth. Money is the tool that allows people to exchange and transact in goods and services. In other words it gives us access to a form of wealth (goods and services) but does not necessarily represent wealth in and of itself. It is important not to confuse the ticket with the performance. Confusing money with wealth is a classic mistake that many people make.

If a society spends money in excess of a nation's underlying productive capacity, it will devalue its money and generate destructive inflation. This would result in too much money chasing too few goods, leading to a potential decline in real living standards. It can help to think of money as the thing with which we chase some forms of true wealth. It gives us access to real goods and services but having a lot of money does not necessarily mean we are wealthy. In fact seeking to accumulate money can often lead people astray as they begin to view money as the end and not the means. After all, as a social construct money is the thing that allows us entry to the show, but entry to the show does not necessarily equate to becoming wealthy. As participants in the economy, we can derive prosperity by being productive within that economy and adding value to the lives of those around us. Wealth, happiness, or prosperity can mean different things to different people so it is unwise to generalize and confuse the accumulation of money with the ultimate end. It is just a means to an end.

THE MONETARY WORLD'S RELATIONSHIP TO THE REAL WORLD

When we begin to understand the monetary system, we have to recognize something that should be obvious to us all but is not always clearly laid out: the financial world represents claims on other financial world assets as well as claims on the nonfinancial world assets. Remember, the theater ticket is not the thing you actually want. The theater ticket simply represents a means to experiencing the end (the show). Financial assets are similar. Therefore the monetary world is the accounting representation of the claims that give us access to the financial world as well as the real world. To understand this thinking it's helpful to remember a general rule of thumb from Professor Marc Lavoie: "Everything comes from somewhere and everything goes somewhere." Once you begin to think in this manner, you can start to think of the financial world in more realistic terms. And this leads to two basic understandings:

One entity's spending is another entity's income.
All financial assets have a corresponding liability.

In the real world we have nonfinancial assets like houses and cars. And in the financial world we have financial assets like stocks, bonds, bank deposits, and the like that give us access to the nonfinancial assets. Remember, the financial world represents claims on the real world. If we look at the aggregate balance sheet of the world, we can arrive at some more basic understandings:

Net Worth = Assets–Liabilities
Assets = Financial Assets + Nonfinancial Assets

But every financial asset has a corresponding financial liability so the aggregate net worth of the world in face value financial terms must be zero. Said differently:

Net Worth = Nonfinancial Assets

Of course this only considers financial assets as trading at face value and not at market value. In the actual financial world many of our financial assets change in value over time, so our financial net worth can be substantially higher than the face value of these instruments.

A medium of exchange or things that serve as money instruments also exists within financial assets. These instruments are unique in that they serve as the medium of exchange at the point of sale. Not all financial assets meet such a demanding requirement. For instance, you might get paid in stock options, but you cannot use your stock options at Walmart to purchase goods. The stock options must be converted into something with a higher level of moneyness. Most financial assets are a claim on things with a higher level of moneyness. In the modern monetary system money is primarily made up of bank deposits, coins, cash, and bank reserves.

A NOTE ABOUT REAL RESOURCES

Unfortunately I don't have enough space here to cover the constraint of real resources in its entirety, but I do want to highlight this very real constraint for the economy as a whole. Many things we rely on in our everyday lives are finite in nature. And there could come a time when we are no longer able to produce or rely on these resources to generate the same standard of living that many of us are accustomed to. The most obvious of these constraints is the energy constraint and the world's current dependence on oil and other sources of petroleum-based fuel. As the world's population and output grow, this has the potential to become an increasingly substantial problem. Will human innovation be able to keep pace with the demand for real resources? The answer is unknown at present but incredibly important. But I do want to emphasize that modern economies are always constrained by the supply of real resources.

UNDERSTANDING INFLATION, DEFLATION, AND DISINFLATION

To understand the relationship of money, output, and living standards, it helps to understand the impact of inflation. Inflation is a continuous rise in the price level. This means the prices for a broad basket of consumer goods continue to rise, usually as measured on a year-over-year basis. For instance, if inflation is 3 percent, a $1 gallon of gasoline will cost $1.03 in one year. Your dollar purchases less gasoline than it did a year ago.

It's important to note that inflation is not merely the rise of a few prices. For instance, if only gasoline prices are rising, the economy may not be suffering from inflation unless the price of the broad basket of goods is also rising. You could have rising gasoline prices and stagnant inflation. Therefore it's important to look at the broad basket to understand whether there is inflation.

CAUSES OF INFLATION

There are two general types of inflation. The first is called demand-pull inflation. The second is cost-push inflation. *Demand-pull inflation* is when demand outstrips supply, resulting in a rise in prices. *Cost-push inflation* is when the cost of business increases, resulting in firms' passing along those costs to their consumers.

A common cause of inflation is an increase in the money supply. This is generally a benign occurrence in a credit-based monetary system because the demand for credit will usually rise over time in a healthy credit-based system. In other words, when the economy is expanding, firms and households will generally be borrowing to consume and invest. This will result in an increase in the broad money supply as banks create more loans, resulting in more deposits, leading to more money chasing (more or less) goods and services. The key to understanding whether this is a positive or negative development requires knowledge of how credit is used within the economy and whether it is increasing our living standards.

INFLATION AND LIVING STANDARDS

Ultimately the real benefit of our labor and output is the time it provides us. In *Wealth of Nations* Adam Smith said,

> The real price of everything, what everything really costs to the man who wants to acquire it, is the toil and trouble of acquiring it.[6]

The value of money is primarily derived from the amount of labor time required to obtain that money. If wages stagnate or decline relative to the rate of inflation, we experience a real decline in our living standards. If, on the other hand, our wages outpace inflation, we experience an increase in our living standards. Said differently, the value of our output, in terms of goods and services produced, is what gives us access to a certain amount of money. To understand this concept a bit better it might help to understand how output, innovation, and the value of money are linked.

Alexander Graham Bell is one of the greatest innovators in American history. So what did Bell do, exactly? He created a more efficient way to communicate by inventing the telephone. Clearly communication is a vital part of human life. And in theory over the long term the demand to communicate is infinite.

At some point in his life Bell sat down and probably said something like, "It would be far more efficient if I could talk to Mr. Smith immediately as opposed to sending him a telegram." Clearly this desire was not peculiar to Bell. And all Bell did was fill a demand by inventing a telephone that helped consumers meet this demand. What Bell really did was give his consumers more time to consume other goods and services. He reduced the toil and trouble of having to acquire things by providing people with a product that made their lives more efficient and productive.

Just imagine all the ways the telephone improves our quality of life and makes us more efficient. Business people in New York no longer had to wait for a telegram from their business partner in Chicago to discuss their new business decisions. Instead, one partner picked up a telephone, and they made a decision in a matter of minutes. There are innumerable (and better) examples of the ways that a simple innovation such as Bell's helps us to improve productivity, efficiency, and ultimately our standard of living. But the point of this is to understand that innovations and productivity improve our living standards even when they might create inflation.

It's important to understand how this process generally occurs in a modern monetary system. Many innovations are financed through the loan process. If Bell had borrowed $1,000 to build his phone system, he might very well have increased the money supply in the process of creating his invention. This might have caused the prices of other products to rise, and it might have even destroyed other jobs (imagine all the telegram delivery services that got destroyed as a result of the telephone). Despite the increase in the money supply, Bell made all his customers better off by giving them more time to consume and produce other things.

This is important when considering the quantity of money within a monetary system relative to the aggregate supply of output and its impact on living standards. For instance, it's not uncommon to hear someone in the mainstream press state that the US dollar has lost more than 95 percent of its purchasing power since the Federal Reserve was created in 1913. This is technically true because inflation has increased substantially (about 3.2 percent per year), but despite the decline in the dollar's purchasing power, our standard of living has increased dramatically because we have become so much more productive. An American in 2013 lives a much higher quality of life than an American in 1913. This is because we have been afforded (through productivity) the luxury to use more time as we please. In other words it takes far less time to purchase one hour of output today than it did in 1913.

Figure 7.3 shows the clear negative relationship of time and the purchasing power of the dollar between 1913 and 2013.

If the purchasing power of the dollar has declined by more than 95 percent, how come the United States is so much better off than it was a hundred years ago? Inflation-adjusted GDP per capita was just $5,300 in 1913 but surged to more than $51,000 in 2013. We are far wealthier as a country than we were a hundred years ago, even though the US dollar has lost substantial purchasing power. This is largely the result of enormous advances in our productivity. Our labor hours produce far more today than they did a century ago because we are much more efficient than we once were. That means our 2013 wages actually buy *more* goods and services than they could in 1913 despite the decline in purchasing power. Our increased productivity makes us better off because it gives us more time to consume and produce other goods and services. This increases our living standards despite some inevitable rise in price.

The key point here is that improvements in our standards of living provide us with the ultimate form of wealth—they give us more time to do the things we think will help us find fulfillment (whatever that might be). This is the ultimate form of wealth. The entrepreneur gives us more

Figure 7.3: US Dollar Purchasing Power

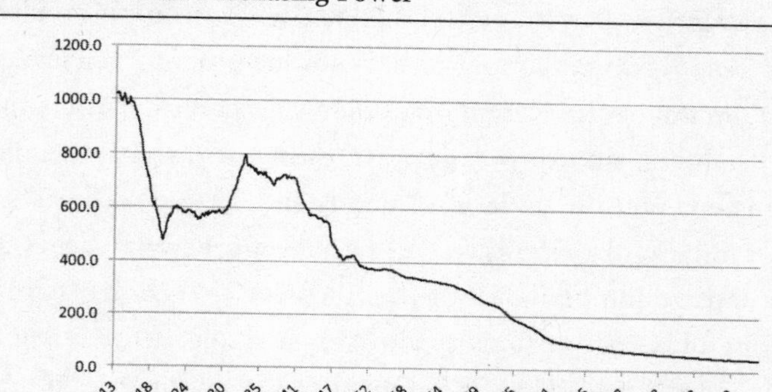

time to consume more goods and services and do the things we want in our lives.

If we look at the modern economy, we can see how streamlined this process has become. For instance, at seven last night I put my laundry in the wash, I put the dishes in the dishwasher, ordered dinner from a local restaurant, and went upstairs into my office, where I did 30 minutes of work. At 8 p.m. my dinner arrived, my laundry was done, I ate dinner on a fresh clean plate, and I had done 30 minutes of work in this period. Imagine trying to do all that a hundred years ago? How long would it take you? Days? Perhaps even weeks? That is a remarkable increase in living standards even though it costs substantially more to do all these things than it would have in 1913. And why are we able to do all these things in such a condensed period of time? Why am I able to consume so much more than I could have a century ago? Because entrepreneurs created a machine that cleans my clothing for me, they created a machine that cleans my dishes for me, they created an oven that cooks my dinner, a car that allows the delivery person to deliver my dinner, and invented a computer that allows me to efficiently and effectively accomplish work.

It is important to understand that consumption and production are two sides of the same coin. We often hear economists arguing about supply-side policies and demand-side policies. The reality is that both are important. Alexander Graham Bell needs customers to buy his phones, just like his customers needed Bell's telephone to communicate more efficiently. Too often the world of economics devolves into a black-and-white story, when the truth generally lies somewhere in between. Supply and demand imbalances can develop, but we must approach each environment as though it is unique and not attempt to apply an ideological perspective to what is certain to be a unique economic environment.

Less common but important price changes include deflation and disinflation. Deflation and disinflation are forms of decreasing inflation. *Deflation* is when the price level of goods and services decreases. This is a rate of inflation below 0 percent. Deflation generally occurs during the credit contraction period of the business cycle when debts are being paid down and economic activity slows as a result of the credit cycle. *Disinflation* is a similar concept but entails a decreasing rate of positive inflation. For instance, a period where inflation declines from 3 percent to 2 percent would be described as a disinflation. Like deflation this generally occurs in a weak economic environment in which the credit cycle is slowing. Deflation and disinflation are rare but important phenomena that occur within any credit-based fiat monetary system.

THE BASIC PURPOSE OF A MONETARY SYSTEM

Understanding the money system, its structure, and its purpose is ultimately about understanding how it is a system of flows from transactions. The money system exists so we can exchange goods and services. Someone spends, another person earns this income, this person invests, the recipient spends, and the cycle goes on. Without the cycle of spending the monetary system essentially dies. That is, if there are no flows, incomes decline, profits dry up, output goes unsold, workers get fired, and so on.

The money system is similar to the way the human body works. The human body is largely based on a system of flows. So long as the blood flows, the body receives the nutrients necessary for survival and every day operation. But the flow is not necessarily enough on its own to sustain the system. The system must be properly nourished and taken care of. A human being who sits on the couch every day eating unhealthy food is likely to experience an interruption in this flow at some point as the system deteriorates in health over time. And when the flow stops (for whatever reason), the system dies.

In the money system the health of the system is based largely on how this flow of funds results in an improvement in living standards over time. Are the economic agents using this flow to create goods and services that improve the overall standards of living for the system as a whole? Are they, as I described earlier, creating goods and services that optimize our time? For the economic system the equivalent of sitting on the couch eating unhealthy food is a period in which economic agents are unable to find productive uses for this flow. In this scenario living standards stagnate, the flow stagnates, and the system deteriorates.

The monetary system is designed to enhance the efficiency of this flow of funds through the system and encourage and reward those who contribute positively to it. In later sections of this book I will focus largely on the institutional design of the system, but it is important to understand that the institutional structure of the system is merely the infrastructure within which the system operates.

THE MYTH OF THE MONEY MULTIPLIER AND BANKING BASICS

The monetary system is designed to cater to the creation of the public's money supply, primarily by private banks by establishing a money supply that is elastic. That is, it can expand and contract as the demand for money expands and contracts. Most modern money takes the form of bank deposits, and most market exchanges involving private agents are transacted in private bank money. As I have discussed, inside money governs the day-to-day functioning of modern fiat monetary systems. The role of outside money, which is created by the public sector, is comparatively minor and plays a mostly facilitating role.

Like the government, banks are also money issuers but not issuers of private sector net financial assets. That is, banking transactions always involve the creation of a private sector asset and a liability. Banks create loans independent of government constraint (aside from the regulatory framework). As I will explain, banks make loans independent of their reserve position with the government, rendering the traditional money multiplier deeply flawed.

The monetary system in the developed world is designed specifically around a competitive private banking system. The banking system is not a public-private partnership serving public purpose, as the central bank essentially is. The banking system is a privately owned component of the system run for private profit. The thinking behind this design was to disperse the power of money creation away from a centralized government and put it into the hands of nongovernment entities. The government's relationship with the private banking system is more a support mechanism than anything else. In this regard I like to think of the government as being a facilitator in helping to sustain a viable credit-based money system.

It's important to understand that banks are not constrained by the government (outside the regulatory framework) in terms of how they create money. Business schools teach that banks obtain deposits and then leverage those deposits ten times or so. This is why we call the modern banking system a fractional reserve banking system. Banks supposedly lend a portion of their reserves. There's just one problem here: banks are never reserve constrained. Banks are always capital constrained. This can best be seen in countries such as Canada, which has no reserve requirements.[7] Reserves are used for two purposes—to settle payments in the interbank market and to meet the Fed's reserve requirements. Aside from this, reserves have little impact on the day-to-day lending operations of banks in the United States. This was recently confirmed in a paper from the Federal Reserve:

> Changes in reserves are unrelated to changes in lending, and open market operations do not have a direct impact on lending. We conclude that the textbook treatment of money in the transmission mechanism can be rejected.[8]

This is an important point because many people have assumed that various Fed policies in recent years (such as quantitative easing) would be inflationary or even hyperinflationary based on the flawed concept that an expansion of the monetary base (reserves) would lead directly to bank lending and higher inflation. Because banks are not reserve constrained, that is, they don't lend their reserves or multiply their reserves, this doesn't necessarily lead to more lending and will not result in the private sector's being able to access more capital.

That banks are not reserve constrained can mean only one thing—banks lend when credit-worthy customers have demand for loans (assuming the banking system is healthy and banks are engaging in the business they are designed to transact). Loans create deposits, not vice versa. In the loan creation process banks will make loans first (resulting in new deposits) and will find necessary reserves *after* the fact (either in the overnight market or through the Federal Reserve).

Understanding the business of banking is rather simple. It's best to think of banks as running a payments system that helps us all transact within the economy. In addition to helping manage this payments system, banks issue money in the form of loans. Banks earn a profit from transacting business when their assets are less expensive than their liabilities. In other words banks need to run this payments system smoothly but will seek to do so in a manner that doesn't reduce their profitability.

Banks don't necessarily use their deposits or reserves to create loans, however. Banks make loans and find reserves after the fact if they have to. But since banking is a spread business (having assets that are less expensive than liabilities), the banks will always seek the least expensive source of funds for managing their payment system. That just so happens to be bank deposits. This gives the appearance that banks fund their loan book by obtaining deposits, but this is not necessarily the case. It is better to think of banking as a spread business in which the bank simply acquires the least expensive liabilities to sustain its payment system and maximize profits. Banks need funding sources to run their businesses, but they do not necessarily need reserves or deposits to make those loans.

To illustrate this point I will briefly review the change in balance sheet composition between banks and households before and after a loan is made. Since banks are not constrained by their reserves, the banks do not need to have X amount of reserves on hand to create new loans. But banks must have ample capital to be able to operate and meet regulatory requirements.

I'll start with a simple money system shown in Figure 7.4. In this example banks begin with $120 in assets and liabilities comprised of currency, reserves, equity, and deposits. Of this, households hold $80 in

Figure 7.4: Banking Example—Before Loan Is Made

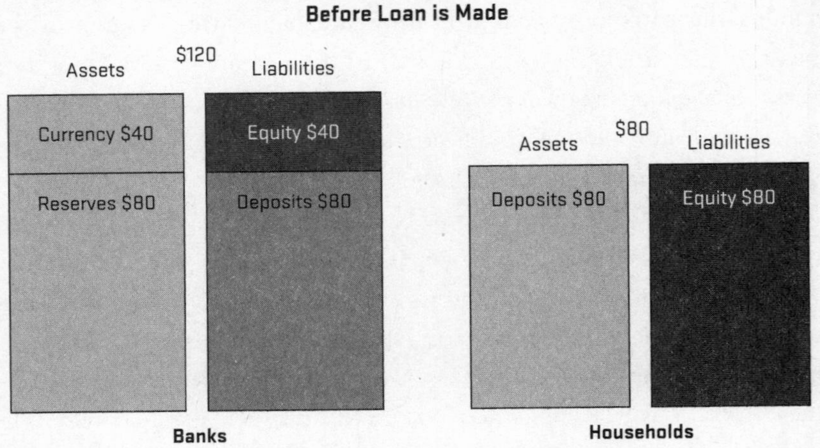

deposits, which are assets for the households and liabilities for the banking system. That is, the bank owes you your deposit on demand.

This banking system has reserves already, but this is not necessary for the bank to issue a loan. It must simply remain solvent within its regulatory requirements. But if the households want to take out a new loan to purchase a new home for $50, the bank simply credits the household's account, as Figure 7.5 shows. When the new loan is made, household deposits increase to $130. Household loans increase by $50. Bank assets increase by $50 (the loan), and bank liabilities increase by $50 (the deposit).

If the bank needs reserves to help settle payments or meet reserve requirements, it can always borrow from another bank in the interbank market, or, if it must, it can borrow from the Federal Reserve Discount Window. The key lesson here is to understand that money in the modern monetary system is largely endogenous and exists through the creation of the loan process within the private sector. The central bank and reserves play a far smaller role in the broad money supply than is often perceived.

Perhaps most important, this example shows that understanding endogenous money means we need to rethink how we teach banking and apply it to our understandings of the monetary machine. Banks and

Figure 7.5: Banking Example—After Loan Is Made

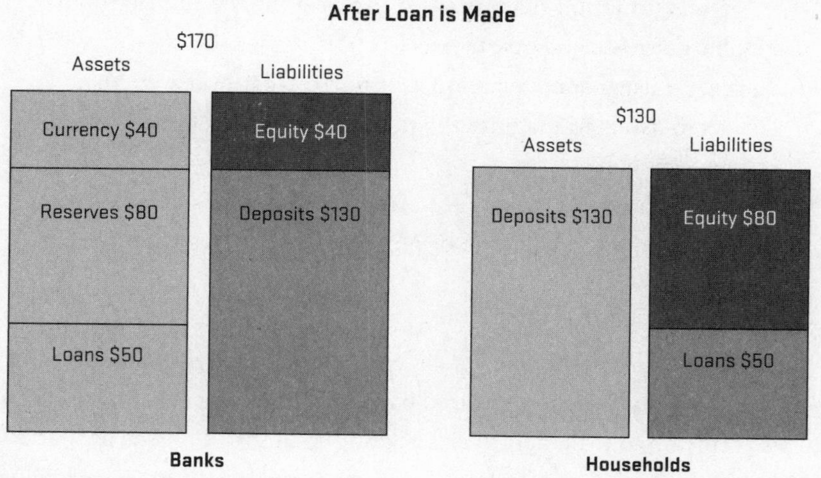

money are much more important than most modern economic models imply.

UNDERSTANDING SHADOW BANKING

Since the mid-1980s banking has evolved from a standard 3–6–3 loan model (that's, borrow at 3 percent, lend at 6 percent, and hit the golf course by 3 p.m.) to a much more sophisticated and opaque business. To understand the modern financial system it's necessary to go beyond traditional banking.

In recent years the concept of shadow banking has become more prominent as banking has evolved. Shadow banks are generally not like traditional banks. They are generally financial intermediaries or non-bank financial institutions engaged in the financial markets by helping to create liquidity in a number of different ways. In its most basic form shadow banking is the use of money market funding for capital market lending. These institutions operate in the shadows because they are not regulated like banks are.

According to the International Monetary Fund a shadow bank operates as a financial intermediary in a number of different ways, including:

Maturity transformation: obtaining short-term funds to invest in longer-term assets.

Liquidity transformation: a concept similar to maturity transformation that entails using cash-like liabilities to buy harder-to-sell assets such as loans.

Leverage: using such techniques as borrowing money to buy fixed assets to magnify the potential gains (or losses) from an investment.

Credit risk transfer: taking the risk of a borrower's default and transferring it from the originator of the loan to another party.[9]

Shadow banks look like banks and operate in a similar fashion to banks but are not issuers of insured bank deposits and do not have access to the central bank's emergency backstop facilities. In essence shadow banks often transform less safe assets into safer assets by repackaging many different instruments into one securitized product, thereby creating an element of reduced risk through diversification and reselling the product. This allows a shadow bank to offer credit by issuing liquid short-term liabilities against less safe longer-term assets.

Shadow banking is an opaque and evolving subsystem in the banking system that will continue to play an important role in the global economy.

UNDERSTANDING THE IMPACT OF THE CREDIT CYCLE

The money supply in most modern monetary systems is largely determined by the credit cycle. And the credit cycle is largely the result of how economic agents perceive the future potential of economic expansion. As I described in Chapter 6, this is, to a large degree, a behavioral effect. In a normal credit cycle the economy expands and contracts around the following stages:

1. As the economy expands modestly, demand for debt leads to increased borrowing and output.
2. Capital expansion improves as balance sheets improve.
3. Risk appetite increases, asset prices increase, a virtuous cycle appears to be in place.
4. As profits and incomes boom, banks relax their lending standards as they compete for more business and demand for debt increases.
5. As a result of leverage or irrational behaviors, asset prices boom, and the perception that nothing can go wrong becomes embedded firmly in the minds of most economic participants.
6. Unsustainable asset price gains lead to more rational perspectives and asset price declines.
7. Lenders tighten standards, causing the debt expansion to slow. The economy begins to slow as businesses become more cautious and unemployment picks up.
8. Risk aversion gains momentum, causing asset prices and the economy to slow further.
9. Deflation or disinflation take hold of the economy.
10. Recession occurs as the economy officially contracts.
11. Defaults surge and the credit cycle grinds to a halt.

Figure 7.6: The Credit Cycle

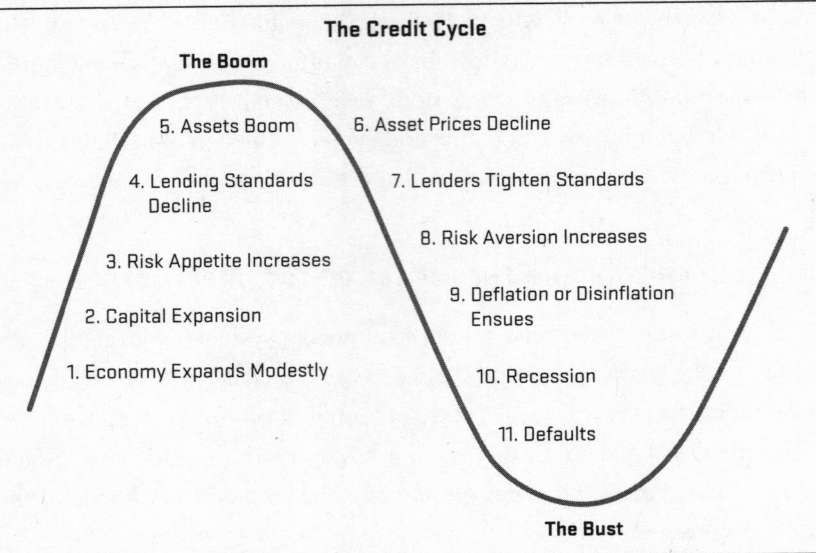

12. Rinse, wash, repeat.

This basic credit cycle (see Figure 7.6) is at the heart of every credit-based monetary system. It is an essential piece of the business cycle and a key driver of the economic system and how it expands and contracts in an elastic form. Understanding this basic outline is essential to understanding how the monetary system functions.

THE DISAGGREGATION OF CREDIT

When studying the potential instability of the credit-based monetary system, it helps to differentiate between good uses of credit and bad uses of credit. In 2009 the economists Dirk Bezemer and Richard Werner referred to such an idea as a "disaggregation of credit."[10] This is the general idea that credit can be used for productive uses and unproductive uses. Credit used entirely for unproductive uses could cause severe imbalances in the economy.

For instance, the use of credit purely for financial transactions by portfolio managers could drive asset prices higher than their fundamental underlying assets can sustain. This could contribute to economic disequilibrium and volatility in the business cycle. Another example is the excessive use of credit for purchases of unproductive assets. If economic participants were to do nothing but purchase unproductive goods and services on credit, the economy could experience an environment in which too much money chases too few goods, causing high inflation and a reduction in living standards.

The disaggregation of credit is a crucial item to understand when thinking about the importance of banking and the credit cycle in the economy.

MONETARY POLICY, FISCAL POLICY, AND THE CONTINGENT CURRENCY ISSUER

Most modern monetary systems are designed around the private banking system, thereby placing private competitive entities in control of the broad money supply. To the surprise of many in the mainstream, and even in the field of economics, the government has far less control over the money supply than most presume. But this system designed around private money issuance has proved terribly unstable at times and in need of a stabilizing force. The aforementioned credit cycle has proved extremely vulnerable to depression at times. What has evolved over hundreds of years is a complex private-public hybrid system. That system involves a complex set of public institutional structures that play a facilitating role for the private banking system.

In addition to the banking system, the monetary system of the United States includes the US Treasury and the Federal Reserve. Together these domestic monetary authorities form a facilitating currency issuer. In modern fiat money systems the government, as the legitimate representation of the people, writes the rules of the game. The term *facilitating currency issuer* is a shorthand way to denote the ability of policy makers to determine macroeconomic policies and development strategies.

Understanding the institutional design of the monetary system is crucial to understanding the roles of monetary and fiscal policy within the money system. The US Treasury, for instance, is the arm of government through which fiscal policy is executed. The Treasury executes policy by managing the tax system and engaging in the sale of bonds in order to procure funds for spending. The Federal Reserve is an independent public-private hybrid that engages in monetary policy through the banking system, primarily by manipulating the levels of inside bank money that exist.

WHAT ROLE DOES THE CENTRAL BANK SERVE?

Central banks worldwide play an important role in helping to support the modern credit-based monetary system that exists in most economies. To emphasize and specify this point I will review the role of the US central bank, although this story is applicable in some form to most central banks.

The US Federal Reserve System was established by an act of Congress in 1913 and can best be thought of as a public-private hybrid. The Fed system created what is known as the interbank market, where banks can settle payments within one centrally regulated market. All member Fed banks are required to maintain reserves on deposit for the purpose of meeting reserve requirements and helping to settle interbank payments. This system was created after a series of banking crises in the late nineteenth and early twentieth centuries exposed the fragility of private banking.

The Federal Reserve System was modeled after the New York Clearing House, which was established in New York in 1853. As its name states, the New York Clearing House was where many of the big banks would come to settle their interbank payments. But it wasn't broad enough to handle the scope and complexity of the US banking system. The Fed system took this private model and expanded it into a public-private hybrid to create a national clearinghouse for interbank payments. You don't hear much talk about this on a daily basis, but that's really what the Fed is—a big clearinghouse to help smooth the payments system.

Before the Federal Reserve System the United States had what was essentially rogue banking dominated by private entities. And when one of these entities experienced a crisis, the system was often thrown into turmoil as Bank A would refuse to settle the payment of Bank B because of solvency concerns. The New York Clearing House and other regional clearinghouses were helpful in times of crisis but far too small to help ease nationwide panics. The Federal Reserve System reduced this risk by creating one cohesive and internal national settlement system. Banks are required to maintain deposit accounts with Federal Reserve banks. You can think of this market as the market exclusively for bank payment settlement as it is not accessible to the nonbank public. This market creates one clean market where banks can always settle payments and where the Fed can intervene and provide aid and oversight when necessary. As the Federal Reserve has explained:

> By creating the Federal Reserve System, Congress intended to eliminate the severe financial crises that had periodically swept the nation, especially the sort of financial panic that occurred in 1907. During that episode, payments were disrupted throughout the country because many banks and clearinghouses refused to clear checks drawn on certain other banks, a practice that contributed to the failure of otherwise solvent banks. To address these problems, Congress gave the Federal Reserve System the authority to establish a nationwide check-clearing system.[11]

The Fed system was created to support the private for-profit banking system, but helps stabilize the entire economy by ensuring that the payments system (or the flow of transactions) remains healthy. So in a sense the Fed is a servant to the banking system as its design is consistent with a mandate to always support the private payments system. This system helps to maintain private competitive banking while also leveraging the strengths of the federal government to create a support mechanism to help keep the banks from imploding because of their inherent inability to properly manage risk at all times.

One point of confusion with the Fed is its ownership. It exists as a result of an act of Congress. But it is also considered an independent entity because it is not part of the executive or legislative branches of government. The Fed exists because Congress created it, but it doesn't execute policy measures with congressional or presidential approval. Politically this makes it a very independent entity.

The regional Fed banks are arms of the Fed system that serve as regional versions of the New York Clearing House. One thing that muddies this discussion of ownership is the issuance of stock by the regional Fed banks to the member banks. Member banks are required to own stock, presumably to ensure that the taxpayer is not the source of capital for the Fed (in keeping with its role as an independent entity). This stock pays a fixed 6 percent dividend and gives the banks a claim on the Fed's annual profits. But it's important to keep this in the right perspective. In 2012 the Fed earned $90.5 billion on its portfolio. Of this, $1.6 billion was paid out in dividends to the banks. The remaining $88 billion was remitted to the US Treasury, as required by law. While the US Treasury doesn't technically own shares in the Federal Reserve, the Fed is required to remit its profits at the end of the year to the federal government. As you can see, remittance often dwarfs any dividends paid to the banks. In other words the US Treasury is the recipient of most of the Fed's profits.

The Federal Reserve System is an imperfect but rather innovative clearinghouse. Its structure as independent within government makes it difficult to determine precisely who owns it. I prefer to think of the Fed as an entity designed to help support the US payments system (which thereby makes it a bank-facilitating entity), which serves public purpose *and* private purpose. In other words it's better to think of the Fed as a public-private hybrid not really owned by anyone.

The Fed's role in the economy and how it influences various actors is widely misunderstood. While the Fed is a facilitating entity for the private banking system, it is also aligned with the US government and has a legislative mandate to achieve price stability and full employment. Confusion about the Fed's role in the economy stems from its primary role in stabilizing the money system, which involves stabilizing and providing liquidity to private banks. The Fed serves as lender of last resort to banks that cannot find sufficient liquidity, so it is often seen as an enabler of bad banking behavior. You can see how this might cause some to conclude the Fed's existence to be a conflict of interest of sorts. It is indeed serving two masters, one private and one public.

THE CENTRAL BANK AND HOW MONETARY POLICY WORKS

Monetary policy involves the use of central bank policy to influence the money supply through interest rates and other channels. The central bank executes monetary policy primarily through influencing the amount of bank reserves in the banking system. The central bank finances its activities by creating money ex nihilo, out of thin air. But it is crucial to understand that the central bank primarily creates money in the interbank market. That is, the central bank can determine the amount of money within the interbank market by buying and selling securities for its own account but does not usually inject or print money for the nonbank private sector, as is commonly believed.

The central bank is the most important bank in any economy because it is the central clearinghouse. The US Federal Reserve is the most important central bank in the global economy because of the comparative size of the US economy in the global economy and also because the US dollar has become the key international currency. In the United States the Fed has a dual mandate to promote full employment and price stability. The key policy lever in the Fed's toolkit is its direct control over the federal funds rate. The *federal funds rate* is the interest rate (i.e., price of money) that private banks pay on overnight loans. This rate can have a substantial influence on the spread at which banks make their loans because it can influence the profits banks earn. For this reason the fed funds rate is widely thought of as having a substantial impact on the credit cycle.

When economists speak of monetary policy, they most often have in mind how the central bank manipulates the federal funds rate. Participating in modern economies is a variety of lenders in addition to private banks (e.g., money market mutual funds, hedge funds, government-sponsored enterprises, issuers of asset-backed securities, etc.) and an array of credit market instruments (e.g., credit cards, mortgage finance, Treasury bonds, etc.). These entities lend money for varying periods of time, from the short term (overnight) to the long term (thirty-years) and much in between. As a result there is a multiplicity of interest rates in the economy. The federal funds rate has the biggest impact on short-term interest rates, with longer-term interest rates and privately related debt instrument–based interest rates determined by what the market can bear. It is important to recognize that the Fed's influence on other rates occurs through arbitrage in other markets against the federal funds rate. The US Federal Reserve achieves the fed funds target rate by engineering changes in the volume of reserve balances and also by open mouth policy. Traditionally this was achieved by changing the quantity of reserves in the banking system, but today the fed funds rate is achieved primarily by setting the interest rate on reserves.

It's important to note that the Federal Reserve could, in theory, control the entire yield curve of government debt. As the monopoly supplier of reserves, the Fed could peg the long end of the US government bond yield just as it pegs the overnight fed funds rate. That is, if the Fed wanted to pin long rates at 0 percent, nothing would stop it from doing so aside from political and public backlash. In this regard it's important to understand that the Fed allows the marketplace to control long rates on US government bonds only to the degree that the Fed permits. In this regard the saying "Don't fight the Fed" is appropriate since the Federal Reserve can always set the price of the instruments it buys. A similar dynamic became clear in Europe in 2011 when the European Central Bank stepped in to backstop the debt of Greece and other countries. Of course, this means it controls the nominal interest rate, but does not necessarily control the real interest rate.

Over the longer term, and when the central bank wants to increase the size of its balance sheet and the volume of reserves, it typically engages in open market purchases of Treasury bonds. In the recent financial crisis, especially the period from September 2008 to the end of 2013, the US Fed grew its balance sheet by purchasing a wide variety of financial assets other than Treasury bonds (e.g., mortgage-backed securities) from depository and nondepository financial firms. In rare instances the Fed also engages in open market sales of Treasury bonds to remove excess liquidity by draining reserves in order to put upward pressure on the federal funds rate. Banks will always try to reduce their holdings of excess reserves by lending them to one another (banks lend reserves only to one another and not to the public). This puts downward pressure on overnight interest rates and helps the Fed control what that rate is because the Fed determines the aggregate quantity of reserves in the banking system. Today the Fed sets a floor on the overnight interest rate by eliminating the desire to lend reserves through the payment of interest on excess reserves (commonly abbreviated as IOER).

It helps to think of the interest rate on reserves as the de facto fed funds rate. The reason why this is important is simple. Were the Fed unable to pay interest on reserves (IOR), the banks would bid down the overnight rate in an effort to rid themselves of reserves. This would put downward pressure on the fed funds rate unless the Fed removed the reserves. By paying interest on reserves, the Fed is able to maintain the size of its balance sheet (thus keeping reserves in the banking system through quantitative easing) while also keeping control of the fed funds rate. In this regard the Fed can always be seen as manipulating the fed funds rate to go higher since excess reserves put downward pressure on the rate.

The Fed's manipulation of short-term interest rates is often called a blunt policy instrument. Why? When the Fed lowers or raises interest rates, the impact on economic activity is indiscriminate. Take, for example, a decision by the central bank to moderate mortgage lending. The policy option of lowering or raising the federal funds rate will influence mortgage interest rates in addition to other interest rates. But the Fed targets only the overnight rate and not the entire curve. So the Fed loosely influences the profit spread that banks earn on their lending, but the Fed does not necessarily control the demand for loans, which is what allows banks to maximize that spread. In this regard monetary policy and interest rate setting are a rather blunt and indirect tool.

Monetary policy is mainly about setting short-term interest rates, although it covers other areas as well, including: liquidity support to financial institutions to fulfill the Fed's role as a lender of last resort; appropriate financial regulation; and maintaining a healthy payments system.

Monetary policy is quite distinct from fiscal policy, although the two do overlap, and there is much coordination by the domestic monetary authorities. Consider that the US Federal Reserve's aggressive interventions during the financial crisis, particularly after the collapse of Lehman Brothers, effectively bailed out financial institutions. Taking distressed assets off the balance sheets of financial businesses in such large volumes meant the Fed's actions had a fiscal component (that did not require congressional approval). By supporting these firms and essentially making a market in illiquid assets (and even removing them from bank balance sheets), the Fed was able to keep asset prices higher than they otherwise would have been and helped make these firms more solvent than they otherwise would be.

THE US TREASURY AND FISCAL POLICY

Fiscal policy involves the use of government taxation and bond issuance to spend money for a public purpose. Understanding the different means through which the Treasury obtains deposits before and in order to finance spending is the most crucial aspect of fiscal policy. It is best to think of all fiscal policy as a redistribution of money. Because banks issue almost all the money in the money system, the government is a self-determined user of bank money (because it has outsourced the right to create money to a private market-based system). Government taxation is a simple redistribution (taking from Paul to pay Peter), whereas bond issuance results in a government budget deficit (spending more than it takes in from taxes).

Deficit spending is also a redistribution of private bank money but involves the sale of government bonds as well as the redistribution of bank money. That is, Paul buys a bond from the government, and the government uses Paul's inside money to pay Peter. Unlike taxation, the private sector (Paul in this case) obtains a net financial asset because a bond is issued to the private sector without a corresponding private sector liability (such as when a corporation makes a loan that results in both a private sector asset and a liability).

The crucial distinction between monetary policy and fiscal policy is that fiscal policy is generally akin to what I would call asset printing. The US government doesn't actually print money in any meaningful sense that expands the private sector's money supply. It does, however, through the implementation of fiscal policy, directly expand the net financial assets of the private sector through the sale of government bonds. These assets for the private sector are liabilities of the public sector without a private sector liability. In other words, they are pure net worth contributions for the aggregate private sector. Monetary policy, on the other hand, generally involves the implementation of asset swaps that change the composition of the private sector's assets but does not always change its net worth (though it can at times, such as in 2008).

THE US TREASURY—A SELF-DETERMINED USER OF BANK MONEY

By law the US Treasury is a user of bank money and reserve money since it settles all its transactions with reserve money in its Federal Reserve bank account, which is initially funded through procuring funds via taxes and bond sales. The Treasury is also the issuer of notes and coins to the banking system. The US Mint and Bureau of Engraving issue notes and coins to the banking system on demand to meet the needs of users of bank customers who have accounts in inside money. For instance, if demand for cash notes is higher than usual, the regional Fed banks will order more notes from the US Treasury.

It's important to note that Congress has *chosen* to make the Treasury a user of reserves and bank money in the modern era; however, that was not always the case and could very well change. Remember, the Federal Reserve is the banker to the US government, so while the current arrangement requires the Treasury to be a user of reserves and bank money, it could in theory simply harness the central bank to always provide a funding source or run its own printing press.

THE GOVERNMENT BALANCE SHEET IS NOT LIKE A HOUSEHOLD OR BUSINESS BALANCE SHEET

It's widely believed that the US government's balance sheet is just like a household's or a business's balance sheet. But this is far from true. A few years ago Warren Buffett noted this, saying:

> The United States is not going to have a debt crisis as long as we keep issuing our debts in our own currency. The only thing we have to worry about is the printing press and inflation.[12]

This important comment has been largely overlooked by many politicians, pundits, and economists. It should be obvious that an entity with a printing press cannot become insolvent. The United States, as an autonomous contingent currency issuer, can fail to pay debts denominated in its currency only if it chooses not to pay those debts. In other words the US government does not have a solvency constraint in the same sense that a household or business does. Households and businesses do not have the authority to tax, cannot issue risk-free debt, and do not have access to a printing press. Households and businesses, in this regard, are all constrained by their ability to obtain money. The US government does not have to worry about running out of money. It has to worry that it is implementing policy that causes spending to outstrip productive capacity, thereby causing high inflation.

THE TRUE CONSTRAINT FOR A CONTINGENT CURRENCY ISSUER

The US Government is a contingent currency issuer.[13] In addition to having the ability to tax 22 percent of all global output, as well as issuing the only risk-free bonds in the economy, the US Treasury could theoretically just print up notes to meet all the debt obligations denominated in dollars. If it were given the legal authority to do so, the US Treasury could literally print up notes in the quantity of the national debt and perform a massive asset swap, thereby retiring the national debt. In this regard it is erroneous to think of the US government as being constrained in the same sense that a household or business is. You and I cannot tax, raise debt through the issuance of risk-free bonds, or print up notes to pay off our debt. The US government, as a contingent currency issuer, does not operate under the same set of constraints imposed on the rest of us.

Now that you understand that an autonomous currency issuer cannot run out of money, it's important to also understand that there are real constraints on a government's ability to operate. Aside from the obvious constraint of real resources, *the true constraint on a contingent currency–issuing government is never solvency but inflation.* Inflation becomes problematic when a nation's spending outstrips productive capacity. This leads to a real reduction in the standard of living and in some cases can lead to a balance-of-payments crisis (currency crisis) and even hyperinflation. Governments must be extremely mindful of their influence on private sector output as misguided government policy could result in reduced private sector output and increased spending on goods and services, thereby leading to a decline in living standards.

It's also important to note that spending by the government must be focused on its efficiency. If spending is misdirected or misguided, there is a very real possibility that this spending will simply result in higher inflation that is not offset by increased production. This could produce both a balance-of-payments crisis that threatens sovereignty and high inflation. If you pay people to sit on their couches all day long, there is no reason to believe that such a government policy will not result in long-term decline in the population's standard of living. Living standards, ultimately, come down to the private sector's ability to produce and innovate. The United States is extremely wealthy not because the government issues financial assets and currency or because the banking system issues bank deposits but because the country is an extremely productive and innovative nation. In other words the United States is extremely productive with the money that is issued within that system.

Thus government cannot just spend and spend or the extra flow of funds and net financial assets in the system could cause inflation, drive up prices, and reduce living standards. It's important to understand that government cannot spend recklessly. This is important, so I'll say it again. *The government cannot spend endlessly as though more money will bring more prosperity.* If the government spends inefficiently or in excess of productive capacity, it can create malinvestment ("bad investment") and inflation, resulting in lower living standards.

Maintaining the correct level of deficit spending or budget surplus is, in many ways, a balancing act performed by the government based on an understanding of the sectors of the economy as well as the health of the economy. We know, by accounting identity, that all nations cannot run simultaneous current account deficits, so it is important to note that the United States is not necessarily the model for the world economy. In fact, depending on specific economic environments in particular nations, the ideal economic strategy could be vastly different from that implemented in the United States or in other developed countries. When we look at the global monetary system, we have to bear in mind that the developed world and many of the US examples I've used in this text are for clarifying purposes and do not always represent the global economy.

When looking at the specific case of the United States, as the reserve currency issuer and a chronic current account deficit country, it is best to think of the government's maintenance of the deficit like a thermostat for the economy. When the economy is running cold, the deficit can afford to be higher. When it is hot, the deficit should be lower. Many variables play into the understanding of whether a government should run a budget deficit, a budget surplus, or a balanced budget. And ultimately voters must decide on the size of government they want and any public purpose that might be necessary.

With regard to the broader money supply, it is important that the government maintain a check on private credit. So while government policy can influence the money supply, the supply of money is primarily determined by private banks. The government should be a good steward of this extension of credit and attempt to execute policy that supports credit extension but does not allow it to run wild, thereby creating systemic instability or private sector malinvestment.

I should also note that not all countries can remain autonomous contingent currency issuers. An exorbitant privilege is bestowed upon a country with substantial output, population growth, and access to natural resources. Some nations, generally less-developed countries, sometimes are forced to peg their currencies to or borrow in a foreign-denominated debt, which can reduce their sovereignty. In the case of the Eurozone all the nations have relinquished their ability to act as a currency issuer because there is no full integration with a central treasury and what is essentially a foreign central bank (the European Central Bank). Therefore it's important to understand each specific economy in its own environment. Exorbitant privilege creates advantages for economic strategy, but it does not create an invulnerable currency.

UNDERSTANDING THE ECONOMIC MACHINE

The economic system is similar to a machine, and understanding that machine requires an understanding of how all these pieces fit together to help the machine operate. Continuing the metaphor of the human body is a good way to better understand this machine.

Monetary policy and fiscal policy help to keep the pace of the flow in the system steady. When the central bank raises the federal funds rate, it does so typically to suppress inflationary pressures by making it less enticing for banks to issue loans (create money). When the Fed increases the federal funds rate (i.e., the short-term interest rate on which monetary policy pivots), borrowing costs rise across the spectrum of credit products, thus slowing economic activity. The reverse is true when the Fed lowers the federal funds rate, typically to counteract a swelling in the number of underemployed. Lowering the rate decreases borrowing costs across the spectrum of credit products (especially loans made on a shorter-term basis), thus accelerating economic activity. Monetary policy is mainly about manipulating short-term interest rates, though other factors also play a role.

Fiscal policy is an alternative way of helping to stabilize the flow in the system. Economists often talk about aggregate supply and aggregate demand. *Aggregate supply* is the total amount of final goods and services produced by an economy during a given period. *Aggregate demand* is the total amount of final goods and services *purchased* by agents in a given period. What we produce as a nation and the market prices at which goods and services are sold can be different; hence, the labels of aggregate supply and aggregate demand. When the economy is booming during an upswing, aggregate demand can exceed aggregate supply and lead to inflationary pressures. When the economy is depressed during a downturn, aggregate supply can exceed aggregate demand and lead to disinflationary or even deflationary pressures. If the economy is suffering from a lack of aggregate demand, the government can, by running larger deficits (i.e., spending in excess of revenues), increase the flow (please note this also can be achieved through lower taxes). In fact, as tax receipts and certain government outlays (e.g., unemployment benefits) both rise and fall countercyclically, much of the government's budget is beyond the control of policy makers and instead is determined by the endogenous performance of the economy. Such receipts and expenditures are known as *automatic stabilizers*—things like unemployment benefits and other automatic forms of spending can rise and fall without any new government action during a downturn or upturn.

Increases in government spending increase the flow of funds in the economy and help to improve private balance sheets. This occurs through two primary functions. The first is the government's power to procure funds and increase the flow of spending in the economy as the taxing authority and seller of risk-free bonds. That is, when the private sector stops spending and investing (for whatever reason), the government can always turn on the flow through the implementation of fiscal policy. The second function occurs in the form of increases in net financial assets, which can help improve the stability of private balance sheets. Remember, when the government is in deficit spending mode, it sells a bond to Peter and redistributes Peter's bank deposits to Pauline. The bond sale to Peter results in a net financial asset for the private sector because there no private sector liability is attached to it. Of course, if government spending is poorly allocated or malinvested, there can be negative long-term consequences through various channels. Do not overlook or underemphasize this effect.

To continue the metaphor of the human body, government regulation can be a nuisance (bureaucratic red tape), but when not overdone it works like the body's immune system, which helps to counteract bad agents, keeping economic activities within acceptable boundaries but without constraining the body from thriving. In some respects the government sector is like a safety net to correct and curb market failures (Though admittedly it can also exacerbate problems if it is abused or misused.).

Everything else in the system can be thought of as the private sector. The nonfinancial business sector is the musculature system and the skeletal system (what we might think of as the core pieces of the system). Nonfinancial businesses are the biggest employers and make most of the products and services essential to increasing living standards. The financial sector is the kidneys and bone marrow, supplying new blood to the system, that is, so it can create liquidity to supply new flow when necessary. The main role of finance is to facilitate the development of the productive capital assets of the economy and to provide the monetary and financial resources that allow us to undertake activities of our own liking (e.g., buy or build homes). The household sector is the brain and comprises the individuals who ultimately make the decisions that steer the economic machine. The drive, ambition, knowledge, and ingenuity of these people ultimately determine the success of the system.

UNDERSTANDING THE FLOW OF FUNDS AND SECTORAL BALANCES

It's important to understand the sectoral relationship within an economy and the ways in which growth is produced by the various sectors and their interdependence through the flow of funds that occurs by means of the transaction chain. Wynne Godley developed the sectoral financial balance approach, which provides a useful way of conceptualizing the macroeconomy and understanding how the different sectors relate to one another. The approach is an ex post facto accounting identity derived by rearranging the components of aggregate demand, and it is typically presented as a three-sector model comprising the private, public, and foreign sectors. This fundamental identity links aggregate demand (i.e., the total amount of final goods and services purchased by agents in a given period) with changes in the positions of the sectors' net financial assets.

The sectoral financial balance approach measures the income of the three sectors' net of spending in a given period. When any sector spends more than its income, it runs a deficit; when a sector spends less than its income, it runs a surplus. It is vital to recognize that only the public sector (in particular the federal government) is able to run large deficits for a prolonged period. This is because the budget constraint of the US federal government is not similar to that of an individual, household, business, or even a state or local government.

The deficit of the entire government (federal, state, and local) is always equal (by definition) to the current account deficit plus the private sector balance (excess of private saving over investment). To be more precise: net household financial income equals current account surplus plus government deficit plus Δ business nonfinancial assets. The surplus of the private sector (households and businesses) represents its net saving of income after spending, whereas the deficit of the public sector is the government's budget deficit. This is the essence of the sectoral balances approach made famous by the late great Wynne Godley. See Figure 7.7 for a visual representation of this approach.

Figure 7.7 shows the three primary sectors of the economy and how they relate to one another. The federal government's position shows how the government's deficit is the nongovernment's surplus. In other words, when the government runs a deficit, the nongovernment is obtaining

Figure 7.7: The Three Sector Financial Balances (percentage of GDP)

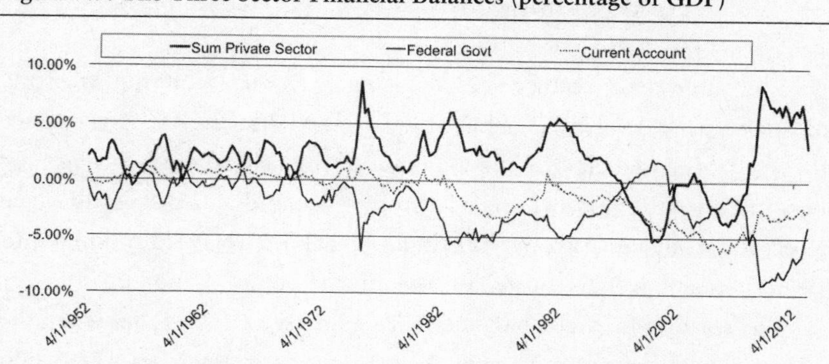

net financial assets as government bonds. This can help to support the private credit structure and strengthen the private sector's financial position. In this depiction the current account position represents a net outflow of income from the United States (as seen in figure 7.7). This means that the rest of the world is running a current account surplus against the United States.

To better understand the sectoral balances view it helps to look into the accounting here in a bit more detail. The sectoral balances can be broken down according to gross domestic product as follows:

$GDP = C + I + G + (X–M)$,
where C = consumption, I = investment, G = government spending, X = exports, and M = imports.

Or, stated differently:

$GDP = C + S + T$,
where C = consumption, S = saving, and T = taxes.

From there we can conclude:

$C + S + T = GDP = C + I + G + (X–M)$.

If rearranged we can see that these sectors must net to zero:

$(I–S) + (G–T) + (X–M) = 0$,
where $(I–S)$ = private sector balance, $(G–T)$ = public sector balance, and $(X–M)$ = foreign sector balance.

The three main sectoral balances *must,* as an accounting identity, add to zero. In Figure 7.7 what stands out is that the US government has run budget deficits for the majority of the last 60 years (in fact for more than two hundred years). Keep this in mind as I discuss the true constraint of the federal government and its ability to avoid running into the perpetual solvency constraints seen in the private sector.

The sectoral financial balance (SFB) approach stresses that when the federal government spends more than it collects in revenues, the deficit spending creates net financial assets for the private sector in the form of government bonds. Private agents benefit from these net financial assets in various ways. Some investors get a safe interest-bearing asset for their portfolios. The thankful recipients of the Treasury's deficit spending receive a payment that enables them to meet their bills and survive. It's important to note that government bonds are an asset of the private sector and a liability of the government. So to pay off the national debt would, by accounting identity, involve the elimination of an important interest-bearing financial asset of the private sector. This does not mean the government can perpetually make the private sector wealthy by providing it with government bonds, but, as I mentioned previously, the public sector's constraint is different than the private sector's constraint (solvency versus inflation), so the notion of paying off the national debt must be placed in the proper context.

THE IMPORTANCE OF UNDERSTANDING S = I + (S–I)

It's important to take the private sector component in the sectoral balances one step further or you might think the true driver of economic growth is the government and not the private sector. Although government can help to drive economic growth (if used properly) never forget that investment is the backbone of private sector equity. After all, investment results in most of the goods and services that help us achieve an improved living standard over time. Most of the private sector's financial claims are against itself and not against the government or the rest of the world. Therefore, when trying to understand the aggregate balance sheet, it helps to look at how the financial assets of firms and households relate to one another within the private sector since this is where the heart of the economy exists.

Rearranging the sectoral balances equation produces an important identity:

$$(S-I) = (G-T) + (X-M)$$
$$S = I + (G-T) + (X-M)$$

rearranges to

$$S = I + (S-I)$$

Don't worry—all that accounting isn't nearly as complex as it looks. What I am saying is really rather simple. Private sector saving is comprised primarily of private investment plus the balance of the government and foreign sector. But remember that the key component of private sector growth and prosperity is derived from the *I* component (investment) because this represents the private sector's innovative and entrepreneurial pursuits.[14]

This shows that wealth creation is not achieved just through government deficit spending or foreign trade but largely occurs independent of these sectors. Remember, net worth equals financial assets plus nonfinancial assets. To highlight this point it's worth looking at the actual private sector balance sheet in the United States (see Figure 7.8). The private sector's balance sheet is comprised of claims primarily against itself in addition to nonfinancial assets. Things like common stock, corporate debt, bank deposits, loans, and real estate all add up to comprise the private sector's balance sheet. You could view these assets as millions of pictures of different smaller sectoral balances by seeing how one sector's assets are another's liabilities. For instance, the Cullen Roche surplus is the non–Cullen Roche deficit. My spending is someone else's income, and my liabilities are someone else's assets. Of this, the government's

Figure 7.8: US Private Sector Net Worth (millions)

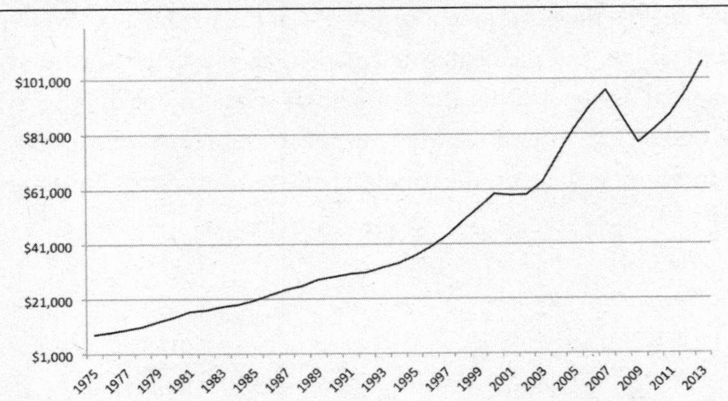

Source: Board of Governers of the Federal Reserve System, Z.1 Financial Accounts of the United States, *December 9, 2013, http://www.federalreserve.gov/releases/z1/Current/z1.pdf.*

net financial assets represent a fairly small portion of the overall balance sheet (domestically held government debt is roughly $11 trillion) on a balance sheet with a net worth more than $100 trillion.

On this point it's important to understand the difference between real wealth and financial wealth since our net worth is comprised of the market value of financial assets plus our nonfinancial assets. A good way to think about all this is to understand that the private sector can create real wealth entirely independent of the government. For instance, a farmer does not need the government or any financial assets to turn two cows into ten. The farmer has achieved real wealth creation regardless of the government's spending position or the financial world's issuance of financial assets. Remember, our financial assets represent claims on goods and services so we should not confuse the theater ticket with the performance. That said, in order to realistically view the monetary system you must understand that we use financial assets to access the nonfinancial asset world. Therefore, if farmers want to engage in the modern economy, they must engage in the modern monetary system by acquiring financial assets. These financial assets will give them the social tool necessary to enhance not only their financial net worth but their nonfinancial net worth. Therefore understanding the modern monetary system is all about understanding this interdependent relationship of financial assets and nonfinancial assets.

UNDERSTANDING FIAT MONEY IN THE INTERNATIONAL SYSTEM

When we talk about fiat money within the global macroeconomic system it is important to note that the system is indeed a globally interconnected system. That Europe, the UK, China, or the United States each has its own currency does not mean these systems are entirely independent. In today's global world we have freely floating foreign exchange, which means that the unit of account in one country floats freely in value relative to the unit of account in another country so while US$1 is always worth one dollar in nominal terms within the borders of the United States, US$1 does not always equal €1 in Europe.

In order to begin thinking in a truly global macroeconomic sense you have to again understand that the international dimension of trade is not all that different from the domestic dimension of trade. In other words one person's income is still someone else's spending. The difference in international trade is the need to transact in the currency of the domestic business, and that generally requires a currency conversion. A country that sells goods and services abroad is said to have exports, while a country that purchases goods and services from abroad is said to have imports. The difference between the amount of exports and imports determines whether a country is running a foreign trade surplus or deficit. One thing you'll notice here again is that one country's surplus is another country's deficit. Everything goes from somewhere and comes from somewhere.

When analyzing the flow of funds, goods, and services between countries, we look at what's called the balance of payments. The *balance of payments* is further defined by three specific accounts—the current account, the financial account, and the capital account.

The most important of these is the *current account,* which shows the "flows of goods, services, primary income, and secondary income between residents and nonresidents."[15] When considering the cross-border flow of funds, it's important to understand the way in which the exchange rates float against one another. In nominal terms the economies in different countries will generally be dynamic in different ways, meaning that what currency buys in one country will not necessarily be equivalent in another country. For instance, a loaf of bread might cost $1 in the United States and €2 in Europe for any number of different reasons (labor markets, resource access, inflation, interest rates, output, etc.). This means the exchange rate is €2 = $1 so goods are generally less expensive in the United States than they are in Europe. This exchange rate floats like the price of any financial asset in any market, based on the supply and demand for the various currencies. In general, less expensive goods in the United States should lead to improved exports because Europeans will import an increasing amount of less expensive goods from the United States.

A lower foreign exchange rate can improve competitiveness for the domestic economy by making it more attractive to foreign investment. As I noted elsewhere, this is often desirable for a nation that cannot compete at the same level with a more developed country, which might lead the domestic government of the less developed country to sometimes engage in policy that improves its domestic economy by making it more attractive to foreign business.

While the most basic elements of foreign trade are common across borders, not all foreign countries have a perfectly similar monetary design or similarly diverse economies. Indeed they are often quite different and limited in extremely different ways.

When I use the term *autonomous contingent currency issuer* in this book, I am referring to the degree to which a country has the ability to remain an autonomous currency issuer. Several elements influence the degree to which a nation is an autonomous currency issuer. This includes reserve currency status, floating exchange rate, foreign debts, and the structure of the domestic monetary system. Figure 7.9 provides a brief overview of the degree to which a nation is an autonomous contingent currency issuer.

Ideally a nation will desire some degree of reserve currency status, floating exchange rates, no foreign debt, and a symbiotic central bank and treasury design. As I discussed earlier, the European Monetary Union (EMU) is an interesting monetary system in that it is a reserve currency with no foreign debt and floating foreign exchange rate, but the monetary design is incomplete in that the central bank is essentially a foreign entity and there is no central treasury. This renders the nations

Figure 7.9: Degrees of Autonomous Currency Issuers

	Reserve Currency	Free Floating FX?	Foreign Debt?	Symbiotic Central Bank & Treasury ?
United States	Yes	Yes	No	Yes
European Monetary Union	Yes	Yes	No	Partial
Japan, UK, & Switzerland	Partial	Yes	No	Yes
Emerging Market Economies	No	Partial	Yes	Yes

Source: Brett Fiebiger, "The International Dimensions of Currency Autonomy," Pragmatic Capitalism *(blog), May 31, 2012, http://pragcap.com/the-international-dimensions-of-currency-autonomy.*

within the EMU users of the euro rather than issuers of the euro. The UK and Switzerland, by remaining outside the euro, have maintained their status as autonomous currency issuers. It's important to note that not all countries can remain autonomous for various reasons. There might not be high demand for their currency on foreign exchange markets, they might not have access to resources, they might not have a developed monetary system, or they might prefer to peg their currency to a stronger trade partner in order to remain more competitive. A certain level of exorbitant privilege is involved in having a diverse economy, access to foreign exchange markets, no foreign debts, a developed domestic monetary system, and resource accessibility.

As the global macroeconomic system grows and becomes increasingly intertwined, it will be more and more important to understand the elements of foreign trade. The relationships between different economies will play an enormous role in the growth and prosperity of the global economy in the decades ahead, so when we view the monetary system as a whole, we should always think of it not only in domestic terms but also in a global sense.

CHAPTER 8

ECONOMIC AND MONETARY MYTHS THAT PERSIST

The biggest impediment to our own progress is often our inability to let go of the past.

IT'S WIDELY ACKNOWLEDGED THAT THE FIELD OF ECONOMICS IS not a hard science. It's often referred to as the dismal science because it is so theoretical. It is also highly politicized. This leaves economics highly susceptible to various emotional biases, political biases, and mythology. Many of these myths are highly destructive and impede our ability to properly understand the monetary system, the financial world, and, perhaps most important, public policy.

There was a time when I used to believe in the myth that the government's balance sheet is just like a household's balance sheet. This led me to all sorts of erroneous conclusions about how the monetary system works and what the potential risks to the system were. If I had maintained this erroneous perspective during the financial crisis I might have believed that I should short US government bonds and bet on a debt default or rising interest rates. But this perspective, which is often politically motivated, would have led to the exact wrong conclusion. Instead, when you try to understand the monetary system through a less biased and more objective lens you come to much more rational and accurate conclusions. In this chapter I will discuss some of the more popular myths in the field of economics with the hope that I can help you formulate a better understanding of the economy, which can help you reach more objective conclusions about the system and how it impacts your portfolio and your life.

MYTH 1—THE UNITED STATES IS GOING BANKRUPT

Few myths are more rampant and pernicious than the idea that the US government is bankrupt or might default on its obligations. We've seen this repeatedly in recent years during the debt ceiling debates and other political discussions about the national debt. This belief pervades the highest level of economics, politics, and the overwhelming majority of the population. But it is highly misleading. The balance sheet of the US government should not be compared with the balance sheet of a household because of the government's status as an autonomous contingent currency issuer.

Remember, the US government has a very different constraint than a household or business. After all, it creates the US currency. Five points are key to understanding the idea that the US government's balance sheet is unlike a household balance sheet:

- The federal government has the authority to tax 22 percent of all global output, giving it access to a revenue stream that is unmatched by any other entity on the planet.
- The US government, as the issuer of the currency and the issuer of the only risk-free bonds in the economy, gives holders of US government debt few other similar options. If you participate in the US economy and you use US dollar-denominated financial assets, you can hold those dollars as either currency or bank deposits in which they will lose purchasing power. You can purchase other assets that include risky private sector–issued assets or you can buy low-risk interest-bearing government bonds. Since all securities issued are always held by someone, this creates a hot potato effect in which some currency holder is always losing purchasing power by saving in dollars and is therefore looking for a risk-free equivalent that protects against the loss of purchasing power. So long as the productive base of the US remains firm and inflation is not spiraling out of control,

we should expect this demand for US dollars and debt to remain strong.

- Congress has the theoretical authority to allow the central bank to buy all bonds issued by the US Treasury. In essence the US government could become entirely self-funded by an entity it created. This eliminates the potential risk of "running out of money." If you had the potential to turn on a press next door to print dollars to fund your credit card payments, I am sure you wouldn't worry about solvency, would you?
- Theoretically in an extreme situation the US government could choose not to issue bonds at all and could instead become the sole issuer of money by circumventing the private banking system and issuing notes for use. Remember the World Cup example in Chapter 7? FIFA doesn't have to outsource the making of soccer balls to Adidas AG, but it chooses to. In the same manner the US government could choose not to let private banks create the primary form of money and could instead simply create it internally.
- The US government has a tremendous asset base that the mainstream media rarely highlight. For instance, the Institute for Energy Research estimates that the US government's fossil fuel resources alone are worth $155 trillion.[1] That's almost ten times the national debt. And that's before we even begin to account for federally owned lands, offshore areas, gold resources, mineral resources, or the trillions of dollars in its own liabilities owned by the Federal Reserve and Social Security Trust Fund. These assets certainly outweigh the government's liabilities by a wide margin.

To further reinforce this point I want to highlight an important quote from the St. Louis Fed researchers Brett Fawley and Luciana Juvenal from 2011:

> As the sole manufacturer of dollars, whose debt is denominated in dollars, the U.S. government can never become insolvent, i.e., unable to pay its bills. In this sense, the government is not dependent on credit

> markets to remain operational. Moreover, there will always be a market for U.S. government debt at home because the U.S. government has the only means of creating risk-free dollar-denominated assets.[2]

None of this means the government can spend as much as it desires without negative consequences. It just means that the government has a different type of constraint than a household. Households can't tax, print US dollars, or borrow funds at a rate our central bank can determine. This is why the US government has been able to run persistent budget deficits for most of its history. Its balance sheet is nothing like a household or business balance sheet.

It is also important to note that the US government's constraint is not that it will run out of funds but that it could supply too much liquidity to the private sector, thereby causing inflation. So the US government's real constraint is inflation and a potential foreign exchange constraint but not solvency. We have to be worried about spending more than our productive capacity or potentially diluting the quality of our domestic output. This is a vastly different issue than the constraint the US media usually focus on with regard to the budget deficit and the US government's ability to afford its spending. For the public policy debate to become pertinent, we need to move from the idea of solvency to government spending's impact on the productive base of the economy.

Is the US the Next Greece?

The recent crisis in Europe has created a great deal of consternation about the potential for the United States to become the next Greece. But Greece is very different from the United States. The European Monetary Union is similar to the United States in that the nations in Europe are all sharing a single currency. The states in the United States are analogous to the nations in Europe. States in the United States cannot create currency, but all are users of the same currency without a floating exchange rate.

The key difference in Europe is that there is no federal government, no central treasury, and no unified central bank. As a result all members of the European Monetary Union (EMU) are users of a currency they cannot create. But because they are users of the same currency, there is no foreign exchange rebalancing. So when Greece runs into an economic downturn, it cannot stimulate its economy by creating the currency, but it also cannot rely on foreign exchange rebalancing. Instead it must rely on wage and price rebalancing through deflation and depression. Likewise, when the Greek economy booms, there is no central bank to raise rates (because the European Central Bank can only raise or lower rates across all of Europe), and there is no foreign exchange rebalancing to make Greece's goods less expensive relative to its neighbors' (again, because there is only one exchange rate across all the trading partners in the EMU).

The thing that has most kept the European Monetary Union from collapsing in recent years has been intervention by the European Central Bank (ECB). The ECB is essentially a foreign central bank but has been acting more like a fiscal backstop in recent years, easing the nerves of bond buyers who are concerned that nations that cannot create their own currency will literally run out of money.

The United States, on the other hand, has a symbiotic monetary union with a unified federal government, a central treasury, and a central bank that all work together. The reason the states in the United States don't run into similar periodic solvency issues is because they receive an extraordinary amount of federal aid. The states that would most closely resemble Greece in the EMU pay far less into the federal pool of funds than they receive. This keeps them solvent and helps keep their economies from collapsing into periodic depressions like we've recently seen in Greece. The EMU has no federal government or central treasury to collect funds and redistribute from the strong to the weak. This means that imbalances will periodically lead to solvency crises that will require a central bank backstop or government bailout. Therefore EMU members benefit from the partial unification and increased efficiencies of the EMU but also suffer as a result of its incompleteness.

China Owns the United States, Right?

Another common extension of this myth is the idea that China or foreigners essentially own the United States because they are holders of substantial amounts of US government bonds. But let's look at the actual allocation of government bonds as of 2012. Foreigners owned about 34 percent of US government debt. The majority of the rest was owned by US citizens. In other words, the US government's liabilities are the nongovernment's assets. If you own a Treasury bill, you own a risk-free interest-bearing asset issued by the US government, and the government has a liability. As we've seen time and time again when discussing a monetary system, we need to focus on both sides of the ledger. As Figure 8.1 shows, most of these bonds are owned by domestic entities. The United States essentially "owns" itself.

So what does China really own and why? When the US government or US businesses do business with foreign governments, the latter obtain US dollars in payment. When these dollars are exchanged for domestic currency, the foreign governments inevitably end up as substantial holders of these dollars. Now, they can hold those dollars, let them earn no interest, use them to bolster their own currency (as many nations do), or they can purchase assets denominated in US dollars. Because the US government issues the safest US dollar–denominated assets, most of these foreign countries end up buying US government bonds. But let's

Figure 8.1: Ownership of US Government Debt in 2012

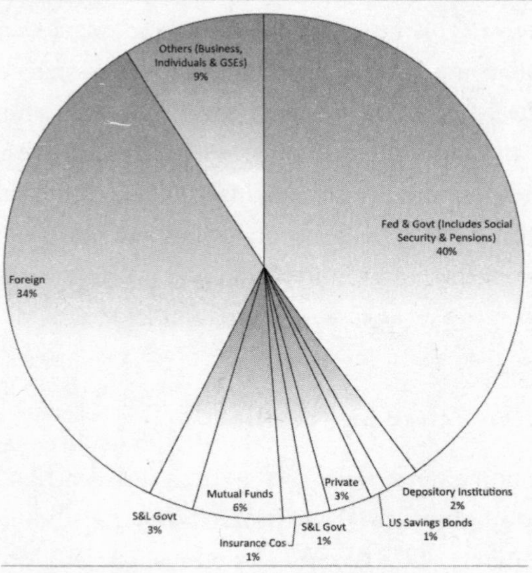

Source: Financial Management Service, "Ownership of Federal Securities," September 2013, http://www.fms.treas.gov/index.html.

remember the causation here. They end up owning dollars by virtue of having done business with the United States. If they don't want to own more bonds, they can simply choose not to do business with the United States. Of course they want to do business with the United States because the United States is the producer of 22 percent of all global output.

Most important, foreign governments could dump US bonds if inflation became a worry, but, again, this is an inflation constraint and not a solvency constraint. The so-called bond vigilantes don't attack a nation that they know can make good on payments and meet solvency needs. They might, however, attack a country perceived as having a balance-of-payments crisis or an inflation crisis. And to keep these conversations in the right perspective we have to understand that a solvency constraint and an inflation constraint are very different things.

What About When We Lose Reserve Currency Status?

Another common concern is that the United States could be losing reserve currency status.[3] But, again, we need to understand the causation here. Reserve currency status is not just something that a nation bestows upon itself. It is primarily earned through sheer economic prowess. Foreign governments hold US dollars because US dollars represent 22 percent of the entire world's output. These dollars are not simply floating into the economy because they are being printed off the presses. They are in foreign economies because foreign governments do a substantial amount of business with the United States and the US dollar is in high demand.

Could we lose reserve currency status? I don't think the question is whether the United States will lose the dominant reserve currency status but when. The United States has a mature economy that has captured a huge and probably unsustainable global market share. As the emerging markets and developed markets converge on one another, the United States will lose market share and dollars will play a less important role in the global economy. But this doesn't necessarily spell impending doom. It's just part of the process of becoming a mature economy. It could very well be problematic if the United States were to become extremely uncompetitive (for various reasons), but that doesn't have to be the case. This is another reason why we need to be focused on the productive base of the economy.

MYTH 2—QUANTITATIVE EASING IS DEBT MONETIZATION AND WILL CAUSE HYPERINFLATION

Quantitative easing (QE) is a form of open market operations that helps the Federal Reserve achieve its policy targets. This policy has garnered a certain mythical prominence in the media and in the investment universe. QE involves open market operations not that different from the way the Federal Reserve always achieves its policy targets. When you hear that the Federal Reserve is changing its target interest rate, this will generally involve open market operations that alter reserves in the banking system. QE involves permanent open market operations, which deviate from standard policy in that the Fed tends to purchase varying assets from the private sector. The New York Fed elaborates:

> The purchase or sale of Treasury securities on an outright basis adds or drains reserves available in the banking system. Such transactions are arranged on a routine basis to offset other changes in the Federal Reserve's balance sheet in conjunction with efforts to maintain conditions in the market for reserves consistent with the federal funds target rate set by the Federal Open Market Committee (FOMC).[4]

Open market operations always involve altering the outstanding reserves in the banking system in order to help achieve a target interest rate. QE is not unique in this regard, although it is believed to have some sort of mythical powers that extend beyond standard open market operations. To better understand how QE works, it's helpful to look at some of the basic accounting behind these operations.

Understanding a QE Transaction

To better understand QE, it's easiest to focus on the two basic ways in which QE transactions occur. The first scenario is when a bank sells bonds to the Fed. The second scenario is when a nonbank sells the bond, and the bank merely acts as an intermediary. In both cases the private sector has the same net financial assets before and after QE occurs (assuming no capital gains). So it's best to think of QE as an asset swap that

Figure 8.2: QE Transaction with a Bank: Bank Sells $100 in T-bonds to Fed

Federal Reserve Balance Sheet:

Change in Assets = +$100
Change in Liabilities = +$100
Change in Net Worth = $0

Banks Balance Sheet:

Change in Assets = $0 (T-bond is swapped for reserves)
Change in Liabilities = $0
Change in Net Worth = $0

alters the composition of the private sector's financial assets but does not add net financial assets.

In the first transaction Figure 8.2 shows that the Fed expands its balance sheet by creating $100 in liabilities (reserves) and swapping those reserves for $100 in T bonds (an asset for the Fed). The bank on the other side of this transaction swaps one asset (T bond) for another (reserves) and experiences no change in net worth as a result.

The second type of transaction is a bit more difficult to follow but not by much. In this case the central bank buys a bond from a nonbank, and the banking system acts as an intermediary. So the nonbank sells a bond to a bank, thereby swapping a bond for a deposit. The bank now has a deposit liability and a new asset (the bond). The nonbank has the same net financial assets as it did before QE. The bank then sells the bond to the central bank, swapping reserves for bonds just like it did in the first scenario. The result of this transaction, shown in Figure 8.3, is again no change in private sector net financial assets.

ISN'T QE LIKE PRINTING MONEY?

QE in the form of buying back government debt is not necessarily money printing. QE through a bank, as shown in Figure 8.3, actually is an asset swap (reserves for bonds). The private sector's net financial assets are the same, although the composition changes. QE through a nonbank results in deposit issuance by a bank, which technically is money creation, but

Figure 8.3: QE Transaction with a Non-Bank: Non-Bank Sells $100 in T-bonds to Fed with a bank acting as an intermediary.

Federal Reserve Balance Sheet:

Change in Assets = +$100
Change in Liabilities = +$100
Change in Net Worth = $0

Banks Balance Sheet:

Change in Assets = +$100 (Reserve Assets Increase)
Change in Liabilities = +$100 (Deposit Liabilities Increase)
Change in Net Worth = $0

Non-bank Public Balance Sheet:

Change in Assets = $0 (Non-bank swaps T-bond for Deposit)
Change in Liabilities = $0
Change in Net Worth = $0

you must also note that the T bond has essentially been "unprinted" because it is removed from the private sector and sits on the central bank's balance sheet, where it has practically zero impact on the real economy (the central bank doesn't buy groceries at Walmart, after all). So QE through a nonbank can change the moneyness of the private sector's assets but won't necessarily change the level of inflation, since spending is a function of income relative to desired savings and QE changes none of the variables in that equation. QE is a lot like changing a savings account (a T bond) to a checking account (deposit).

Additionally, as I discussed in Chapter 7, banks never lend reserves (except to one another) so more reserves don't mean the money supply expands. Loans create deposits. The money multiplier is a myth. This is the primary reason why QE does not cause a surge in loans or inflation.

So What Does QE Do?

QE has various side effects that stem from this change in private portfolio composition. The main effect is known as the wealth effect. This occurs when the central bank removes the interest-bearing safe assets and forces savers to look for other safe interest-bearing assets. This can drive up prices and demand for private credit but does not necessarily drive up the fundamentals underlying those assets. It's not unlike a stock buyback and its immediate effects, which drive up price but have no impact on the underlying corporation's fundamental operations.

QE can directly alter the value of private sector assets, which can have wide ranging portfolio effects, including the improvement in private sector net worth and balance sheet health. One could even argue that QE is a case of widespread misinformation that contributes to asset bubbles and potential market disequilibrium. I think those fears are probably somewhat valid as QE has powerful behavioral effects on the markets' irrational participants.

QE's primary mechanism is through its ability to alter psychology, thereby keeping rates lower than they might otherwise be. The magnitude of the rate effect is hotly debated and almost impossible to quantify. I think QE has some effect on interest rates and therefore positively impacts private investment and debt burdens. These are positive overall outcomes for the economy but difficult to quantify.

QE could drive down the value of the currency relative to other currencies, which could alter foreign trade balances. This would be particularly helpful for a country trying to boost exports. A specific foreign exchange rate target relative to other currencies could be more effective than the way many central banks have implemented QE in recent years.

On the whole QE is widely misunderstood and remains the subject of many different myths. In reality it depends precisely how and where the central bank implements this policy to be able to gauge its efficacy. There are certainly risks in such a policy mainly because the behavioral response tends to be so extreme. But the likelihood of money printing, hyperinflation, and general fears of QE have tended to be overblown.

MYTH 3—CENTRAL BANKS EXIST SOLELY TO ENRICH THE BANKERS

James Carville once said: "I want to come back as the bond market. You can intimidate everyone."[5] Carville was wrong, though. You really don't want to be a bond market. If you come back, you really want to come back as a central bank because then you can intimidate everyone.

Not only does the central bank have enormous powers, but the myths surrounding the central bank give it the appearance of having even more power than it really does.

A lot of these myths are rather misleading and some are downright conspiratorial. For instance, many people think the Federal Reserve is a secret entity owned purely by the banks and in existence entirely to enrich the banks that enslave the rest of us in their debt-based money system. That's not entirely false, but it's mostly false.

The Fed is actually a relatively simple entity, as I explained in Chapter 7. It is, in essence, just a big clearinghouse modeled after the New York Clearing House, which was begun in the mid-nineteenth century. The Fed's primary purpose is to ensure the payments system functions properly. The economy needs a healthy functioning payments system to operate, so allowing the payments system to periodically crash and send the economy into depression because a few banks made lending mistakes is simply inexcusable. The Fed system helps substantially to mitigate this risk.

Of course central banks have become more than just clearinghouses, and this is the cause of much of the conspiracy talk. Today central banks are best known for implementing monetary policy by changing interest rates and executing policies like quantitative easing. In addition the central bank is often the lender of last resort, helping to stabilize banks during crises by supplying liquidity when needed. But this doesn't change the central bank's primary role, which is to oversee the payments system. In the United States the Fed has a dual mandate. But I like to think of the Fed as having a triple mandate. The official dual mandate calls for price stability and full employment, but the Fed can't achieve these targets if it doesn't first ensure that the payments system is running smoothly at all times. After all, if the banking system doesn't work, the payments system doesn't work, and if the payments system doesn't work, the economy doesn't work. And if the economy doesn't work, the Fed can't even begin to think about price stability and employment targets.

So, yes, the central bank is there to serve the banks (they must, by operating as a clearing house). But the central bank exists in large part because the alternative to that setup is letting the banks run a nineteenth-century payments system in which their risk management goes largely unregulated or unmanaged by any outside body. And the alternative to an entirely free banking system is to nationalize banking and let the government run the entire monetary system. So pick your poison—you can have a purely free banking system run by risk takers and capitalists, a purely nationalized system run by a government bureaucracy, or some variant of the modern system in which private banks compete to issue money under the supervision of the central bank and the government serves as regulator and facilitator. This public-private hybrid system has the appearance of a conflict of interest because the central bank serves not only the banks, but also the government. But on the whole the design is a fairly rational compromise between a purely public or purely private system. It's by no means perfect, but it's also not the conspiracy theory some make it out to be.

MYTH 4—A CREDIT-BASED MONETARY SYSTEM IS UNSUSTAINABLE

Many people talk about debt as though it is always a bad thing but generally fail to understand how the credit-based monetary system is mainly just records of accounting. So it's important to understand the essential accounting here. Someone's liabilities are someone else's assets. When corporations issue corporate bonds, they take on liabilities in the form of corporate debt and issue assets for the holder of the bond. When governments spend more than they tax, they sell bonds in the form of government debt, and these government liabilities are held as assets of the bond buyer. When you want to spend more than your income, you might take on debt from the bank, in which case you take on a loan liability and the bank obtains a loan asset. In addition you have a deposit asset and the bank has a deposit liability. Is this always a bad thing? Not necessarily.

For example, if you borrowed money to buy a house that is more expensive than your current liquid assets allow you to purchase, your mortgage represents your choice to own an asset that represents something that provides you with a living standard that is superior to what your liquid assets could otherwise attain. This isn't always a bad thing. In fact, as I discussed in connection with the example of the MacroSoft

Corporation in Chapter 2, liability issuance could be a good thing for everyone involved. By allowing us to bring our future spending into the present, debt can allow us to also bring future production or a superior living standard into the present. There is a cost for this (the loan), but the overall impact of the debt really depends on how wisely you're using the debt.

This doesn't mean debt can't be a bad thing. A credit-based monetary system can be highly unstable at times. If lenders issue more credit than borrowers can pay back during periods in the credit cycle, this could result in substantial economic instability. We experienced this during the housing boom and bust when banks relaxed lending standards and borrowers took on more debt than their future incomes could service. Additionally, as I touched on earlier, a disaggregation of credit can occur in a credit-based monetary system in which credit is used largely for unproductive purposes. This can drive up prices or the price of assets without creating sustainable output to support the credit structure.

The bottom line is that debt is not always a bad thing. You have to explore both sides of the ledger to understand the full picture, and, perhaps more important, you need to understand not only the flow of funds in the economy but also the stock of assets and liabilities in the economy to fully understand how these variables relate to one another and steer the credit cycle.

MYTH 5—THE FREE MARKET CAN SOLVE ALL OUR PROBLEMS

Political biases often lead to extremist opinions about the efficacy of socialism as well as capitalism. The reality is that both systems, if taken to an extreme, can be extremely dangerous. I've stressed the potential dangers of government regulation and government spending to the system, but we should also be wary of the risk inherent in capitalism. Capitalism is an incredibly powerful and beneficial system when it is properly implemented; however, we should be wary of extremists who think we need to tear down capitalism or let capitalism run entirely free. To understand this it helps to think about the inherent nature of a capitalist system.

Capitalists are, by nature, monopolists. A good capitalist will try to monopolize as much of the means of production as possible. This means that capitalism, if left entirely unchecked, will naturally lead to corporatism: the economy will be dominated by a few substantial capitalists who monopolize the means of production. In fact this nearly happened in the United States in the late nineteenth and early twentieth centuries when John D. Rockefeller, J. Pierpont Morgan, Cornelius Vanderbilt, and Andrew Carnegie owned the vast majority of the US economy.

The problem with allowing such a system to develop unfettered is that capitalists by their nature are profit maximizers. And in the process of profit maximization they will tend to minimize wages, minimize employment, and inevitably increase inequality as a few capitalists accumulate the majority of the nation's wealth. In a credit-based monetary system this could also lead to excessive borrowing by the least creditworthy participants as they try to achieve a living standard that their current incomes don't offer. This can result in substantial instability in the economy as the balance sheet of the middle class and working poor deteriorate. A properly run government can actually help create balance within a capitalist economy. There's a balance to be found here, and throughout history the US economy has maintained a balance that has tended to work well.

As with any powerful system, if left to its own devices, capitalism, just like unchecked government, has the potential to become corrupted. This doesn't mean we should chain down capitalists and make it undesirable or exceedingly difficult to pursue business activities, but I think we have to be careful about the idea that unchecked capitalism will necessarily serve the best interests of society as a whole through a purely free-market system.

MYTH 6—CONSUMERS MATTER MORE THAN PRODUCERS

At the core of much of modern economics is a relatively simple question—who matters more to the economy: consumers or producers? This is a nearly impossible question to answer because, like so much of what I've discussed, there are two sides to the coin. Consumers need producers and producers need consumers. Producers create goods and services that enhance the lives of the consumers, while consumers provide the demand that helps drive income, revenue, and future business expansion.

Perhaps more important to the discussion is understanding the relationship between aggregate supply and aggregate demand. When supply is low and demand is high, we experience an economy that is operating above capacity. When supply is high and demand is low, we experience an economy that is operating below capacity. The economy rarely operates at the economic holy grail of an equilibrium point because the economy is generally swinging between excess supply and excess demand. Markets rarely clear. And depending on where we are in the business cycle and the credit cycle, this story will look different at different points, and producers will at times look more important than consumers and vice versa.

The answer to this question about consumers and producers is not that one is more important than the other but that both matter throughout the business cycle, and understanding potential policy or economic needs is mostly about understanding where we are in the cycle. Additionally we should view producers and consumers as two sides of the same coin. To multiply that coin we need not only healthy consumers but vibrant and innovative producers.

MYTH 7—SAVING FINANCES INVESTMENT

It's common in our everyday lives to extrapolate the microeconomic from the macroeconomic without realizing that we're falling victim to a fallacy of composition. The classic example of a fallacy of composition is when one person stands up at a football game in order to gain a better view. Of course you'll ruin the view of the people behind you, forcing them to stand up and subsequently requiring everyone behind them to stand up. If everyone stands up, everyone has this better view, which is almost exactly the same as the view sitting down. Your position is better only if viewed in isolation, but in the aggregate the group is not better off.

This commonly occurs in economics where we view the microeconomic as an accurate representation of the macroeconomic. This is why it's so important to think in a macroeconomic sense. There are two sides to all financial transactions. Thinking of a financial transaction's impact on the economy from the perspective of yourself and yourself alone is ignoring a big part of the picture. One of the most common errors in economics is the misuse of the accounting identity $S = I$, or saving equals investment. This overly simplistic view of the macroeconomic world leads many to claim that "saving finances investment." That seems obvious, right? After all, if you don't have any savings, how could you possibly invest? But it's actually backward most of the time. Investment creates saving.

The idea that saving finances investment has two major flaws. The first is based on the idea that the savings of the aggregate economy is some sort of "loanable funds" market that investors must bid on in order to be able to create output. But a modern monetary system is not a barter system or a loanable funds system. We use a medium of exchange that exists primarily in the form of loans that have created deposits. And as I noted in Chapter 7, these loans are not created by banks that necessarily have some previous savings (although they must meet capital requirements). But that's precisely what this sort of thinking about the world implies. It implies that the supply of credit is constrained only by what has been saved. But banks create loans and deposits by simply expanding their balance sheet. In other words, when you borrow from the bank, the bank will simply mark up its assets (the loan) and its liabilities (the deposit), and you will mark up your assets (the deposit) as well as your liabilities (the loan). When a bank extends credit, it does not necessarily decrease its revenues, consumption, or income. It is a pure balance sheet change created from thin air. Bank loans, of course, don't in and of themselves increase private sector saving but are often used to finance investment.

The second major flaw in the idea that saving finances investment is it doesn't realistically account for the causation of saving. We know that output equals income because we earn income by creating output. We also know, in the immediate timeframe, that all income is saved. If you get paid $100, whether you like it or not, you are saving $100, if only for the briefest of moments. This is your income, and it has not yet been consumed. Let's say you now consume a $50 dinner. You consume your dinner and you've dis-saved $50. But that $50 becomes someone else's saving immediately. In the aggregate, saving has not increased; it has merely been transferred. But what if, instead of consuming your $50, you purchased a $50 production line (that is one inexpensive production line!). Then you own a productive $50 nonfinancial asset. You have not consumed your income and it has not declined; your level of investment has increased by $50. In addition the seller of the production line will experience an increase in saving. Their saving has increased without your having dis-saved. Therefore in the aggregate investment often creates saving.

This once again highlights the importance of investment in the economy. It is investment that generally results in most of the great advances in the goods and services we use that help us attain a better living standard. In addition, while saving and investment are two sides of the same coin, investment is primarily what grows the coin.

MYTH 8—THE IS-LM MODEL CAN PROPERLY EXPLAIN THE ECONOMY

A nefarious extension of myth 7 is the continued use of the IS-LM model in modern macroeconomics. Modern macroeconomists often use the investment-saving, liquidity-money (IS-LM) model to try to better understand the relationship between real output and interest rates. But the model is not just a poor reflection of reality; it also is based on several myths. John Hicks, who devised the IS-LM model, later referred to it as a "classroom gadget."[6] Despite this, the model, which is a terribly oversimplified and unrealistic view of the actual economy, lives on.

The primary flaw in the IS-LM model is that it is based on the same loanable funds model I discussed earlier in this chapter. In other words, it is based on the idea that saving finances investment and that a big pool of saving sits around waiting to be tapped by investors. The model is often used to argue that credit is constrained only by the amount of loanable funds or saving that exists. As I've shown repeatedly, this is simply not how modern finance operates. The loanable funds model of the world does not correctly portray a world with endogenous bank money.

Additionally the IS-LM model, with its loanable funds–based approach, assumes that if we save more, less competition in this loanable funds market will drive down interest rates and stimulate investment.

This same argument is often made to claim that government borrowing taps into this pool of loanable funds, thereby driving up interest rates as more people compete for fewer loanable funds. Therefore it is automatically assumed that lower consumption and smaller government budget deficits would lead to more loanable funds. This cannot be true, however, because lower consumption by one party means lower saving by another party. If you save more on clothing than you did last year, some clothing store has less income. And as I've shown, government deficits most certainly don't steal from the pool of loanable funds. In fact they add to the net financial assets of the nongovernment sectors.

The IS-LM model simply does not reflect the reality of the modern monetary system. It is actually worse than just a classroom gadget. Unfortunately it's still being used as a cornerstone in many economic curricula, perpetuating many of the myths that muddy people's understanding of the way banking, money, and the economy actually work.

MYTH 9—GROWTH OF MONEY EQUALS INFLATION

If you take a course in macroeconomics, you're likely to encounter what's called the equation of exchange at some point. This equation states: $MV = Py$, where M is the money supply, V is the velocity of the money supply (how many times a dollar is spent), P is the price level of goods and services, and y is the quantity of goods and services sold. Much like $S = I$, $MV = Py$ is a tautology. You can't reject it, but you can misrepresent it. And the interpretation of this tautology is often flawed or filled with general assumptions that are misleading.

First, let me be clear that inflation, as it is commonly used in economics today, is a rise in the price level. Defining inflation as a rise in the money supply, as some heterodox economists do, tells us a lot less about the economy than we need to know. The reasoning is simple. The most basic error in the equation of exchange and the "more money equals inflation" thinking is the definition of *money.* Many modern macroeconomists do not even include banks in their models of the world and do not account for the varying degrees of moneyness across different types of financial assets. In general economists start with bank reserves and cash and simply assume that the central bank has some sort of direct control of the entire money supply through control of reserves and cash. Of course, as I've discussed here, banks are not reserve constrained so reserve levels have only an indirect impact on bank lending, and cash is merely a facilitating form of money. The central bank does not shoot dollar bills out the front door or print money in the capacity that many assume. In reality, *M* is primarily driven by demand for loans by credit-worthy bank customers. Therefore the equation of exchange is based on an extremely vague definition of what is arguably its most important component.

Additionally the equation of exchange ignores the reality that spending is a function of current income relative to desired saving. Our savings are made up of many financial assets as well as nonfinancial assets. Money is not the only factor driving the financial asset component. But the equation of exchange has such an unrealistic definition of money that it is practically rendered meaningless when applied to the actual monetary system we have.

Could more money lead to higher inflation? Of course. As we've seen, the money supply in the United States tends to rise because we reside in a credit-based monetary system in which consumers and producers are usually borrowing from the future so they can consume and produce today. Does an increasing money supply automatically mean we are worse off or experiencing a decline in our living standard? It most certainly could, but the assumption that "more money equals inflation" won't really tell you whether more money and potential inflation are actually good or bad.

The reality is that inflation is more than a monetary phenomenon. The economy is a complex nonlinear dynamic system that cannot be mapped out with overly simplistic models based on extremely vague and even inapplicable inputs. The equation of exchange does not shed a lot of light on the inflation story and the idea that more money (depending on what that is in your model) equals more inflation is often misleading as a result.

MYTH 10—HYPERINFLATION IS CAUSED BY PRINTING MONEY

It's commonly believed that hyperinflation is just a very high level of inflation that results from excessive money printing. But hyperinflation is poorly understood by modern economists in large part because they do not have a substantial data set of developed economies from which to fully understand the phenomenon. My research shows that hyperinflation is not merely the result of printing money or an expansion of the money supply and in fact tends to occur around specific and severe exogenous economic circumstances that *lead* to an increase in the money supply, ultimately leading to hyperinflation.[7] In other words hyperinflation is not merely high inflation or a collapse in confidence but is actually the result of *severe* exogenous shocks with real and provable transmission mechanisms. Historically, these causes tend to be

- A collapse in production.
- Rampant government corruption.
- Loss of a war.
- Regime change or regime collapse.
- Ceding of monetary sovereignty generally through a pegged currency or foreign-denominated debt.

A quick review of the modern cases of hyperinflation shows striking similarities. Most notably they involved war (the losing end of a war), regime change, or foreign-denominated debt. All resulted in catastrophic hyperinflations, as Figure 8.4 shows.

Figure 8.4: Modern Hyperinflation Causes (post-1900)

1. WW1 Hyperinflations	**Cause**
a. Austria	Foreign denominated debt, regime change
b. Hungary	Foreign denominated debt, regime change
c. Weimar Republic	Foreign denominated debt, regime change
d. Poland	War with Russia, regime change,
e. Russia	Regime change, civil war
2. Post WW2 Hyperinflations	
a. China (1948)	Civil war, regime change
b. Greece (1944)	Civil war, regime change
c. Hungary (1945)	Foreign denominated debt, war
d. Argentina (1975–1991)	Foreign denominated debt
e. Zimbabwe (2004)	Regime change, foreign denominated debt

Hyperinflation is not merely high inflation. Hyperinflation is a disorderly economic progression that leads to collapse of the currency. While government debts and deficit spending can exacerbate a hyperinflation, they have not generally been the cause of hyperinflation but rather the result of other political and economic events. Understanding hyperinflation is not necessarily about understanding the effect of money printing but about understanding environments that can lead to such a policy response.

MYTH 11—ECONOMISTS HAVE ALL THE ECONOMIC ANSWERS

In his excellent book *The (Mis)behavior of Markets,* Benoit Mandelbrot tells a joke that goes like this:

> The engineer, the physicist and the economist find themselves shipwrecked on a desert island with nothing to eat but a sealed can of beans. How to get at them? The engineer proposes breaking the can open with a rock. The physicist suggests heating the can in the sun until it bursts. The economist's approach: "first assume we have a can opener."[8]

Economic models are often filled with vague assumptions based on a false representation of reality. Models are often fun to look at, but if they don't represent our reality, they're a lot less useful than we think. Take, for instance, what we all commonly know as actual models—the beautiful men and (mostly) women who strut around modeling the various things we might wear. These models are constructed as completely unrealistic portrayals of the average reality. When actual consumers put the clothes on, they do not resemble those models in any way. These models look great in theory, but the model does not always translate well into reality. The model really only gives us a vague idea of what reality might look like.

Economic models of course were created to simulate reality. But much like our average clothing model, economic models are based on a version of the world that is largely fictitious as it applies to the average reality. And unlike doctors or biologists, who can perform experiments over and over again to test theories, economists cannot implement a test model on an entire economy. When you combine this with the enormous amount of guesswork in the inputs (such as erroneous definitions of money, for instance), you tend to get a lot of failed theorizing.

Making matters even worse, much of modern-day economics has become politicized as economists are called on to advise on major policy using only theory and conjecture. Much of economics involves conforming a political bias with a worldview. For instance, most Keynesians start with government spending and taxing and how those government policies can influence the economy and then interpret a model in a way that confirms their political bias. Monetarists start with the central bank and interpret a more laissez-faire view of a model to predict how an independent central bank policy can impact the economy. Austrians start with the private sector and build a model that seeks to eliminate or reduce government. So on and so forth. Every school of economics has a specific ideology, and the political lines are clearly drawn. This doesn't even approach science. It's more like religion.

If economics were more of a science, it would start with operational realities and build out from there. It would start purely with how the system works and how it functions at the operational level instead of looking at how a certain political entity can use certain policies to conform to a particular worldview. The flaw in this approach is that it doesn't actually result in any agreed-upon understanding of the actual inner workings of the monetary system. So you have a lot of economists who all essentially disagree on policy *and* their understanding of the way the monetary system works. Can you imagine if all the surgeons in the world didn't work from similar understandings of the way the human body functions and instead just experimented on the body with various hammers, scalpels, and other toys?

In Chapter 7, I talked about a da Vinci approach to modern economics. Leonardo da Vinci was famous for his work in anatomy. But da Vinci didn't take bodies apart so he could fix them. He took them apart so he could understand them. Leonardo knew that you couldn't even begin to fix a system until you understood it. Curiously modern macroeconomists still haven't undergone this process of discovering an agreed-upon understanding of the system. There has been no da Vinci approach in modern macroeconomics. Plenty of surgeons pretend to have the best tools. But what we need are more da Vincis. Until then the state of modern macroeconomics will remain fairly dismal.

It's also interesting to note that John Maynard Keynes, Wynne Godley, Adam Smith, and Karl Marx were not trained economists. Often the best contributions to economics are made by those outside the profession because they are providing an unbiased and alternative perspective. Of course this doesn't mean that economists have nothing to contribute or have been detrimental to the progress of economics, but we should be willing to look beyond the sphere of the theoretical in search of something more closely resembling reality if we are to find better answers for using this system more effectively. Economists are an important part of the development of our thinking and understanding, but that development is often impeded by the heavy political bias and theorizing that deters us from coming to sound conclusions.

CHAPTER 9

ESSENTIAL PRINCIPLES OF PRAGMATIC CAPITALISM

If we can't agree on the basics, we can't agree on anything.

I OFTEN TALK ABOUT A FOUNDATION OF "PLAIN FACTS," OR things we can prove for understanding the new macroeconomic world we live in. Focusing on plain facts helps us establish a foundation from which we can understand and interact in the financial world. From there we can disagree on many things, but a macroeconomic view requires an understanding of observable truths and things we can verify through real-world understandings. Economics will never be a hard science, but that doesn't mean there are no observable truths. Yet, for some reason, many myths hold sway in this field. When viewing this new macroeconomic world and why it matters more than ever, we have to establish a set of understandings that we can work from. This includes what I view as the 20 essential principles that I have outlined in this book:

> *The big picture matters more than ever.* As the world's population expands, technological advances grow and the emerging market's middle class demands a higher living standard, the global economy will become an increasingly interconnected and tiny place. This will force changes in the use of global resources, the way governments engage in the economy, and a shift in the way we all interact and engage in the economy and in the markets.

Modern money is a social construct that serves primarily as a medium of exchange. Modern money exists primarily as a record of account and a medium of exchange that allows for its highly socialized users to more easily interact in the economy. This money is not necessarily a physical thing and is likely to further evolve as an electronic record of account. As technology continues to change, we should expect money to evolve with it.

One person's spending is another person's income. At the most basic level the economy is made up of millions of individual transactions that involve spending. As Professor Marc Lavoie likes to say, "Everything comes from somewhere and everything goes somewhere." Our spending is someone else's income. Someone's assets are someone else's liabilities. One entity's deficit is another entity's surplus. To think in a macroeconomic sense we must always keep both sides of the ledger in mind.

Spending is a function of current income relative to desired saving. Spending drives the economy because it is the flow that feeds all consumption and production. When we think about how that flow occurs in the economy, it's helpful to think of how our stock of financial assets relates to the current flow. Most of us are generating some source of income from which we choose to save, consume, or invest. Our savings is a crucial stock item that helps us better prepare and plan for future spending needs. Therefore our spending is a function of current income relative to the amount we desire to save.

Investment is spending not consumed for future production. Saving is income not consumed. Investment and saving are not necessarily what we commonly think of them as. Investment is spending not consumed for future production. And saving is income that has not been consumed.

The best investment you'll ever make is likely to be in yourself. The best investments do not always involve the purchase of a claim on someone else's business. Instead the best return on investment you are likely to generate is an investment in yourself and improving the way you can provide value to other economic participants, thereby maximizing the income stream that drives your total portfolio.

Secondary markets are where most of us allocate our saving. Our income flows into a total portfolio. After choosing how much to allocate toward future production (investment), we then allocate our savings to various financial assets with the goal of protecting that savings from the risk of permanent loss and the risk of purchasing power loss. This is done in large part on secondary markets where existing securities are exchanged. Primary markets are where real investment occurs. This is where corporations obtain funding for future production. Secondary markets are where we primarily allocate savings.

We are often our own worst monetary enemy. Although we created money to simplify our economic lives, we are ill equipped to handle many of the behavioral problems that come with having a monetary system. Our inherent biases and deficiencies will often make us our own worst enemies. Identifying potential errors and flaws is the best way to protect yourself from yourself.

In being wrong we can learn to be right. The monetary system is a complex dynamic system. It is constantly evolving and changing, and our understandings of it are constantly trying to keep up. You will make mistakes interpreting and engaging in this system, but learning from these mistakes can vastly improve future interaction within this system. Being wrong can be a good thing if you learn from your mistakes.

The money multiplier is a myth. Banks are not reserve constrained. They are capital constrained. Remember, modern money is primarily endogenous money, meaning that it comes from within the private sector and not from the public sector or the government. Money comes mainly from within the private sector when banks make loans, which create deposits. And they do so without constraint from their reserve position. Banks do not check their reserve positions before making a loan. If they require reserves, solvent banks can always find reserves in the interbank market or borrow from the central bank. The money multiplier, which is taught in almost every mainstream economics text, describes a strict reserve constraint on banks that is purely mythical. This idea should be eliminated from the way we understand modern banking.

Banks matter as the primary issuers of money in the modern monetary system. Understanding banking matters because banks issue the primary medium of exchange, which makes up an incredibly important component of private sector balance sheets. The banking system is an important cog in the economic machine, and its health and stability are absolutely vital to sustaining a healthy monetary system and economy.

Double-entry bookkeeping matters. Accounting matters for understanding macroeconomics, finance, and money. To avoid falling victim to your own biases and fallacy of composition, you must view both sides of the ledger in order to obtain a full understanding of the workings of the monetary system. A basic understanding of accounting provides clarity and a broader perspective. As my friend JKH likes to say: "If you can't explain it with accounting, you can't explain it."

Investment is the backbone of private sector equity. One of the key takeaways from this text is the importance of the private sector in the chain of production. At the heart of this production chain is private sector investment. Investment is not only a key driver of private saving; it is also the primary driver of sustainable output as well as innovation. To understand the future health of the monetary system and the improvement of our financial living standards, we must remember that investment is the backbone of private sector equity.

Business investment is driven primarily by demand for goods and services. While investment is the backbone of private sector equity, businesses cannot exist without customers. Businesses expand investment when they are seeing demand for their goods and services. Your spending is someone else's income, and it's this income that helps businesses expand and operate so they can produce and invest in the economy. Remember, there are two sides to the coin of consumption and production. Investment can increase the number of coins but only if there is strong demand from consumers.

Deficit spending by government redistributes existing money and creates net financial assets as government bonds. The idea that governments print money in a modern monetary system is misleading. Instead we should think of taxation and deficit spending as a mere redistribution of existing bank money. I am not using *redistribution* in a pejorative sense, although this redistribution could certainly be negative at times. Instead we should understand the government as an entity that helps to sustain the flow in the monetary system and that it also is an entity that provides net financial assets to the nongovernment sectors. At times these are highly beneficial policy responses that can both contribute to corporate profits and incomes and help support the nongovernment balance sheet. The efficacy of government spending is about understanding its impact on investment and inflation and not about understanding whether an autonomous currency-issuing government can afford that spending.

An autonomous contingent currency–issuing nation has an inflation constraint, not a solvency constraint. A country that remains autonomous and controls its own currency should never run out of that currency unless it so chooses. Therefore comparing this type of government to a household or business is highly misleading. We need to think of the true constraint in these nations as the inflation constraint. These nations do not suffer from a lack of liquidity but rather the risk of too much liquidity. The national debate needs to refocus on the risk of inflation from government spending and other policies and move past the risk of not being able to meet the payments on a debt that is denominated in a currency we could just create by passing laws enabling us to do just that.

Outside money exists primarily to facilitate inside money. Our monetary system is designed primarily around the private banking system and inside money (money created inside the private sector). This private banking system is supported and regulated by the role of outside money (cash, coins, and bank reserves, or money that comes from outside the private sector). When we discuss the importance of money in our monetary system, we should recognize that the inside money predominates because this is the money that most influences output, employment, and transactions at the point of sale.

We have a fiat monetary system, not a hard money or barter-based system. Analyzing and understanding the modern monetary system means we must understand the system we have and not the system we want. We do not reside in a commodity-based monetary system or a barter system. Therefore when we analyze and understand the system we must always approach it from the reality that we reside in a fiat monetary system that is credit based. Any discussions about barter or commodity money are largely inapplicable to our modern monetary reality. If we're going to resolve the issues we have with our current system, we must understand it for what it is and not what we want it to be.

Money is not the same as "true wealth." Money is the medium of exchange. It is the thing that gives us access to the show that is the economy. Mistaking money for wealth is like mistaking the theater ticket for the performance. The reality is that the ticket is the means to the end. For most of us true wealth includes things like shelter, food, water, security, companionship, family, and things that money may or may not give you access to.

Good capitalists serve themselves best by serving others. The capitalist system is most efficient and productive when its users are providing goods and services that enhance the lives of other participants within this system. The private, profit-motivated, and competitive nature of the capitalist system is operating best when its users understand that good capitalists serve themselves best by serving others.

CHAPTER 10

PUTTING IT ALL TOGETHER

Understanding the global macroeconomic puzzle is all about understanding how the pieces fit together.

WE'RE NOW LIVING IN A NEW MACROECONOMIC WORLD. THIS IS a place that is becoming smaller and more interconnected by the minute. And understanding that world matters more than ever to everyone in it, whether you're a consumer, producer, investor, or saver. This interdependent world requires an understanding of how all its smaller components fit into the much larger and interconnected puzzle.

THE NEW MACROECONOMIC WORLD AND ECONOMICS

The new macroeconomic world is changing the way economists interpret the world and build an understanding of it. This is a global system that is connected by banks, central banks, government agencies, and enormously complex global marketplaces. To understand the economics of this new macroeconomic world, we have to think of the big picture and understand how the global macroeconomic picture is influencing all its participants. Economists have to adapt and evolve from the old microeconomic world and start thinking in terms of the big picture.

THE NEW MACROECONOMIC WORLD AND EVERYDAY LIFE

We all live in communities that are simply smaller components of a much larger and interconnected world. The new macroeconomic world is changing the way we all interact, do business, consume resources, and benefit from the economy. You don't have to be a market participant or an economist to care about why the big picture matters to you. As global citizens we have a responsibility to understand this system so we can ensure that we are putting it to good use and engaging within it as efficiently as we can.

THE NEW MACROECONOMIC WORLD AND POLITICS

The new macroeconomic world is altering the political landscape and forcing governments and politicians to be more cognizant of the way their policies impact the global economy. This is forcing increased government involvement and cooperation. Politicians must become increasingly aware of the ways this global macroeconomic world is changing and becoming more interconnected so they can formulate policy that not only benefits domestic economies but ensures that the global system as a whole remains healthy. And perhaps more important, the people of the world must grow increasingly aware of the new macroeconomic world so they can ensure that their political representatives are enacting policy that best promotes the health of the global macroeconomic system.

THE NEW MACROECONOMIC WORLD AND MARKETS

The new macroeconomic world is shifting the landscape of world markets and is forcing market participants to adapt to the changing global macroeconomic world. Market participants have to be aware of what's going on at the big-picture level so they can better interpret potential future market outcomes and position themselves appropriately. The financial markets are no longer made up of separate domestic stock, bond, or commodity markets. They are all interconnected at a global macroeconomic level, and the big picture is changing the way all markets operate. Benefiting from the new macroeconomy requires a change in the way we approach this global system.

WINNERS IN THE NEW MACROECONOMIC WORLD

Those who are prepared and understand the new macroeconomic world will be better prepared to benefit from the seismic shift that is occurring in the global economy. These people will recognize the massive changes occurring at the government level, the household level, and the corporate level, and they will begin to think many moves ahead about how this changing macroeconomic landscape is altering the playing field that is the economy. These winners will identify the macroeconomic trends, including

- Huge changes in foreign trade and the emergence of the truly global corporation.
- Massive growth of the middle class in emerging markets and the way this is changing our consumption and production of almost everything.
- An aging developed world that will change the way we care for our elders and cater to a society that is living increasingly long lives (in large part a result of the medical and technology boom).
- Greater cooperation and coordination at the government level as economies become interconnected and interdependent.
- Another technology boom whose rapid growth is met with ferocious demand for better living standards.
- A boom in innovation and entrepreneurialism arising from the increasingly interconnected and technologically advanced global economy.
- A changing resource landscape in which all economic participants are going to become more cognizant of increasing competition for limited resources.
- An energy race emerging from demand from an increasingly wealthy population that requires more efficient and better availability of energy.

The big picture matters more than it ever has, and it is my hope that this book has provided you with some of the building blocks that will help you better navigate the new macroeconomic world.

CHAPTER 11

WE NEVER STOP LEARNING

The costliest lesson is ignorance.

CHARLIE MUNGER ONCE SAID, "IF YOU KEEP LEARNING YOU HAVE a huge advantage."[1] I hope by now I've convinced that you should approach the world of money and finance with an open mind. The monetary system is always evolving and extremely new relative to human existence. The system is complex and dynamic. And our understanding must reflect this. Our ability to adapt, evolve, and learn from the system over time is crucial to being able to use it to our best abilities. In order to benefit the most from the new macroeconomic world, you must keep adapting and evolving with it.

We should also realize that much of what we think we know is based on inherent biases and could very well be wrong. That said, you should recognize that this book does not pretend to be an all-encompassing view of this world of money, finance, and economics, but I hope it provides you with a solid foundation for understanding that world. The answers to the monetary puzzle are much bigger than you'll find in any book. Additionally the puzzle is evolving, and we're just trying to keep up with it. And that evolution requires constant vigilance for new information and ideas as they become available.

SUGGESTED READING

Here is a list of books, websites, and resources that I have found particularly useful over the years. The Internet is a veritable gold mine of information these days. You should scour it, find people who disagree with you, engage them kindly, gorge yourself with their knowledge, and come to your own conclusions. The answers are all out there for the taking if you're willing to make the effort. I try to encourage people to read a variety of different authors and views. It shouldn't matter if you consider yourself a Keynesian, monetarist, Austrian, liberal, or conservative. To maintain an all-encompassing and open-minded view of the world, it's best to keep your sources varied. That said:

- I am very active on the Internet and try my best to respond to readers at my primary website, *Pragmatic Capitalism* (www.pragcap.com). I maintain an "ask me anything" forum as well as a general discussion forum at pragcap.com where I try to answer any question you might have. I love to answer questions and help out where I can, so don't hesitate to reach out.
- My good friends Michael Sankowski, Carlos Mucha, JKH, and Brett Fiebiger, founders of the website *Monetary Realism,* are always busy discussing high finance and monetary theory at *Monetary Realism* (www.monetaryrealism.com).
- I always tell people to read all of Warren Buffett's Letters to Berkshire Shareholders as well as the Warren Buffett Letters to Partners. There is an enormous amount to learn there from Buffett's career. You can find them online for free by using Google search.

Here are some books and other texts I also highly recommend:

Against the Gods: The Remarkable Story of Risk by William Bernstein

The Alchemy of Finance: Reading the Mind of the Market by George Soros

All About Asset Allocation by Rick Ferri

Animal Spirits by Robert Shiller and George Akerlof

The Black Swan by Nassim Taleb

Debt—The First 5,000 Years by David Graeber

The General Theory of Employment, Interest and Money by John Maynard Keynes. I particularly recommend Chapter 12.

How We Know What Isn't So by Thomas Gilovich
Influence by Robert Cialdini
Just About Anything by Daniel Kahneman
The Intelligent Investor by Ben Graham
Irrational Exuberance by Robert Shiller
Memos to Oaktree Clients by Howard Marks (can be found online for free)
The (Mis)Behavior of Markets by Benoit Mandelbrot
Monetary Economics by Marc Lavoie and Wynne Godley
The New Paradigm of Macroeconomics by Richard Werner
The Only Guide to a Winning Investment Strategy You'll Ever Need by Larry Swedroe
The Only Investment Guide You'll Ever Need by Andrew Tobias
Think Twice by Michael Mauboussin
Trend Following by Michael Covel
Why Smart People Make Big Money Mistakes by Gary Belsky and Thomas Gilovich
Why Stock Markets Crash by Didier Sornette
The Winner's Curse by Richard Thaler
Winning the Loser's Game by Charles Ellis
You Can Be a Stock Market Genius by Joel Greenblatt

One of the best ways to keep up with financial content and education is through the financial blogosphere, where many of the world's experts in economics, finance, and money write daily. There are hundreds of superb blogs. I recommend scouring the larger blog aggregators like Seeking Alpha and Business Insider as well as the blog rolls of various large websites like the *Wall Street Journal*'s *Real Time Economics* blog and *FT Alphaville*. Among the blog aggregators, I highly recommend Abnormal Returns and Real Clear Markets. If you tracked just those two websites every day, you'd get more than your fill of financial news, opinions, and research. For mainstream news you can't go wrong with Bloomberg, Reuters, *Financial Times*, CNBC, and FOX Business, and Yahoo Finance is always a great resource.

PARTING THOUGHTS

In his classic text *Meditations* Caesar Marcus Aurelius said: "The only wealth you will keep forever is the wealth you give away." As I wrote this book I kept that in mind, as I hoped to provide you with a series of principles and understandings that can help you navigate the new macroeconomic world. After all, while this book is about money, finance, and economics, it's really about much bigger things. For money is just the means to some other end. And when you realize that you serve yourself best by serving others, then you will, I hope, begin to think of money a bit differently. If there's one lesson I hope you take away from this book, it is that.

GLOSSARY

Acceptance value: Acceptance value represents the public's willingness to accept something as the nation's unit of account and medium of exchange. This is achieved mainly through the legal process and democratic vote. That is, the government and the people deem a specific thing (such as the US dollar) the accepted unit of account and medium of exchange. *Acceptance value is only one facet of currency demand.* See also **quantity value.**

Autonomous contingent currency issuer: An autonomous contingent currency issuer is a nation that is politically and monetarily unified in a manner that affords it the ability to issue currency in contingent environments. Additionally the nation must maintain its status as an autonomous currency issuer by maintaining debts denominated in the currency it can create and by sustaining a floating exchange rate. These nations are generally developed economies with access to resources and strong private sector economies. Not all nations have the ability to remain, or sustain their status as, an autonomous currency issuer.

Equity: Equity represents an ownership interest. Discussions of equity generally refer to stocks.

Federal Funds Rate: The overnight lending rate in the interbank federal funds market.

Fiat money: Fiat money is money organized under the rules and regulations of a government and sustained through the productive base of the private sector. Fiat money has no value in and of itself but affords its users a convenient and simple medium for exchange. When quantifying the value of fiat money, it is best to study the living standards of the society as a whole rather than the more misleading and more commonly used rise in inflation over time. Rising inflation can be perfectly consistent with both the existence of fiat money and rising living standards, as evidenced by the experience of the United States in the twentieth century.

Fiscal policy: Fiscal policy is government policy geared at changing the size of federal spending and taxation.

Hyperinflation: Hyperinflation is a disorderly economic environment caused by unusual exogenous shocks to an economy. Contrary to popular opinion, hyperinflation is not caused by money printing but generally occurs after an exogenous shock to an economy that results in money printing or a collapse in the tax system. The primary historical causes of hyperinflation are lack of monetary sovereignty, war, regime change, production collapse, and government corruption.

Inflation: Inflation is a consistent rise in the general level of prices for goods and services in an economy. Low inflation is usually consistent with healthy economic growth in a credit-based monetary system.

Inside money: Inside money is bank-issued money. The term comes from the idea that it is money created inside the private sector by private competitive banks.

IOR or IOER: This is the common abbreviation for interest on reserves or interest on excess reserves.

Monetary policy: Monetary policy is policy formulated and executed by the central bank of a country in an attempt to influence the money supply and economy. Specifically monetary policy is executed by interacting in various ways with the private banking system in an attempt to influence the cost and use of inside money.

Monetary realism: Monetary realism (MR) is a set of understandings and principles that seek to describe the operational realities of the monetary system through the specific institutional design and relationships that exist in a particular monetary system.

Money: Money is a social tool with which we primarily exchange goods and services. Technically anything can serve as money, but in modern societies money is most commonly organized under the rules and regulations of government. In a credit-based monetary system most money is issued by banks through the loan creation process. It is important to note that different assets within the monetary system can have differing levels of "moneyness" in that they serve to varying degrees as a medium of exchange.

MR: See **monetary realism.**

Outside money: Outside money is government-created money. This includes notes, coins, and bank reserves. It is called outside money because it is created outside the private sector. Outside money exists to facilitate the use of inside money.

Quantitative easing: Quantitative easing is a form of monetary policy, implemented through open market operations in which the central bank tries to influence the cost and use of inside money by altering bank reserves. Specifically this is achieved by swapping reserves for Treasury bonds (in most cases). It results in no change in private sector net financial assets and is often confused with money printing or debt monetization. It's really just an unusual form of standard Federal Reserve policy or open market operations, and its effectiveness is highly debatable.

Quantity value: Quantity value describes the medium of exchange's value in terms of purchasing power, inflation, exchange rates, production value, and so on. This is the utility of the money as a store of value. While acceptance value is generally stable and enforceable by law, quantity value can be quite unstable and result in currency collapse in a worst-case scenario.

Reserves: Bank reserves are a form of outside money used as the means of settling payments and meeting reserve requirements. Reserves (and the Federal Reserve System) exist to help streamline the banking system into one cohesive unit while maintaining the private competitive banking system.

S = I + (S–I): Monetary realists use this important equation to emphasize that an economy is based on private production. The equation emphasizes the role of private investment in the economy and the idea that living standards are maximized when a nation is highly productive and creating goods and services that increase overall living standards.

Sectoral balances approach: The sectoral balances approach was created by Wynne Godley to show the flows through an economy. It is a useful way of understanding the way that various economic agents generate gross domestic product.

Social construct: Social construct is another term for money. See **money**.

Unit of account: A standard monetary unit for measuring the value of goods, services, and financial assets. In the United States the unit of account is the dollar; in the European Monetary Union the unit of account is the euro; in the UK it is the pound sterling; and in Japan it is the yen.

NOTES

WHAT I HOPE TO ACCOMPLISH

1. Office of Investor Education and Advocacy, Securities and Exchange Commission, *Study Regarding Financial Literacy Among Investors* (Washington, DC: Securities and Exchange Commission, August 2012), 3.

CHAPTER 1: WHAT IS MONEY?

1. John Maynard Keynes, "Theorie des Geldes und der Umlaufsmittel." *Royal Economic Journal* 24 (1914), 417-419.

CHAPTER 2: WHY THE NEW MACROECONOMY MATTERS MORE THAN EVER

1. Benjamin Graham, "A Conversation with Benjamin Graham," *Financial Analysts Journal,* Vol. 32, No. 5, September, 1976, 55-84.
2. Francois Trahan and Katherine Krantz, *The Era of Uncertainty: Global Investment Strategies for Inflation, Deflation, and the Middle Ground* (New Jersey: Wiley, 2011).
3. Arvind Subramanian and Martin Kessler, *The Hyperglobalization of Trade and Its Future,* Global Citizen Foundation, June 2013 (Washington, DC).
4. National Intelligence Council, *Global Trends 2030: Alternative Worlds,* Office of the Director of National Intelligence, December 2012 (Washington, DC), http://globaltrends2030.files.wordpress.com/2012/11/global-trends-2030-november2012.pdf.
5. Trahan and Krantz, *The Era of Uncertainty.*
6. Richard Dobbs et al., *Urban World: The Shifting Global Business Landscape,* McKinsey Global Institute, October 2013, http://www.mckinsey.com/insights/urbanization/urban_world_the_shifting_global_business_landscape.
7. BlackRock, "A Look at Emerging Opportunities," August 7, 2013, https://www2.blackrock.com/us/financial-professionals/market-insight/daily-stat/a-look-at-emerging-opportunities?
8. "Economic Principles," Bridgewater Associates, LP, 2013, http://www.economicprinciples.org/

CHAPTER 3: ARE YOU AN INVESTOR, SAVER, OR BOTH?

1. Boyd Erman, "For Warren Buffett, the Cash Option Is Priceless," *Globe and Mail,* September 24, 2012, http://www.theglobeandmail.com/globe-investor/investment-ideas/streetwise/for-warren-buffett-the-cash-option-is-priceless/article4565468/.

CHAPTER 4: MARKET MYTHS THAT PERSIST

1. S&P Dow Jones Indices, *S&P Indices Versus Active Funds (SPIVA) Scorecard,* US midyear 2013, http://us.spindices.com/resource-center/thought-leadership/spiva/.
2. Russel Kinnel, "Mutual Fund Expense Ratios See Biggest Spike Since 2000," *Morningstar Advisor,* January 31, 2011.
3. Brad Barber and Terrance Odean, "Trading Is Hazardous to Your Wealth," April 2010, http://papers.ssrn.com/sol3/papers.cfm?abstract_id=219228; Brad Barber and Terrance Odean, "The Behavior of Individual Investors," September 2011, http://papers.ssrn.com/sol3/papers.cfm?abstract_id=1872211.
4. James Montier, "I Want to Break Free, or, Strategic Asset Allocation ≠ Static Asset Allocation," *Retail Investor,* May 25, 2010, http://www.retailinvestor.org/pdf/Montier.pdf; Grantham Mayo Otterloo, https://www.gmo.com/America/Research/AssetAlloc/.
5. *Contango* A situation where the futures price of a commodity is above the expected future spot price. Contango refers to a situation where the future spot price is below the current price, and people are willing to pay more for a commodity at some point in the future than the actual expected price of the commodity. This may be due to people's desire to pay a premium to have the commodity in the future rather than paying the costs of storage and carry costs of buying the commodity today. "Definition of *Contango,*" *Investopedia,* http://www.investopedia.com/terms/c/contango.asp.
6. Thornburg Investment Management, *A Study of Real Real Returns,* July 2013, http://www.thornburginvestments.com/pdfs/TH1401.pdf.
7. "American Housing Survey for the United States: 2009," US Census Bureau, March, 2011, http://www.census.gov/prod/2011pubs/h150-09.pdf.

CHAPTER 5: HOW THE NEW MACROECONOMY IS CHANGING PORTFOLIO CONSTRUCTION

1. Francois Trahan and Katherine Krantz, *The Era of Uncertainty: Global Investment Strategies for Inflation, Deflation, and the Middle Ground* (New Jersey: Wiley, 2011), 5.
2. Rebecca Patterson, *A New Fiscal World Order,* JP Morgan, August 2011.
3. Daniel Burnside, "How Many Stocks Do You Need to Be Diversified?" *AAII Journal,* July 2004, http://www.aaii.com/journal/article/how-many-stocks-do-you-need-to-be-diversified-.touch.
4. US Small Business Administration, "Frequently Asked Questions," http://www.sba.gov/sites/default/files/sbfaq.pdf.
5. Jeremy Siegel, *Stocks for the Long Run* (New York: McGraw-Hill, 2002), 36.

6. Hyman Minsky, "The Financial Instability Hypothesis," Levy Economics Institute of Bard College, Working Paper No. 74, May 1992, http://www.levyinstitute.org/pubs/wp74.pdf.
7. Benjamin Graham and David Dodd, *Security Analysis,* 6th ed., foreword by Warren Buffett (2008).
8. Mary Buffett and David Clark, *The Tao of Warren Buffett* (New York: Simon & Schuster, 2006).
9. Rob Arnott, "The Biggest Urban Legend in Finance," Research Affiliates, March 2011, http://www.researchaffiliates.com/Our%20Ideas/Insights/Fundamentals/Pages/F_2011_March_The_Biggest_Urban_Legend.aspx.
10. David Levy, Martin Farnham, and Samira Rajan, "Where Profits Come From," 1997, http://www.levyforecast.com/assets/Profits.pdf.
11. Marc Lavoie and Wynne Godley, "Kaleckian Models of Growth in a Coherent Stock-Flow Monetary Framework: A Kaldorian View," *Journal of Post Keynesian Economics,* Winter 2001–2.
12. Arthur Kortweig, Roman Kraussl, and Patrick Verwijmeren, "Does It Pay to Invest in Art? A Selection-Corrected Perspective," October 2013, http://papers.ssrn.com/s013/papers.cfm?abstract_id=2280099.
13. I would recommend reviewing the following websites for more information about how to construct your own lazy macroeconomic portfolio:

    The Bogle Heads website (http://www.bogleheads.org/wiki/Lazy_portfolios)
    MarketWatch Lazy Portfolios (http://www.marketwatch.com/lazyportfolio)
    AssetBuilder Lazy Portfolios (http://assetbuilder.com/lazy_portfolios/)

14. BarclayHedge, Barclay Global Macro Index, October 2013, http://www.barclayhedge.com/research/indices/ghs/Global_Macro_Index.html.
15. Eugene Fama and Kenneth French, "Why Active Investing Is a Negative Sum Game," Fama/French Forum, June 2009, http://www.dimensional.com/famafrench/2009/06/why-active-investing-is-a-negative-sum-gain.html.

CHAPTER 6: THE IMPORTANCE OF UNDERSTANDING BEHAVIORAL FINANCE

1. Ralph Sawyer, *Sun Tzu's Art of War* (Boulder, CO: Westview, 1994), 15.
2. Andrew Lo, "Fear, Greed, and Financial Crises: A Cognitive Neurosciences Perspective," *Handbook on Systemic Risk,* August 28, 2011.
3. Daniel Kahneman and Amos Tversky, "Prospect Theory: An Analysis of Decision Under Risk," *Econometrica,* Vol. 47, No. 2, March 1979, 263-292.
4. Robert Hagstrom, *The Warren Buffett Way* (New York: John Wiley, 2013), 148.
5. "Laurie Santos: A Monkey Economy as Irrational as Ours," TED, July 2010, http://www.ted.com/talks/laurie_santos.html.
6. "Mixed Opinions and Maxims: Aphoristic Insights by Friedrich Nietzsche," University of Southern California, March 29, 1995, http://www.usc.edu/schools/annenberg/c/faculty/thomas/mixed.html.
7. Adam Smith, *The Money Game* (New York: Random House, 1967), 135.

8. Federal Reserve Bank of St. Louis FRED Economic Data, NBER based Recession Indicators, http://research.stlouisfed.org/fred2/series/USREC.
9. Justin Kruger and David Dunning, "Unskilled and Unaware of it," *The Journal of Personality and Social Psychology,* December 2009, http://citeseerx.ist.psu.edu/viewdoc/summary?doi=10.1.1.64.2655.
10. John Maynard Keynes, *The General Theory of Employment, Interest, and Money* (New York: Classic Books America, 2009), 140.

CHAPTER 7: UNDERSTANDING THE MODERN MONETARY SYSTEM

1. "Legal Tender Status," U.S. Department of the Treasury, January 4, 2011. http://www.treasury.gov/resource-center/faqs/currency/pages/legal-tender.aspx
2. Aleia Van Dyke and Beth Robertson, "Retail Point of Sale Forecast 2012–2017: Cash Is No Longer King; Cards and Mobile Payments Likely to Rise," Javelin Strategy and Research, June 2012.
3. Ricardo Lagos, "Inside and Outside Money," Research Department Staff Report 374, Federal Reserve Bank of Minneapolis, May 2006, http://www.minneapolisfed.org/research/sr/sr374.pdf.
4. Hyman Minsky, "The Financial Instability Hypothesis," Working Paper No. 74, Jerome Levy Economics Institute of Bard College, May 1992, http://www.levyinstitute.org/pubs/wp74.pdf.
5. John Maynard Keynes, "Theorie des Geldes und der Umlaufsmittel," *Royal Economic Journal* 24 (1914), 417-419.
6. Adam Smith, *The Wealth of Nations* (Blacksburg, VA: Thrifty Books, 2009), 21.
7. Kevin Clinton, "Implementation of Monetary Policy in a Regime with Zero Reserve Requirements," Bank of Canada, Canada, April, 1997.
8. Seth Carpenter and Selva Demiralp, "Money, Reserves and the Transmission of Monetary Policy: Does the Money Multiplier Exist?," Washington, DC, May, 2010: 28
9. Lauara Kodres, "What Is Shadow Banking?," International Monetary Fund, June 2013, http://www.imf.org/external/pubs/ft/fandd/2013/06/basics.htm.
10. Dirk Bezemer and Richard Werner, "Disaggregated Credit Flows and Growth in Central Europe," Munich Personal RePEc Archive, May 2009, http://mpra.ub.uni-muenchen.de/17691/1/MPRA_paper_17691.pdf.
11. Board of Governors of the Federal Reserve System, "The Federal Reserve in the US Payments System," *The Federal Reserve System: Purposes and Functions,* 83.
12. Cullen Roche, "Buffett's Silly Talk About the US Debt," *Pragmatic Capitalism* (blog), May 18, 2011, http://pragcap.com/buffetts-silly-talk-about-the-u-s-debt.
13. Jeff Howlett, "Treasury and the Central Bank—A Contingent Institutional Approach," May 29, 2012, http://monetaryrealism.com/treasury-and-the-central-bank-a-contingent-institutional-approach/.
14. Jeff Howlett, "Briefly Revisiting $S = I + (S-I)$," *Monetary Realism,* February 25, 2013, http://monetaryrealism.com/briefly-revisiting-s-i-s-i/.
15. International Monetary Fund, "Primary Income Account," *Balance of Payments and International Investment Position Manual,* 6th ed. (Washington,

DC: International Monetary Fund, 2009), http://www.imf.org/external/pubs/ft/bop/2007/pdf/chap11.pdf.

CHAPTER 8: ECONOMIC AND MONETARY MYTHS THAT PERSIST

1. Institute for Energy Research, "Federal Assets Above and Below Ground," January 17, 2013, http://www.instituteforenergyresearch.org/?p=15346.
2. Brett Fawley and Luciana Juvenal, "Why Health Care Matters and the Current Debt Does Not," Federal Reserve Bank of St. Louis, October, 2011.
3. Barry Eichengreen, "Why the Dollar's Reign Is Near an End," *Wall Street Journal,* March 2, 2011, http://online.wsj.com/news/articles/SB10001424052748703313304576132170181013248.
4. "Permanent OMOs: Treasury," Federal Reserve Bank of New York, September 2013.
5. John Greenwald, "Greenspan's Rates of Wrath," *Time Magazine Online Edition,* November 28, 1994, http://content.time.com/time/magazine/article/0,9171,981879,00.html.
6. John Hicks, "IS-LM: An Explanation," *Journal of Post Keynesian Economics* 3 (1980–81), 152.
7. Cullen Roche, "Hyperinflation—It's More Than Just a Monetary Phenomenon," *Social Science Research Network,* (March 30, 2011), 6-7.
8. Benoit Mandelbrot, *The (Mis)Behavior of Markets* (New York: Basic Books, 2004), 83.

CHAPTER 11: WE NEVER STOP LEARNING

1. Patricia Sellers, "Warren Buffet and Charlie Munger's Best Advice," *Fortune,* October 31 2013, http://postcards.blogs.fortune.cnn.com/2013/10/31/buffett-munger-best-advice/.

INDEX